Anonymous

My mother's Bible stories,

Told in the language of a gentle loving mother conversing with her children

Anonymous

My mother's Bible stories,
Told in the language of a gentle loving mother conversing with her children

ISBN/EAN: 9783337775391

Printed in Europe, USA, Canada, Australia, Japan

Cover: Foto ©ninafisch / pixelio.de

More available books at **www.hansebooks.com**

My Mother's Bible Stories

TOLD IN THE LANGUAGE OF A GENTLE, LOVING
MOTHER CONVERSING WITH HER
CHILDREN

Designed for family use during "the children's hour" around
· · · the evening lamp · · ·

INTRODUCED BY

Bishop JOHN H. VINCENT, D. D.

Chancellor of Chautauqua Institute

Tell me a story, mother,
Tell it to your little child.

Embracing all the wonderful, romantic, beautiful and tender incidents and events
of the Scriptures, related in the form of stories to please
and instruct the little ones

VERY BEAUTIFULLY ILLUSTRATED

with two hundred steel etchings, wood engravings and colored photogravures

PEOPLE'S PUBLISHING CO.,
PHILADELPHIA, PA.   ST. LOUIS, MO.

✦✦✦ INTRODUCTION ✦✦✦

BY BISHOP JOHN H. VINCENT.

THE Book of Books is a book for the babe as well as for the full-grown man; a book for the babe and for the babe's mother. Best of all, the child's growth never carries him beyond the Book. Its stories and its songs hold and charm him when he is so small as to sit or lie in mother's lap. "That sweet story of old" is a joy to him then—the Babe of Bethlehem, and how He lay in a manger, and how the shepherds came to Him and the wise men with their gifts of gold and frankincense and myrrh; the flight into Egypt through the fear of Herod; the warning and the guiding angels—how all these things make baby's eyes grow bright! When he is big enough for "trousers with pockets," and for high top boots on a snowy morning, his eyes will flash at the story of David, the shepherd boy, as he braved the bear, slew the lion and swung the sling that made the giant bite the dust. And the stories of Joseph and of Moses and of Joshua, of Samuel and of Samson and of the brave Daniel—well, he loves to hear them over and over. Or, if told him at the right time his face will grow serious under the account of the fine lad from Nazareth who, when He visited the temple in Jerusalem, lingered in the school of the wise doctors to listen to what they had to say, and to say things that made even the doctors wonder.

When the boy gets to be a big boy—almost a man, if he be skilfully dealt with, he will take a lively interest in the journeys and deeds and wise words of Bible men; and while he may not *seem* to give much attention, and while he may really care a great deal more for one of Scott's stories or for some bright book of travels or of battles, than he does for anything to be found in the Bible, he will still read his daily chapter or study his Sunday-school lesson, or give reverent attention to his father's voice in the morning reading and pick up now and then an idea from it all, which will make him a sturdier boy and a manlier man.

If ministers and mothers (and why not fathers) were wise with ordinary wisdom, the Bible might be made so fascinating. It is a book of History—graphic, brilliant, in a good sense sensational, and if rightly taught has captivating power in it. Why are not parents and pastors wiser?

In the later years, when the boy is a man with a home and children of his own, the cares of life upon him and the home of his childhood a memory, he will find strength in the big Book. And later on, in old age, when the frosts are in his hair and a dimness in his eyes, he will turn to the same great and gracious volume for comfort and consolation. He will recite over again more slowly and reverently now than when he was a boy—the words he learned in boyhood but which he is now just beginning to appreciate: "The Lord is my Shepherd, I shall not want," and " In my Father's house are many mansions." He said these things glibly once as mere feats or tasks of memory. He repeats them now with a clinging heart, putting its love into the memory. His tremulous voice makes music of these divine words. A book with so much in it, for so many stages in one's career, cannot be too early or too carefully taught. And the best place for the early teaching is at home. And the best teachers are mother and father. It is a great thing to connect God's words of history and poetry and promise with the voices and faces of those whom we love earliest and best. Therefore whatever helps to make home teach God's word, and do it well, is a blessing which one cannot overvalue.

This then is the mission of the present volume: To turn the attention of parents to the simple and wonderful lessons of the Holy Bible; to help them in winning the interest of the little folks; and thus to build up memories in which the love and light and joy of home are connected with the law and love and precious promises of the sacred Scriptures.

The compiler of this book of Bible stories has availed herself of the helps which other works in the same line have furnished, believing that in this new form they will invite the parents of our times to a renewal of effort in the reading of the Bible and in the repeating of its matchless stories to the children of our land and age.

The truth of the Bible forms the basis of the republic. The God of the Bible is the hope of its future prosperity. The laws of the Bible must be the laws of the land. Therefore this home help to Bible study has no mean or unimportant part to play in training a generation of American citizens who shall make God their trust, His love their inspiration, His laws their standard, His Son their Redeemer, His grace their strength, His heaven their eternal home.

John H. Vincent

BUFFALO, N. Y.

THE BOW OF PROMISE.

The Author's Purpose in Writing This Book.

HILDREN are children, the wide world over. In many things they widely differ. In color they are black, or white, or brown, or yellow, for there are many races among the children of men.

In character they are greatly unlike, for while some are gentle and good, others are wild and wayward, and downright little savages.

But in one thing they are all agreed, they all delight in stories.

"Tell us a story," is the ceaseless cry that comes from the children's lips, as they sit on papa's knee, or at mother's feet, or stand beside grandpa's chair.

In Germany or Japan, in Calcutta or Chicago, there is the same close clustering and the same eager listening when the story-teller is present and the story is about to be begun. Nor is this true of the little children only. We are all but children of a larger growth, and we never lose our relish for pictured truth, and that is what a story is, if it be a story that is worthy of the name. There are many stories afloat that are not true, and cannot be, they are so absurd; and many that are true that ought not to be told, they are so utterly silly, or so abominably bad.

Our Father in Heaven knew just what kind of a book would please and profit His children most, and so He has given us a story book. The most wonderful story book in the world is the Bible—more wonderful than the Arabian Nights, or Grim's Fairy Tales, or any other book that ever was written by the pen of man: the story of Creation and the story of Eden; the story of the Fall; the story of the Flood; the story of Abraham, Isaac and Jacob;

the story of Joseph and Moses, and on through all the range of Old Testament history.

And when we come to the New Testament it is brimming and beautiful with stories most wonderful. The Great Teacher taught the people in parable, and what are parables but stories intended to picture the truth? What story was ever told of such beauty and tenderness as that of the Babe of Bethlehem and the Man of Calvary?

And the lives of such followers of Christ as Peter and Paul— what could better stir the blood and warm the heart? And the best of it all about these stories is that they are absolutely true, and not only full of deepest interest, but shed the clearest light upon the path that leads us on from earth to heaven.

The Bible Stories that are told in this book are not intended to draw the children away from the Bible, which after all is "the Book of Books," but are intended to draw them to it. The Bible is for all ages, and in it are many words that are sometimes hard to be understood, at least for the younger sort of readers. This story book is intended for the younger sort, and it is to be hoped will give them a clearer light upon God's holy pages, and will also be a help for those busy parents and other friends of children who wish they "had the knack" of interesting children by the telling of Bible Stories but hardly know how to set about it. This book will furnish a delightful guide, and we do not doubt will warm many a heart, brighten many a home, cheer many a lonely hour, and lift up many a life into a higher plane of usefulness and happiness.

CONTENTS

	PAGE
How God Made the World	33
The Wonderful Things that God made to Grow out of the Ground	34
The Wonderful Living Things that God Created	36
The Story of Creation	39
The Story of How Adam and Eve Sinned	42
The Sad Story of Cain and Abel	47
Story of Enoch, the Good Man, Who did Not Die	49
Story of the Great Flood that Covered the Whole Earth	50
Nimrod the Mighty Hunter, and the Building of the Tower of Babel	54
The Beautiful Story of Abraham	56
Abraham Receives a Promise from God and Entertains Three Angels	58
Abraham is Commanded to Sacrifice Isaac	60
The Story of Isaac and Rebecca	64
Jacob's Wonderful Dream	67
Jacob's Love for Rachel	69
The Wonderful Story of Joseph	71
Joseph's Brothers Sell Him as a Slave	76
The Strange Things that Happened to Joseph in Egypt	79
The Butler and the Baker	81
The Wonderful Story of How Joseph was Released from Prison and Became a Great Ruler	83
Joseph's Brothers Come to Egypt to Buy Corn	88
Joseph Makes a Great Feast for his Brothers	91
Joseph Makes Himself Known to his Brothers	96
Jacob and His Family Remove to Egypt	99
The Story of Moses, and How He was Found in the Bulrushes by the King's Daughter	103
How Moses Slew the Task-master	110
Story of the Wonderful Burning Bush	112
A Description of Some of the Terrible Plagues that God Sent Upon Egypt	116
Other Great Plagues that Fell Upon the Egyptians	119

CONTENTS.

	PAGE.
How Moses and the Children of Israel Crossed the Red Sea	126
Story of the Manna, and the Rock in the Desert	130
The Terrors of Mount Sinai	133
The Building of the Tabernacle	136
The Wonders and Beauties of the Tabernacle	142
Story of the Twelve Spies	145
The Story of Baalam	151
The Sin of Moses and Aaron, and Aaron's Death	154
The Brazen Serpent	157
The Death of Moses	159
Joshua, the Great General	163
The Children of Israel Cross the River Jordan	167
The Walls of Jericho Fall Down	171
Conquest of Canaan and Death of Joshua	175
Story of Samson, the Strong Man	178
The Beautiful Story of Faithful Ruth	181
Ruth Gleans Corn in the Fields	185
The Wedding of Ruth and Boaz	189
The Story of Gideon	193
The Story of Job	197
The Story of Samuel and His Mother	202
Eli and His Wicked Sons	203
The Israelites Ask Samuel to Give Them a King	205
Saul is Chosen King	206
King Saul Conquers the Amalekites	209
God's Punishment of King Saul	211
The Story of David	213
David Plays the Harp Before King Saul	214
Story of the Giant Goliath	217
David's Battle with Goliath	219
Saul Tries to Kill David	221
The Death of Saul	225
David Becomes King	227
Nathan Rebukes David	228
Absalom is Found Hanging on an Oak Tree	232
David's Grief for the Death of Absalom	234
David's Farewell to His People	236
Story of Solomon, the Wise Man	236
Story of the Two Women and the Dead Child	237
Solomon Builds a Beautiful Temple	239

CONTENTS.

	PAGE
Story of the Queen of Sheba	243
Solomon Forgets God and Worships Idols	245
How Jeroboam was Punished for His Wickedness	246
Story of Elijah and the Ravens	248
Story of the Widow and Her Son	250
Elijah Goes on a Long Journey to See King Ahab	253
Elijah and the Prophets of Baal	255
Story of the Little Cloud No Larger than a Man's Hand	257
What Happened to Elijah in the Wilderness	260
Elijah is Taken Up to Heaven in a Chariot of Fire	262
Story of the Bears and the Wicked Children	264
Elisha Restores Life to a Little Boy Who Had Died	265
Story of Naaman the Leper	269
The Wonderful Story of Jonah	272
The Story of King Hezekiah	274
The King of Babylon Captures Jerusalem and Burns the Temple	278
Story of the Three Men Who Were Thrown into a Fiery Furnace	280
Story of the Handwriting on the Wall	282
Daniel in the Lion's Den	285
Story of Esther, the Beautiful Queen	289
Story of the Wicked Haman	292
God Saves the Jews, and Haman is Hanged on His Own Gallows	295
Cyrus, the Great King	296

PART TWO—THE NEW TESTAMENT.

Zacharias and His Wife Elisabeth	301
Mary the Mother of Jesus	303
Birth of John the Baptist	305
Jesus is Born in Bethlehem in a Manger	307
Simeon, and Anna the Prophetess	310
Story of the Wise Men of the East	312
Herod Sends His Soldiers to Kill the Little Boys Who Lived in Bethlehem,	315
Jesus Talks with the Priests in the Temple	318
John the Baptist Preaches in the Desert	320
Satan Tempts Jesus in the Wilderness	321
The Disciples of Jesus	324
How Nathaniel Became a Disciple of Jesus	327
The Miracle at the Wedding Feast	328
Story of the Woman of Samaria	330

CONTENTS.

	PAGE.
The Men of Nazareth Try to Kill Jesus	332
The Miraculous Draught of Fishes	333
Jesus Heals a Man Who Was Insane	336
Jesus Heals a Sick Man	338
A Wonderful Thing that Happened at the Pool of Bethesda	340
Jesus Chooses Twelve Apostles	342
Something More About John the Baptist	345
John Sends Messengers to Jesus	346
Herod Causes John to be Beheaded	348
Jesus Restores Life to a Young Girl Who Had Died	350
Herod, on Hearing of Jesus, Supposed He Was John the Baptist Come to Life Again	351
Jesus Walks on the Water	353
Jesus Preaches to the People	355
Glories of the Mount of Transfiguration	358
Jesus Teaches Humility	360
The Story of Mary and Martha, Who Loved Jesus	361
Story of the Blind Beggar	364
Story of the Lost Sheep	367
Jesus Blesses Little Children	370
Story of the Humble Publican and the Proud Pharisee	374
The Wonderful Story of Lazarus	376
Mary and the Precious Ointment	380
Christ's Royal Entry into Jerusalem	383
Jesus Weeps Over Jerusalem	384
Story of the Widow and Her Mite	388
The Evening on the Mount of Olives	390
Judas Betrays His Master	392
The Feast of the Passover	395
Jesus Accuses Judas of His Treachery	397
Jesus Rebukes Peter	399
The Sacrament	400
The Agony in the Garden	403
Peter Draws His Sword in Defence of His Master	406
The Trial and Mockery of Jesus	408
Peter Denies His Master	410
Pontius Pilate	411
Death of Judas the Traitor	413
Pilate Tries to Save the Life of Jesus	414
The Jews Ask for the Release of a Robber	417

CONTENTS.

	PAGE.
The Roman Soldiers Mock Jesus	420
The Crucifixion	421
The Agony on the Cross	424
Death of Jesus	426
The Seven Sayings of Jesus on the Cross	429
Truly, This Was the Son of God	430
Joseph of Arimathea	432
The Women and the Angel at the Tomb of Jesus	434
Jesus is Risen and Glorified	436
Jesus Appears to His Disciples	440
Doubting Thomas	443
Jesus Ascends Into Heaven	444
The Disciples Receive the Promised Comforter	447
The Lame Man at the Beautiful Gate	450
The Stoning of Stephen, the First Martyr	451
Story of Philip and the Ethiopian Prince	454
The Wonderful Vision of Saul	456
Ananias Appears to Saul in a Vision	458
An Angel Delivers Peter from Prison	461
Story of Paul and the Wicked Sorcerer	464
Paul and Timothy	466
Paul's Wonderful Dream	467
Story of a Great Earthquake	468
Paul's Visit to Greece	470
Paul and Titus	472
A Great Uproar in the Temple and on the Castle Stairs	473
Paul's Escape from Scourging	476
Paul Speaks Before King Agrippa	477
Paul's Life in Rome	480

∴ ILLUSTRATIONS ∴

	PAGE
The Building of the Pyramids	Frontispiece
The Bow of Promise	6
Women of Babylon	32
In the Beginning the World was Void and Without Form	35
The Giving of the Law	37
Some of the Beasts that God Created	38
Adam and Eve in the Garden of Eden	41
The Beautiful Home Lost Through Sin	43
Adam and Eve Driven from the Garden of Eden	44
Eve and her Two Boys	45
Cain Slays Abel	46
The Flood	51
Going Into the Ark	52
Noah's Sacrifice and the Rainbow	53
Ham Deriding His Father	54
Building of the Tower of Babel	55
Abraham Building an Altar to God	57
Lot's Wife Turned Into a Pillar of Salt	59
Sara, Abraham's Wife	61
The Angel Appearing to Abraham	62
Rebekah Gives Abraham's Servant Water to Drink	64
Hagar Driven from Home	65
Esau Sells His Birthright	66
Isaac Blesses Jacob	68
Rachel at the Well	69
Jacob Arrives at the House of Laban	70
Meeting of Esau and Jacob	72
Jacob's Wonderful Dream	73
Merchants Barter for Joseph	75
Merchants Traveling in Palestine	77
The Wicked Brothers Sell Joseph	79
A Prison in Egypt	81

ILLUSTRATIONS.

	PAGE
Jacob's Well	85
Destruction of Pharaoh's Army	87
On the Road from Canaan to Egypt	93
Jacob and His Family Remove to Egypt	99
Death of Jacob	102
The Egyptian Well	105
Hagar and Ishmael	106
The Princess Finds Moses	107
A Home in Bible Land	109
Moses at the Home of Laban	113
Travelers in Palestine	115
The Rods Turned to Snakes	117
The Storm of Fire and Hail	120
The Pest of Locusts	121
Eating the Passover	122
The Angel of Death Passing Over Egypt	123
The Children of Israel Preparing to Depart	124
Pharaoh's Army Pursuing the Children of Israel	127
Pharaoh's Rage on Learning that the Children of Israel had Fled	128
The Song of Triumph	129
Gathering Manna in the Wilderness	131
Water Gushes from the Rock	132
Moses Brings the Book from Mount Sinai	135
The Golden Calf	137
The Children of Israel Delivering their Treasures to Moses	139
The Altar of Incense	140
The Brass Altar	142
The Brass Basin for the People to Wash In	143
Aaron Blessing the People	146
The River Jordan	147
The Return of the Spies	148
The People Threaten to Stone Caleb and Joshua	150
Balaam Sees the Angel	152
The People Murmur Against Moses and Aaron	155
Death of Aaron	156
The Brazen Serpent	158
Moses Blesses the People	161
Burial of Moses	162
Joshua, the New Leader of the Israelites	164
Escape of the Spies	166

xvi ILLUSTRATIONS.

	PAGE.
The Priests Bearing the Ark	169
The Angel Appearing to Joshua	171
Destruction of Jericho	173
Joshua Commanding the Sun and Moon to Stand Still	176
Destroying Idols	177
Samson Kills the Lion	179
Samson Slaying the Philistines with the Jawbone of an Ass	180
Samson Thrown into Prison	181
Samson and Delilah	182
Samson Destroys the Temple of Dagon	183
Orpah Returns Home	184
Ruth Before Boaz	187
Boaz and the Kinsman of Naomi	191
The Angel Departing Out of Gideon's Sight	194
Gideon Wringing the Water from the Fleece	195
Robbers Attacking the Servants of Job	198
Job's Anguish When Told of the Death of His Children	199
Fire Falls from Heaven and Consumes the Shepherds	201
Samuel Anoints Saul	207
"God Save the King!"	208
Saul Defeats the Amalekites	210
Return of Saul's Army with the Sheep and Oxen	211
Samuel Departs from Saul	212
Bethlehem, the City of David	215
David Slays Goliath	220
David Fighting the Philistines	222
Saul Tries to Kill David	223
Saul and the Witch of Endor	224
Death of Saul	226
Nathan Rebuking David	229
David Fleeing from Jerusalem	230
Death of Absalom	232
The Messengers Tell David of the Death of Absalom	234
Solomon and the Two Women	238
Building the Temple	240
Bringing the Ark to the Temple	241
The Queen of Sheba Visits Solomon	244
Jezebel Comes from Sidon to Meet Ahab	249
Jezebel and Ahab	251
Killing the Prophets of Baal	256

ILLUSTRATIONS

	PAGE
Elijah and the Angel	258
Dogs Eat the Body of Jezebel	261
Elisha Restores the Child to Life	267
The Dead Man Restored to Life	268
The King of Assyria and His Army	275
The Angel of the Lord Destroying the Assyrians	277
The Soldiers of Babylon Capture Zedekiah	279
The Fiery Furnace	281
The Hand-Writing on the Wall	283
The Soldiers of Darius Kill Belshazzar	284
A Hungry Lion Attacking a Traveler	285
Casting the Wicked Men and their Families Into the Lions' Den	287
People Came from All Parts of the World to the Feast	289
Esther is Brought to the Palace	291
The Vision of the Cross	297
Rebuilding Jerusalem	299
Of Such is the Kingdom of Heaven	300
The Star of Bethlehem	301
Blessing the Holy Child	304
Salome Dancing Before Herod	305
The Angel Appears to Mary	306
The Angels and the Shepherds	307
Angels Appear to the Shepherds	309
The Wise Men Worship Jesus	311
The Shadow of the Cross	314
The Childhood of Jesus	316
Death of Herod	317
On the Way to Jerusalem	319
The Voice of One Crying in the Wilderness	321
"Thou Art My Beloved Son"	321
Alone in the Desert	322
The Angels Serve Jesus	323
Jesus and His Disciples	326
The Miracle at Cana of Galilee	329
Jesus and the Woman of Samaria	335
Jesus Careth for the Sick	337
Jesus Sows the Good Seed in Every Heart	341
The Winds and the Waves Obeyed Him	343
Street Leading to Herod's Palace	347
Beheading of John the Baptist	349

ILLUSTRATIONS.

	PAGE
Jesus Walking on the Water	354
Jesus Talking with His Disciples	359
Jesus Loves Little Children	361
Jesus at the Home of Mary and Martha	363
The Lost Sheep	365
Jesus the Friend of Sinners	368
Jesus Blesses Little Children	369
The Road to Samaria	371
The Rich Young Man	373
Modern Jericho	375
Zaccheus in the Sycamore Tree	376
The Raising of Lazarus	378
The Sisters at the Tomb of Lazarus	379
Mary Anointing the Feet of Jesus	381
Pity for the Unfortunate	385
And the Door was Shut	387
The Evening on the Mount of Olives	389
God's Care for Us Taught by the Beautiful Lily	391
A Water Carrier in the Streets of Jerusalem	393
Peter's Denial of Christ	401
Angels Ministering to Jesus	405
The Jews Reject Christ	419
The Crucifixion	423
The Friends of Jesus Watching the Procession to the Cross	425
At the Foot of the Cross	427
The Basin of Vinegar	428
Jesus Giveth the Water of Life	431
The Women at the Tomb of Jesus	433
The Cross of Christ	435
The Burial of Christ	437
Jesus and Mary Magdalene	439
Jesus Ascends Into Heaven	445
Jesus Shows Himself to the Two Marys	449
The Gate Near Which Stephen Was Stoned	453
The Chariot of the Ethiopian Lord	455
Interior of a House in Damascus	457
A Street Scene in Bible Land	459
Released by the Angel	463
Paul Expels the Evil Spirit	465
A Street Scene in Damascus	471
The Shipwreck of Paul	475

WOMEN OF BABYLON.

My Mother's Bible Stories.

How God Made the World.

THIS large place we live in is called the world. It is very beautiful. If we look up we see the blue sky; if we look down we see the green grass.

The sky is like a curtain spread over our heads; the grass like a carpet under our feet, and the bright sun is like a great beautiful lamp to give us light. It was very kind of God to make such a beautiful world for us to live in.

How did God make the world? By simply speaking the word. First of all, He made the light. God said, "Let there be light," and there was light. No one can make things by speaking but God:—God made everything out of nothing. He only spoke and the light came.

Then God made the air. You cannot see the air, but you can feel it. The air is everywhere. You can sometimes hear the noise it makes, for you hear the wind blow, and the wind is air.

Then God said, "Let the waters under the heaven be gathered together into one place, and let dry land appear," and it was so. The clouds are full of water, and sometimes it comes down, and we call it rain.

God made a large, deep place, and filled it with water, and this He called the sea. Ships and boats sail on the sea, and it is filled with fishes and whales and living things; but men cannot live in the sea.

So God made the dry land for us to walk upon, and for the trees and the grass and the flowers to grow upon, and the land is very beautiful. We could not walk upon the sea, nor build houses in it; but the ground is hard and firm and dry.

Now I have told you of five things that God made: 1, the Light; 2, the Air; 3, the Clouds; 4, the Sea; 5, the Dry Land.

Let us praise God for making such a large and beautiful world.

The Wonderful Things That God Made to Grow Out of the Ground.

When God made the dry land there was nothing on it; it was bare. So He spake, and immediately the whole earth was covered with many wonderful and beautiful things.

Trees came out of it; they were covered with green leaves of different shapes. Some were called oak trees, some elm trees, and some beech trees; and some trees bore nice fruit.

Vegetables grew upon and in the earth, such as beans, lettuce, potatoes, and the many other nice things that we cook and put on our tables to eat.

Corn came up out of the earth. Some corn is called wheat, and some barley, and some is called oats. The maize or Indian corn was not known until Columbus discovered America, but God made it the same time He made the other corn. The ears of corn bend down when they are ripe, and look yellow, like gold.

God made the soft, green grass to spring up, and flowers to grow among the grass—flowers of all colors and of the sweetest smell— the yellow buttercup, the white lily, the blue violet, and the queenly rose, the most beautiful of all flowers.

The world looked very beautiful when it was covered with grass and trees, and bright and lovely flowers; but only God and the angels saw its beauty, because there were no other living creatures at that time.

Afterward God placed the sun in the sky, and bade it shine all day. Then He made the moon to shine at night, and filled the sky with stars.

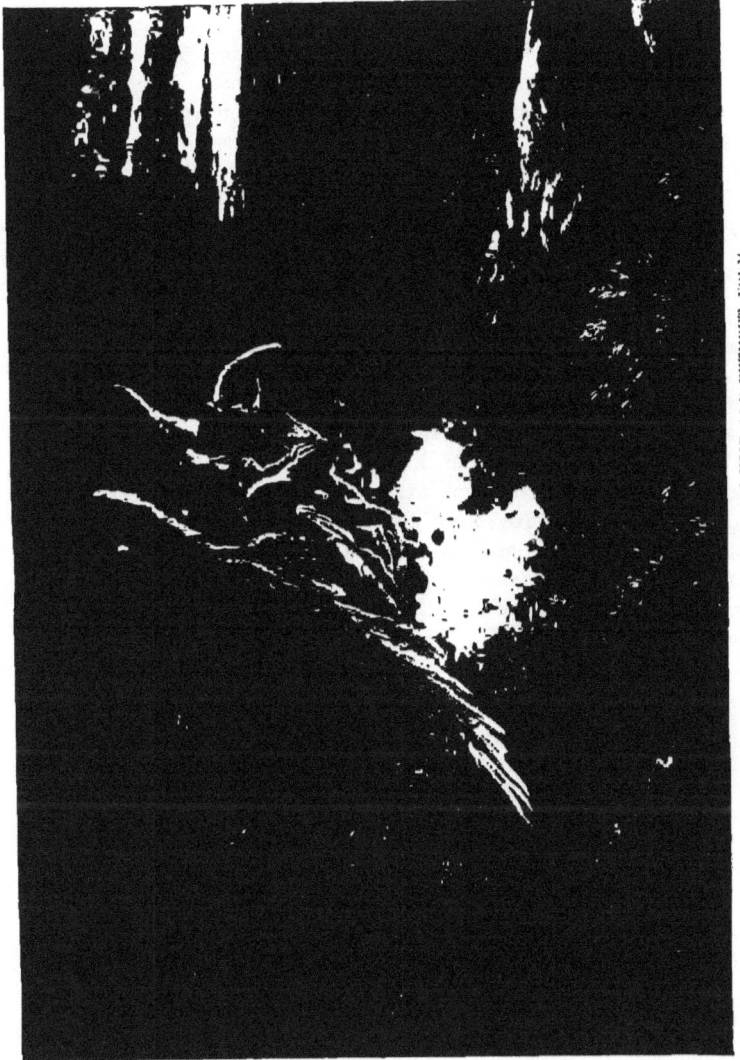

IN THE BEGINNING THE WORLD WAS VOID AND WITHOUT FORM.

You never saw anything as bright as the sun. It is very large, and is like a blazing ball of fire, but it looks small, because it is a great way off. It can never fall, for God holds it up.

The moon does not shine as brightly as the sun. It only shines by reflection from the light of the sun, so that if God should take the sun away we could not see the moon at all. God lets it be dark at night, that we may rest and sleep soundly.

Who could count the stars? No one but God. He alone knows their names and their number. Each star is a great round world like the one we live upon; and all of these mighty worlds go whirling and spinning night and day on the courses God has marked out for them. They rush through space faster than any bird can fly. There are many thousands of these bright and beautiful worlds, all whirling round and rushing forward on the paths that God has fixed for them; but they never come together or strike one another, because God keeps each one in its own path. It is said that as the worlds turn round and spin along on their courses they sing a glad song of praise to God, and this song is called the "music of the spheres," because each world is round like an orange or a sphere. When we look at the moon and stars let us think, "how great God is! Yet He cares for the little birds and loves little children."

The Wonderful Living Things That God Created.

Among all the wonderful and beautiful things God had made up to this time, none of them had life. At last He made living things. He spoke, and the water was filled with fishes, more than could be counted.

Some were very small, and some were very large. Have you heard of the great whale? It is a fish as long as a church. Fishes are cold and they have no feet, and they cannot sing or speak.

God made the birds, more beautiful than the fishes, to fly about in the air. They also perched upon the trees and sang among the branches, and the woods seemed alive with the music of their songs.

THE GIVING OF THE LAW.

Birds have wings, and are covered with feathers of many beautiful colors. The robin has a red breast, the goldfinch has some yellow feathers, and the jay some blue ones, but the peacock is the most brilliant of birds. It has a little tuft upon its head and a long train that sweeps behind; sometimes it spreads out its feathers, and they look like a large fan.

The thrush, the blackbird and the linnet can sing sweetly; but there is one bird that can sing more sweetly still—it is the nightingale.

Some birds swim upon the water, such as the duck and the beautiful swan, with its long neck and feathers, like the snow.

The eagle builds its nest in a very high place. Its wings are very strong, and it can fly as high as the clouds.

The gentlest of the birds is the dove. It cannot sing, but it sits alone and cooes softly, as if it were sad.

SOME OF THE BEASTS THAT GOD CREATED.

I cannot tell you the names of all the birds, but you can think of the names of some other kinds.

There are other sorts of living creatures, called insects. God made them come out of the earth, and not out of the water, like fishes. Insects are small and creep upon the earth, such as ants. Some insects can fly also, such as bees and butterflies. The bee sucks the juice of flowers, and makes wax and honey. How gay are the wings of the butterfly! They are covered with little feathers, too small to be seen. All the insects were good and pretty when God made them.

At last God made the beasts. He commanded the earth to bring them forth, and at once they were everywhere, in all parts of the world. They walked upon the land, and it was wonderful to see them all suited to the climate and the country where they lived. You know the names of a great many kinds of beasts. Sheep and cows, dogs and cats are beasts. But there are many others besides: the squirrel that jumps from bough to bough, the rabbit that lives in a hole under ground, and the goat that climbs the high hills; the stag, with its beautiful horns; the lion, with its yellow hair; the tiger, whose skin is marked with stripes. The elephant is the largest of the beasts, the lion is the strongest, the dog is the most sensible, the stag is the most beautiful, but the lamb is the gentlest. The dove is the gentlest of the birds, and the lamb is the gentlest of the beasts. Now God had filled the world with living creatures, and they were all good; even lions and tigers were quiet and harmless when they were first created. I have told you of four sorts of living creatures:

1. Fishes.
2. Birds.
3. Insects.
4. Beasts.

All these creatures have bodies, but they have not souls like you. They can move and breathe. God feeds them every day and keeps them alive. He is good to all His creatures.

The Story of Creation.

God had nothing to make the world of. He only spoke, and it was made.

Making things of nothing is called "creating." No one can create anything but God.

Do you know why God is called the Creator? It is because He created all things. There is only one Creator. Angels cannot create things, nor can men. They could not create one drop of water, or one little fly.

You know that God was six days in creating the world. I will tell you what He did on each day.

I.

On the first day God said, "Let there be light," and there was light.

II.

On the second day God spoke again, and created the waters which existed everywhere. Then He said, "Let there be a firmament

40 MY MOTHER'S BIBLE STORIES.

in the midst of the waters," and immediately the firmament appeared and divided the waters that were above from those that were below. He called the firmament heaven, and it remains to this day.

III.

On the third day God spoke, and the dry land appeared from under the water; and the water ran down into one deep place that God had prepared. God called the dry land Earth, and He called the water Seas. We walk upon the dry land. We cannot walk upon the sea. God spoke, and things grew out of the earth. Can you tell me what things grew out of the earth? Grass, and corn, and trees, and flowers.

IV.

On the fourth day God spoke, and the sun, and moon, and stars were made. God ordered the sun to come every morning, and to go away in the evening, because He did not choose that it should be always light. It is best that it should be dark at night, when we are asleep. But God lets the moon shine in the night, and the stars also; so that if we go out in the night, we have a little light. There are more stars than we can count.

V.

On the fifth day God began to make things that are alive. He spoke, and the water was filled with fishes, and birds flew in the air, and perched upon the trees.

VI.

On the sixth day God spoke, and the beasts came out of the earth: lions, sheep, cows, horses, and all kinds of beasts, came out of the earth, as well as all kinds of creeping things.

At last God made man. He said, "Let us make man in our likeness." So God made man's body of the dust, and then breathed the breath of life into his nostrils. The man had a soul as well as a body; and God called him Adam.

God put him in a very pretty garden, full of trees covered with fruit. This garden was called the Garden of Eden. God showed Adam all the beasts and birds, and let him give them what names he pleased. He said to Adam, "I give you all the fishes, and insects, and birds, and beasts; you are their master." So Adam was king over everything on the earth.

But he had no friend to be with him; for the beasts and birds could not talk to him.

Then God said He would make a woman to be a friend to Adam. So God made Adam fall fast asleep, and He took a piece of bone and flesh out of his side, and made it into a woman. When Adam awoke he saw her. He knew that she was made of his flesh and bone, and he loved her very much. Her name was "woman," and afterward she was called Eve.

ADAM AND EVE IN THE GARDEN OF EDEN.

When God had finished all His works, He saw they were very good. He was pleased with the things He had made. They were all very beautiful. The light was glorious; the air was sweet; the earth was lovely, clothed in green; the sun and moon shone brightly in the heavens; the birds, and beasts, and all the living creatures, were good and happy, and Adam and Eve were the best of all, for they could think of God and praise Him.

VII.

You know there are seven days in the week. Now, on the seventh day God did not make anything; but He rested from all His works. He called the seventh day His own day, because He rested on it. This is the reason people rest on the seventh day, and call it God's day. It is the Sabbath day. It is the day for praising God.

None of the creatures that God had made in the six days could praise him with their tongues, except Adam and Eve.

Angels in heaven can praise God, and men upon earth.

Angels always praise God with their hearts, and so should we.

Let us now count the things that God made on each day:—

First day, Light.
Second day, Air and Clouds.
Third day, Earth and Sea, and the things that grow.
Fourth day, Sun, Moon and Stars.
Fifth day, Fishes and Birds.
Sixth day, Beasts and Creeping Things, and Man.
Seventh day, Nothing. God rested.

The Story of How Adam and Eve Sinned.

You remember that God put Adam and Eve in a pretty garden. There they lived very happily. They never quarreled with each other; they were never sick nor in pain. Adam worked in the beautiful garden, but not so hard as to tire himself.

But there was one tree of which they were forbidden to eat the fruit. It was called "The tree of knowledge of good and evil."

God had said, that if Adam ate of it he should die. Adam and Eve might eat of all the other trees in the garden.

THE BEAUTIFUL HOME LOST THROUGH SIN. (43)

Do you not think that they had fruit enough without eating of the tree of knowledge of good and evil? They did not wish to eat of it, as God had told them not. They loved God. He was their friend, and used to walk and talk with them in the garden. Now you shall hear how Adam and Eve grew wicked

ADAM AND EVE DRIVEN FROM THE GARDEN OF EDEN.

You know that there are a great many wicked angels; one of them is called "Satan," and he is the prince of the wicked angels. Satan hated Adam and Eve, and wished to make them unhappy; so he thought, "I will try and persuade them to eat that fruit which God has told them not to eat." Then he disguised himself in the body of a serpent and came into the garden.

He saw Eve; he pretended to be kind, and said to her, "Hath God indeed said, you shall not eat of every tree in the garden?"

But she said, "God has told us not to eat of the fruit of the tree in the midst of the garden, and that if we do we shall die."

EVE AND HER TWO BOYS. (45)

46   MY MOTHER'S BIBLE STORIES.

But the serpent said, "No; you shall not die: but this fruit will make you wise like God."

The woman was afraid to eat; but she looked, and thought the fruit good; she looked again, and thought it beautiful; and she said to herself, "I should like to be wise." So she took the fruit and gave some to Adam.

Sad was that hour! no more happy days for Adam and Eve! They had grown naughty; they knew they had done wrong; they were afraid of God. Soon they heard His voice in the garden and they went and hid themselves among the thick trees.

But God saw them, for He can see everywhere.

So He called and said, "Adam, where art thou?" Then Adam and Eve came from under the trees. God said to Adam, "Have you eaten the fruit that I told you not to eat?" And Adam said, "It was this woman who asked me to eat the fruit."

CAIN SLAYS ABEL.

And God said to Eve, "What is this thou hast done?"

And Eve said, "The serpent deceived me and I did eat."

God was angry with them, but most of all with the serpent, and said he should be punished forever, and that he should always crawl upon the ground and eat dust.

And God said to Adam, "You shall work hard, and dig the ground: thorns and thistles shall grow: you shall have bread to eat; but you shall be obliged to work so hard that drops of sweat shall often stand upon your forehead: you shall be sad while you live, and at last you shall die: your body was made of dust, and it shall turn into dust again."

What great punishments these were! How sad Adam and Eve must have felt when they heard them! But this was not all; they were not allowed to stay in the pretty garden. God drove them out, and would not let them come into the garden again; so He placed an angel with a fiery sword to stand near it; yet God showed His pity by giving them clothes made of skins of beasts. They had tried to make clothes of the leaves of the trees, but God gave them better clothes.

It was not so pleasant outside of the garden. A great many weeds and thistles grew there, while in the garden were fruits and flowers.

Adam was forced to dig the ground till he was hot and tired, for he could not always find fruit on the trees.

The Sad Story of Cain and Abel.

After Adam and Eve were turned out of the garden they had two little children; their names were Cain and Abel.

They were obliged to work hard, like Adam their father. Cain dug the ground, and planted trees, and reaped corn. Abel took care of the sheep; he was a shepherd.

Now I will tell you how Cain and Abel behaved toward God.

God did not walk and talk with people then, as he had done in the garden; but He did speak sometimes, and He allowed people to pray to Him.

He told them to heap up stones (this heap was called an altar), and then to put some wood on the altar; then to take a lamb, or a kid, and to bind it with a rope to the altar; then to take a knife, and to kill the lamb; and then to burn it on the altar. Doing this was called "offering a sacrifice," and God commanded this because of the sin of Adam and Eve in eating the forbidden fruit.

Abel brought lambs and offered them up to God; and he thought of God's promise, so God was pleased with Abel, and with his sacrifice But Cain did not obey God, he brought some fruit instead of a lamb; and God was angry with Cain, and did not like his sacrifice.

Then Cain was very angry and hated Abel, because he was envious of him.

Then God spoke to Cain and said, "Why are you angry? If you will love and serve Me, I shall be pleased with you; but if not, you shall be punished."

Still Cain went on in wickedness. Now, hear what he did at last. One day he was talking with Abel in a field, when he rose up and killed him.

Abel's blood was spilt upon the ground, and he was the first man that ever died. So Cain began by hating Abel, and ended by killing him, though he was his brother.

Soon Cain heard the voice of God calling him. God said, "Where is your brother Abel?"

"I know not," answered wicked Cain; "am I my brother's keeper?"

But God said, "I have seen your brother's blood upon the ground; and you are cursed. A fugitive and a vagabond shalt thou be on the earth."

Then Cain said unto God, "My punishment is greater than I can bear! Oh, let me not be killed!"

God said, "You shall not be killed, but you shall go to a place far off."

So Cain went and lived a great way off, and built houses for himself and his children.

MY MOTHER'S BIBLE STORIES. 49

So Adam and Eve lost both their sons; for Cain went a great way off, and Abel died.

But God had pity on Adam and Eve, and gave them another son, who was made good by God's Spirit; he was called Seth.

Story of Enoch, the Good Man, Who Did Not Die.

The children of Seth feared God; and God loved them, and called them His children.

Seth had a son, and he had a son, and he had a son, and so on—till at last Noah was born.

How many fathers and sons—one after another—came between Adam and Noah?

There were ten.

Adam was the first father in this line, and Noah was the last son.

All their names are written in Genesis V.

Here is a list of these ten. They all lived to be very, very old. No one lives now as long as they did.

	Years he lived.
Adam,	930
Seth,	912
Enos,	905
Cainan,	910
Ma-ha-la-le-el,	895
Jared,	962
Enoch,	365
Me-thu-se-lah,	969
Lamech,	777
Noah,	950

Of all these, who lived the longest?
Look and see.
Methuselah.

If he had lived only thirty-one years more he would have been a thousand.

Lamech and Noah were both prophets. When Noah was a baby, Lamech prophesied that he would be a comfort, and called him Noah, which means "Rest;" and Noah was indeed a "REST," or comfort, for through him the Saviour was born at last.

Who lived the shortest time on the earth of any of the ten?

It was Enoch, the seventh from Adam. The life of Enoch was very holy. He walked with God. This means that his heart was with God wherever he went and whatever he did. It was just as if he had been walking beside God, with his hand in His, listening to what God said and trying to please Him and obey Him.

Observe, it is said of all the ten but one, "He died." But this is not said of Enoch. It is said of him, "He was not, for God took him." He took him up to heaven without dying.

Story of the Great Flood that Covered the Whole Earth.

Cain had a great many children; and so had Seth.

At last Adam and Eve died, and Cain died, and Seth died; but still there were a great many people in the world, and they became very wicked.

God was very angry with the wicked people, and He determined to punish them.

God said to Noah, "I shall make it rain so much that all people shall be drowned, except you, and your wife, and your children." Then God told Noah to make a great ark. An ark is like a boat or a ship. Noah made a very great ark, which would float upon the top of the water when God should drown the wicked people.

Noah made the ark of wood. He cut down many trees, and cut boards, and fastened them together. He made one door in the ark, and one little window at the top.

Noah told the people that God was going to drown the world, and advised them to leave off their wickedness.

But they would not mind. Still they went on eating and drinking, and not thinking of God nor trying to please Him.

God did not choose that all the beasts, and birds, and insects should be drowned; so He desired Noah to get some birds of every sort, and some beasts of every sort, and some insects of every sort, and to bring them into the ark.

All these went into the ark; for God made them gentle and obedient. Then Noah himself went in, with his wife, his three sons and their wives. This made eight people in the ark, and they alone were saved from the flood. But Noah did not shut the door: God shut the door, and Noah knew that he must not open it till God bid him.

Then it began to rain. It rained all day and all night. What did the wicked people think now? How they must have wished that they had minded Noah! If they climbed trees, the water soon reached to the tops; if they went up high mountains, as high as the clouds, the water rose as high as they: for it rained forty days and forty nights. All beasts, and birds, and men, and children died, except those that were in the ark.

GOING INTO THE ARK.

At last nothing was to be seen but water, and the ark floating

52 MY MOTHER'S BIBLE STORIES.

upon the top of the water. Noah and his family lived in the ark almost a year.

A long while after it had left off raining, Noah wished to know whether the waters had dried up. He went among his birds, and chose a raven and let it out of the window. A raven is a fierce bird. It did not like the ark, and though there were no trees to be seen, nothing but water, yet the raven would not go back to Noah, but went on flying night and day over the water.

When Noah saw that the raven did not come back, he went again among his birds, and chose a dove. The dove is a very gentle bird. Noah put it out at the window; and when it saw nothing but water, the dove came back to the ark. Noah knew when his bird had come back (perhaps it pecked at the window), and he put out his hand and pulled it in. Noah waited seven days, then he sent the dove out again; and this time it saw some trees: yet it did not

THE FLOOD.

stay, but plucked off a leaf with its beak and came back to Noah. Noah must have loved this good little dove.

He waited seven days more, and then he sent out the dove again, and this time it did not come back. Now Noah knew that the earth was dry, but he waited in the ark till God told him to go out.

At last God said, "Go out of the ark, you and your wife, your three sons, and their three wives, and the birds, and the beasts, and all the creeping things."

When the door was opened the beasts came out. How glad the sheep must have been to lie down again upon the soft grass, and the goats to climb the high hills!

Noah saw the green hills and fields again; but where were all the wicked people? He would never more

NOAH'S SACRIFICE, AND THE RAINBOW.

see their faces. Noah remembered God's goodness in saving him from being drowned. He made a heap of stones for an altar, and took some beasts and birds, and offered a sacrifice to God. God was pleased with this sacrifice. Then God made a very kind promise to Noah. He said, "I will never drown the world again. When it rains do not think there will be a flood. Look up in the sky after the rain, and you will see a bow. That shall be the sign that I remember my promise."

Nimrod the Mighty Hunter, and the Building of the Tower of Babel.

Noah had three sons, whose names were Shem, Ham and Japheth. After the flood, they had many children, and the earth became full of people again. But these people were no better than those before the flood, who had been drowned.

The most famous man in those times was Nimrod. He was the grandson of Ham, the wicked son of Noah. Nimrod was a very brave, strong and clever man. His delight was hunting wild beasts. Many men followed Nimrod in his hunting, and they called him, "The mighty hunter before the Lord."

HAM DERIDING HIS FATHER.

Though they said this, Nimrod was a great enemy of the Lord.

These hunters went about the earth far and wide. At last they came to a great plain, very flat and wide, near the great river Euphrates.

The plain was called the land of Shinar. There this multitude of men settled themselves to dwell. No doubt it was a fruitful, pleasant and shady place, or they would not have chosen it for their dwelling-place.

Of course they must at first have lived in tents on the plain. But they soon wished to build houses. They found no stones there; but they knew how to make bricks of the clay under their feet. They said to one another, "Let us make bricks, and burn them well." They dug up the clay, made them in the shape of bricks, and then piling them together, made a fire in the midst.

BUILDING THE TOWER OF BABEL.

There was a sticky substance on the ground called slime, or bitumen, and this served instead of mortar to join the bricks together.

The builders set about very diligently to build their houses. But all the time they had a very wicked thought in their hearts; it was a proud and rebellious thought. They wished to build a great city, and live altogether in that place. They hoped that they should be counted very great, and that all people would be afraid of them. To make their city look terrible, they meant to build a very high tower, that might seem to reach into the clouds.

But the Lord had determined that they should be scattered abroad, and what the Lord determines must be done.

He knew that it would be a bad thing for so many wicked people to live together, and to help each other in doing wickedness.

God's plan for stopping the building of the city was by making the men forget their own language, and speak different words which the others could not understand. On this account they could not help each other in their work. The Lord had put confusion in their minds, and then all was confusion and disorder in their doings. They were obliged to leave off building the city. But they had already built some of it, and that part they called "Confusion," or "Babel."

They went different ways, and settled in different countries.

Thus the Lord scattered them abroad upon the face of all the earth.

This city of Babel was afterward called Babylon, and became a very wicked city. It is believed that the tower was called the temple of Belus, or Baal; and that Baal was worshiped there.

It was a long while before this city became very great. At last it became the greatest city in the world, and the most wicked.

But where is Babylon now? It is utterly destroyed.

Where Babel was built, there is nothing but a heap of rubbish; and where wicked men dwelt, there is now nothing but owls and ravens, and the wild beasts of the desert.

Turn to Isa. xiv. 23, 24, and read God's sentence upon Babylon.

The Beautiful Story of Abraham.

Noah's sons had many children, and they had many children, and at last there were a great many people in the world.

Most of the people in the world worshiped idols instead of the true God. Sometimes the idols were made of wood, sometimes of stone, or silver, or gold.

Then God said, "I will choose one man, and teach him to love Me, and to be My servant." Now there was a man called Abraham. His father and his friends worshiped idols. God said to Abraham, "Leave your home and your friends, and go to a country which I will show you, and I will bless you and take care of you."

Abraham did not know where God would tell him to go, yet he went because God told him to go. Abraham was obedient.

Abraham lived in a tent, moving from place to place; for he had to travel a great many miles over high hills and wide rivers. At last he came to a beautiful country, full of trees and flowers, and grass and corn. This was the place that God chose Abraham should live in. It was the country called Canaan.

ABRAHAM BUILDING AN ALTAR TO GOD.

Abraham still lived in a tent. Sometimes he made a heap of stones, called an altar, and offered sacrifices of beasts to God. He never worshiped idols; but all the people in Canaan did.

God often spoke to Abraham, and said, "I will bless you, and take care of you, and no one shall hurt you." God was pleased that Abraham had left his own home when He told him; and God called him His friend.

Abraham had a nephew, named Lot, who went to live in Sodom. This Sodom was a very wicked city, and God determined to destroy it for its wickedness. One evening He sent two angels to warn Lot to flee from that city before it was burned. They even took him by the hand and hurried him away, as also Lot's wife and daughters. When they led them out of the city, they pointed to a mountain and said, "Escape for thy life; look not back." But Lot's wife did look back, and God punished her disobedience by turning her into a pillar of salt. Sodom, and three other cities of the plain, were destroyed by fire from heaven.

Abraham Receives a Promise from God and Entertains Three Angels.

Abraham's wife was named Sarah, and they lived in a tent in the land of Canaan. They had no little child. Abraham was a very old man, and Sarah was a very old woman. Abraham was almost one hundred years old, and Sarah was nearly ninety.

One night God said to Abraham, "Come out of your tent, and look up at the sky. What do you see?"

The sky was full of stars, more than could be counted. And God said, "You shall have a great many grandchildren, and great-grandchildren, and they shall have more children, and they shall have more children, till there are as many children as there are stars in the sky; and they shall live in the land of Canaan, and the wicked people shall be turned out of it."

Now Abraham had not even *one* little child; yet he believed that God would do as He had promised. It was very right of Abraham to believe all that God said: for God always speaks the truth and keeps His word.

One day Abraham was sitting in his tent. It was about twelve o'clock in the day, and it was very hot indeed; but the tent was under a tree. Abraham looked up, and he saw three men a little way off. He ran to meet them, and bowed down, and said to one of the men, "My lord, pray come and rest yourself, and let me bring a little water to wash your feet, and a little bread for you to eat, and then you can go on your journey." And the men said that they would rest themselves. Who

LOT'S WIFE TURNED INTO A PILLAR OF SALT.

do you think these men were? They were angels, though they looked like men. They had come from heaven with a message from God to Abraham. Angels are often near us though we cannot see them.

The angels sat outside the tent, under the shade of the tree. Sarah was in the tent. Abraham said to Sarah, "Take some flour, and make some cakes, and bake them very quickly." Then Abraham ran to his cattle, and took a fat calf, and said to one of his servants, "Kill it, and roast it quickly."

When it was ready, Abraham brought some butter, and some milk, and the cakes, and the calf, and spread the dinner under the tree. The three men began to eat, and Abraham stood by them.

While they were eating, they said to Abraham, "Where is Sarah, your wife?" And Abraham said, "She is in the tent." Then one of the men said, "Sarah shall have a son."

Sarah heard what the angel said, and she could not believe that she would *really* have a child now she was so very old: so she laughed to herself.

Do you think that God remembered His promise? The next year Sarah had a son. His name was Isaac. He was a good child, and God loved him. Abraham and Sarah were much pleased with their little son.

Abraham is Commanded to Sacrifice Isaac.

Isaac grew up to be a fine lad. He lived in a tent, as his father and mother did.

They all three loved God, and loved each other very much. It was a happy little family.

Now you know that Abraham had a great many things. He had cows and asses, sheep and goats, tents and servants, silver and gold. But he had one thing that he loved more than any of these. What was that? His son, his dear son, Isaac. He loved him more than everything else that he had.

Yet there was one person whom Abraham loved better, even better still, and that was God. Why ought Abraham to love God better than all? Because God had given him all he had.

At last, God said He would try Abraham, to see whether he loved Him more than anything in the world; more even than he

SARAH, ABRAHAM'S WIFE.

loved his son Isaac. You have heard how Abraham used to burn lambs upon altars. Now God said to Abraham, "Take your dear son Isaac, and offer him up on an altar in a place that I will show you."

Was not this a very hard thing for Abraham to do? But Abraham wished to do all God told him; because he loved God so much. So Abraham cut down some wood to burn; he put the wood upon an ass, and he told two of his servants and Isaac to come with him. He left Sarah in the tent at home. They all four walked on for three days; at last they saw a high hill a great way off. Abraham knew that was the place where he was to build the altar. So he said to his servants, "Stay down here with the ass, while I and the lad go and worship God on the top of the hill." He took the wood off the ass, and bound it round Isaac with a rope. Then he took some fire in one of his hands, and a knife in the other, and Abraham and Isaac walked up the hill together.

THE ANGEL APPEARING TO ABRAHAM.

Isaac did not know that his father was going to offer him as a sacrifice; he thought that his father would offer a lamb. So he said, "Father," and Abraham answered, "Here am I, my son." And Isaac said, "Here is fire, and wood; but where is the lamb?" "My son," said Abraham, "God will find a lamb;" but Abraham did not tell Isaac that he was to be the lamb.

At last they came to the top of the hill. Then Abraham took stones, and built an altar; and he took the wood off Isaac's back, and laid it on the altar. Now the time was come when Isaac must know who was to be the lamb. The rope that had bound the wood was fastened round his hands and feet, and he was laid upon the wood like a lamb.

Then Abraham took the knife, and lifted up his hand to kill Isaac; when he heard a voice calling, "Abraham, Abraham!" It was an angel speaking from heaven. The angel said, "Do not kill your son, nor hurt him at all; for now God knows that you love Him, because you have given Him your only son."

How glad was Abraham to untie the rope that bound Isaac, and to find that he need not sacrifice him!

Abraham saw a ram caught in the bushes by the horns; and he went and took it, and offered it up as a sacrifice instead of Isaac.

Abraham thanked God very much for having given him back his son, and the angel called to him out of heaven again and said, "God is much pleased with you, and He will bless you, and all your children, and grandchildren, and their children, and one of your children's children shall make all people happy."

Whom did the angel mean? He meant that Jesus would one day be a child, and make people happy and take them to heaven.

When the angel had done speaking, Abraham and Isaac went down the hill together; there was no wood now on Isaac's back.

They found the servants where they had left them with the ass; then they all went back together to Sarah.

The Story of Isaac and Rebekah.

Abraham and Sarah were now very old. At last Sarah died, and Abraham wished to bury her, but he had not a piece of ground in Canaan to bury her in; so he gave some of his silver to the people of Canaan and bought a field. The field was full of trees, and there was a cave in it. Abraham took the dead body of Sarah and put it in the cave. At last Abraham died, and Isaac his son buried him in the same cave where Sarah lay.

But before his death, Abraham sent his servant to the city of Nahor, to look for a wife for his son; for he wanted Isaac to get a wife from his own country and kindred. So this servant went on his errand, taking with him ten camels. It was evening when he reached Nahor, and he stopped near a well, outside the city walls. Many young women were just then coming to draw water from this well.

REBEKAH GIVES ABRAHAM'S SERVANT WATER TO DRINK.

Then Abraham's servant prayed that God would show him which one was to be Isaac's wife; and he prayed that it might be the one who was willing to give him a drink and also to water his camels. Even while he prayed, a beautiful young woman, named Rebekah, came to the well. When the man asked her, she freely gave him a drink from her pitcher, and she also watered his camels. He knew then that the Lord had sent her. So Rebekah became Isaac's wife, and lived in the tent where Sarah used to live.

Isaac and Rebekah had two sons. They were called Esau and Jacob. They were twins; but they were quite different from each other. Their faces were unlike, and their hearts were unlike. Esau was wicked from a child; but Jacob was good, and loved God.

HAGAR DRIVEN FROM HOME.

When Esau was a man he became a hunter. He had a bow and arrows; and he would go into the woods and shoot birds and stags; he used to bring them home and dress them for dinner; and he gave some of the nice meat to his father Isaac. It was not wrong in Esau to hunt, and to cook the meat; but his heart was wicked: he did not care for God; and he loved meat and drink more than God.

ESAU SELLS HIS BIRTH-RIGHT.

Jacob was a shepherd; he stayed at home near his tent with his father and mother, and his sheep and goats. He loved God, and prayed very often.

Isaac loved Esau better than he did Jacob, because he was sorry for his wickedness and wanted him to repent and be a good boy.

But Rebekah loved Jacob, and God loved him; but God did not love Esau. Do you think that Esau and Jacob loved one another?

They did not; Jacob sometimes behaved unkindly to Esau; and so Esau hated Jacob and wished to kill him. One day Esau said, "My father will soon die, and then I will kill my brother Jacob." Rebekah heard that Esau meant to kill Jacob some day, so she was frightened, and called Jacob and said to him, "Your brother Esau means to kill you.

This is what you must do: go to your uncle, who lives a great way off, and stay with him. Soon Esau will leave off being angry: then I will send for you to come home."

Jacob's Wonderful Dream.

Jacob did as his mother advised. He took leave of his father Isaac, and Isaac blessed him before he went. Jacob did not ask his father to give him anything. He took no servant with him, no sheep, nor goats—not even an ass to ride upon. He took only a stick in his hand, and he set out upon his journey. Jacob felt very sad. He was a poor stranger, and he was going to a far country which he had never seen.

He had no tent nor house to sleep in by the way; so when night came he took some stones for a pillow, and lay down to sleep on the ground. There were bears and wolves in that country; but God took care of him. God knew how sad he was; and He made him dream the sweetest dream that you ever heard.

In his sleep, Jacob saw a great many steps reaching up to the sky, and on the steps beautiful angels; some going up, and some coming down; and at the top he saw God Himself. Then Jacob heard a voice, and God spake to him and said, "I am the God of Abraham and of Isaac, and I will take care of you wherever you go; and I will bring you home again; and your children shall live in this land of Canaan, where you are sleeping."

Then Jacob awaked out of his sleep, and now his heart was glad: he knew that God and His angels were watching over him. He wished never to forget the place where he had dreamed this sweet dream; so he took the stones which had been his pillow and made them into a heap. "Now," he thought, "I shall be able to find the place when God lets me come back to Canaan, as He has promised." He could not offer a sacrifice upon the stones, because he had no lambs, but he poured some oil upon them, and he prayed to the Lord, and said, "Since God will take care of me, and give

68   MY MOTHER'S BIBLE STORIES.

me bread to eat, and clothes to wear, and bring me home again, He shall be my God, and this stone shall be God's house."

Jacob felt sure that God would take care of him, and bring

ISAAC BLESSES JACOB.

him home again, because He had promised that He would. God takes care of you and all good little children. He sends His angels down from heaven to watch over you, as they did over Jacob.

Jacob's Love for Rachel.

Then Jacob went on his journey. He traveled for a great many days; at last he came to a place where there was a great deal of grass. In that place there was a well, and a great stone upon the top of the well. Many sheep were round the well; and some men were with the sheep. These men were shepherds. There was very little water in that country, and Jacob was glad to see a well and plenty of good, cool water.

He said to the shepherds, "Do you know a man called Laban?" — (That was the name of Jacob's uncle.)

"Yes," said they, "we do."

Then Jacob said, "Is he well?"

The shepherds answered, "He is well; and here is his daughter Rachel coming with the sheep."

RACHEL AT THE WELL.

Jacob was very glad to hear this, for Rachel was Jacob's cousin. He ran to her and kissed her, and he sobbed and wept for joy.

70   MY MOTHER'S BIBLE STORIES.

People sometimes cry for joy. Jacob had not seen a friend for a long while, and he was glad to see his beautiful cousin. Rachel did not know who Jacob was till he said, "I am your cousin, and have come from a great way off."

Then Rachel ran, and said to her father Laban, "My cousin Jacob has come: I found him sitting by a well."

Then Laban was glad, and ran out to meet Jacob, and kissed him and said, "You must come to my house: I am your uncle." Jacob told Laban that he would take care of his sheep: and so Jacob was Laban's servant. Jacob was a good shepherd, and sat up to guard the sheep at night from lions and bears. He cared not for the heat by day nor the cold by night.

JACOB ARRIVES AT THE HOUSE OF LABAN.

Laban had another daughter named Leah, and he gave both Leah and Rachel to Jacob to be his wives. So Jacob had two wives. No one may have two wives now, but then it was permitted. God gave Jacob a great many little children. I will not tell you their names because they were so many. Jacob lived a long while in tents with his wives and his little children. At first he took care of Laban's sheep only. At last Laban gave Jacob some sheep and goats of his own. Jacob had plenty of bread to eat and raiment to wear, as God had promised; for God always keeps His promises.

But Jacob could not forget his father and mother, and Canaan, where he had lived when he was a little boy. He knew that God had promised to give the land of Canaan to Abraham's children, and Isaac's children, and to his own children; and he wished to live there again.

I will now write down the names of the good men who first lived in Canaan, and I will write down the names of their wives.

Abraham,——Sarah.
|
Isaac,——Rebekah.
|
Jacob,——Leah and Rachel.

The Wonderful Story of Joseph.

Jacob saw his old father Isaac again: and then Isaac died, and Jacob and Esau buried him in that same cave where Abraham and Sarah had been buried. They will all rise together at the last day: for Isaac wished to live in the country that is better than Canaan; that is, in heaven.

Esau did not live in the land of Canaan; but Jacob chose to live there with his children and his cattle.

All the sons were grown up to be men when Benjamin was still a baby. Joseph was next youngest to Benjamin. He was a big boy, and he was the best of all the children.

Jacob gave a beautiful present to this dear son. It was a very pretty coat made of many colors,—yellow, blue, green, pink, red, purple; and Joseph used to wear it. The brothers were very envious when they saw this coat.

72   MY MOTHER'S BIBLE STORIES.

One night Joseph had a strange dream. He thought he was in a field of corn with all his brothers, and that they were making up large bundles of corn called sheaves. He thought that each of his brothers made a sheaf, and that all his brothers' sheaves bowed down to his sheaf. Joseph thought this a very strange dream, and he told it to his brothers.

MEETING OF ESAU AND JACOB.

But when they heard it they were very angry and said, "We suppose you mean that we shall bow down to you, though you are younger than we are!" And so they hated him more than they had done before.

Soon after Joseph had another strange dream. He thought he saw the sun, moon and eleven stars in the sky, and that they bowed down to him.

This dream was more strange than the other; and he told it to his father, as well as to his brothers. His father was surprised, and said, "Does the sun mean me, and the moon your mother, and the stars your brothers, and we shall bow down to

JACOB'S WONDERFUL DREAM.

you?" Yet Jacob thought that God had sent the dream to Joseph, and would make it come true; but the brothers were more and more angry.

Now Joseph's brethren had a great many sheep and goats to take care of, and there was not enough grass for them all near the tents, so they took their flocks a great way off, that they might eat fresh grass. Joseph stayed at home with his old father; and Benjamin stayed at home, because he was quite a little child.

At last Jacob wished to know how his sons were; so he said to Joseph, "Go and see your brothers, and come back and tell me how they are, and how the flocks are."

Joseph was always ready to do what his father wished; so he set out on his way. He took no ass to ride upon, and no servant; but putting on his pretty coat, he wished his dear father good-bye. He little thought how long it would be before he should again see that dear father's face.

Joseph went a great way, but could not find his brothers. At last a man saw him, and said, "Whom seek you?"

And Joseph answered, "I seek my brethren. Can you tell me where they are feeding their flocks?"

Then the man told him which way they had gone.

Joseph took a great deal of pains to find his brothers.

Now the brothers saw Joseph coming when he was very far off. They knew that it was Joseph; and they said to each other, "Here this dreamer comes: let us kill him and throw him into a deep hole, and tell our father that a lion or a bear has eaten him up!"

The brothers were going to kill him, but one of them, named Reuben, said, "Do not kill him, but only throw him into a pit." This brother was a little kinder than the rest, and meant to take him out of the pit and bring him back to Jacob. The brothers agreed not to kill him. But first they took off his pretty coat.

They threw him into the deep, dark pit; and there he lay, hungry and thirsty and weary—without one drop of water to quench his thirst. How it must have grieved Joseph to think that he should not return to his dear father, and that his father perhaps would think he was dead.

JOSEPH SOLD BY HIS BROTHERS.

(75)

The wicked brothers cared not for his groans, but they sat down and began to eat their dinner.

God saw them from His throne in heaven, and was much displeased.

Joseph's Brothers Sell Him as a Slave.

While the brothers were eating their dinner they looked up and saw some people coming along. As the people came nearer they saw camels, and men riding on them. I will tell you who these men were.

They lived in a country a great way off, and they had been to some hills, where very sweet things grew, called spice and balm. They were going to carry them to a country a great way off, and sell them for money.

This was their way of getting their living, and it was a good way; yet they were wicked men, as you will see.

One of the brothers, called Judah, said, "Let us sell Joseph to these men: for it would be better to sell him than to kill him: we shall get some money if we sell him: and it would be very cruel to kill Joseph, as he is our brother."

Yet, was it not very cruel to sell Joseph? This brother was not really kind. The other brothers said that they thought it was a good plan to sell Joseph. So they called to the men, and asked them if they would buy a young boy.

And the men said, "Yes."

"How much will you give us for him?" said the brothers.

"We will give you twenty pieces of silver," said the men.

Then Joseph's brothers pulled him out of the pit. Perhaps he thought they were going to let him return to his father.

Ah! poor Joseph! He soon found that his brothers were not going to be kind. The men and the camels were waiting outside the pit. The men paid the money to the brothers, and then they took Joseph and carried him away with them.

MERCHANTS TRAVELING IN PALESTINE.

When he was gone the brothers said, "What shall we tell our father when he asks us where Joseph is?—we will not say we have seen Joseph, but we will say we have found his coat on the ground!"

Then the brothers killed one of their young goats, and dipped the pretty coat in the blood. "We will show our father this bloody coat," said they. So they carried the coat home, all covered with blood; and they took the money also for which they had sold Joseph.

Old Jacob had been thinking of his sons while they were gone. How glad he must have been when he heard the bleating of their sheep, and knew they had come home! He must have looked to see whether Joseph was with them. But no—his sons came up to him. In their hands they held the bloody coat. They showed it to Jacob, and said, "We have found this—do you think it is your son's coat, or not?"

Jacob knew that coat, and said, "It is my son's coat: a lion or a bear has torn Joseph to pieces, and has eaten him up!"

How Jacob wept for his darling child! How sorry he was that he had sent him alone to seek his brothers! The wicked brothers tried to comfort Jacob, and said, "Do not weep so much;" but Jacob would not hear.

"No; I shall die: and then I shall be with Joseph: for I never shall be happy any more!"

How sad it was to see this poor old man, leaning on his stick, his gray hair, and his face full of sadness, while he thought that his dear boy was eaten up by the lions or the bears! His little Benjamin was a comfort to him. Jacob would never let him go away, nor would he trust him with his brothers, though he did not know how wicked they had been. These brothers first had envied Joseph, then they had sold him, and then they had told a lie to hide their sin.

Children sometimes try to hide their faults by telling lies, and so they make God more angry than He was before. My dear children, remember that God always sees you: and that He hates liars, and will not let them live with Him in glory.

MY MOTHER'S BIBLE STORIES.   79

The Strange Things That Happened to Joseph in Egypt.

The men who had bought Joseph took him to a country a great way off. It was called Egypt. When they got to Egypt they tried to sell him, as if he had been a horse or a cow. In this country, where we live, no one sells men. In some countries men are sold, and are called slaves: they are beaten and made to work very hard, but are not paid any money for their labor.

Poor Joseph was sold as a slave. Do you not hope that a kind man bought him? And it was a kind man who bought him. There was a very rich man who knew the king, and he bought Joseph to be his slave. His name was Potiphar. He took Joseph home

THE WICKED BROTHERS SELL JOSEPH.

with him, and Joseph had not very hard work to do. He tried to be a good servant. Though he wished very much to be with his father, he did not waste his time in fretting, but took great pains to please his master. When he was told to do anything, he did it so well that his master was quite pleased with him. It was God that made Joseph able to do his work so well; and Joseph's master knew that it was God that helped him to do things well. I suppose that Joseph had told him; for his master did not know the true God, but worshiped idols.

So Joseph had the care of everything, and all the other servants minded what he said: and he might do what he liked when his master was out. But Joseph behaved the same as if his master were watching him; for he knew the eye of God was always upon him. There are many children who behave ill as soon as their parents go out of the room; such children do not fear God.

So Joseph had now all he could wish for: but he could not forget his father, and his little baby-brother Benjamin. As for his mother, Rachel, she had died some time before.

Now you shall hear what a sad thing happened to Joseph.

Potiphar had a very wicked wife. She wished Joseph to be turned out of the house, for Joseph had found out how bad she was; so she did not like to see Joseph.

This wicked woman said to Potiphar, "Your slave, Joseph, that you think so good, is very wicked, and when you are out he behaves very ill." Then she told Potiphar of bad things that she said Joseph had done.

Potiphar was so foolish as to believe her, and he fell into a great rage and said, "Joseph shall be put into prison."

So some men took Joseph and brought him to the prison, which was in Potiphar's house.

A prison is a dark place with very little windows, and bars of iron before the windows, and gates and bolts.

Joseph was put into prison; and his feet were hurt by great iron chains, which were fastened round them.

There were a great many men in the prison, and most of them had done very bad things, but Joseph had done nothing wrong. God still loved Joseph, and He could make him happy even in a prison.

There was a man who kept the keys, and took care of the prisoners: he was called the keeper of the prison. Sometimes keepers are very unkind, but God put it into the keeper's heart to love Joseph.

At last the keeper took the chains off Joseph's feet, and allowed him to walk about the prison, and take care of the prisoners. The keeper found that he could trust him, and that Joseph managed

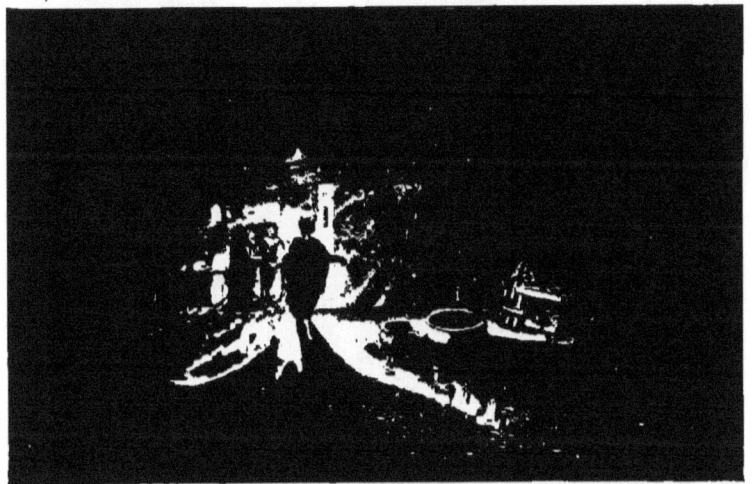

A PRISON IN EGYPT.

And Joseph's master took him, and put him into the prison, a place where the king's prisoners were bound: and he was there in the prison.—GENESIS xxxix: 20.

things well. It was God who made Joseph do everything so well; for God was Joseph's friend, and was always watching over him to comfort him.

Joseph hoped that God would some day let him get out of prison.

The Butler and the Baker.

The prison, you remember, was in the house of Potiphar. One day Potiphar brought two men to Joseph, and said to him, "Take great care that these men do not get out of prison. I give them under your charge." So you see Potiphar thought Joseph could be trusted; perhaps he had found out that Joseph was not so bad as he had once thought,—still he did not let Joseph out of prison.

Pharaoh's butler and the baker had both offended the king; I do not know how, but they had made the king so angry that he had said they should be shut up in prison.

So the king said to Potiphar, the great captain, "Put these men into prison."

Then Potiphar brought them to Joseph, and told him to keep them safe. Joseph shut them up in a room together, and gave them bread and water every day, and took great care of them.

One morning, when Joseph came to see them, he observed that they looked very sad indeed. So Joseph said to them, "Why do you look so very sad?"

Then they answered, "We have each had a very strange dream to-night, and we think our dreams have some meaning, but we cannot find it out; and there is nobody in the prison who can tell us."

Then Joseph said, "But my God knows all things: He could tell me the meaning. Only tell me your dreams."

The butler told his dream first. He said, "I thought I saw a tree such as grapes grow upon—a vine. It had three branches, but no grapes. While I was looking, I saw little buds, and they turned into grapes, and they grew ripe. I picked the grapes, and squeezed them into a cup, and made wine, and then brought the cup to the king for him to drink, as I used to do."

This was the butler's dream, and God told Joseph the meaning of it.

"You saw three branches," said Joseph; "something will happen to you in three days. The king will send for you to be his butler again."

When the baker heard this pleasant meaning he thought that his dream would be pleasant too; so he began to tell it. The baker said, "I dreamt that I was carrying three white baskets on my head, the one on the top of the other. In the baskets there was baked food, and birds came and picked the food out of the top basket."

The baker thought that Joseph would say, " In three days you shall be baker again to the king." But this dream had a sad meaning.

"Something will happen to you in three days," said Joseph. "The king will send for you, and will hang you upon a tree, and the birds will pick your flesh off your bones."

So, while the butler was pleased with what Joseph had told him, the poor baker was very sorry, because he knew that he must die.

In three days the king sent some men to the prison to fetch the butler and the baker. It was the king's birthday, and he had made a feast for his servants, and he had thought of the butler and baker, and had said, " Let the butler come back to me; and let the baker be hanged; I will not forgive him." So now both the butler and the baker knew that Joseph had told them the truth.

But the butler forgot Joseph when he was restored to his place in the king's house. I suppose he was thinking of the fine things he saw, of eating and drinking, of money and fine clothes, and forgot that poor Joseph was in a prison. The butler was unkind, and worse than unkind—he was ungrateful. Joseph had been kind to him, yet he was not kind in return; therefore I call him ungrateful.

Poor Joseph waited in vain. No one came to let him out of prison. One day passed, then another; summer came, and then winter: but Joseph was still a prisoner. Yet God had not forgotten him. Why did God make him wait so long? That he might learn to be patient.

The Wonderful Story of How Joseph Was Released from Prison and Became a Great Ruler.

I have told you of the great king of Egypt. He was the king of the country where Joseph was. His name was Pharaoh. He had a great many servants, as I told you. He sat upon a throne, wore beautiful clothes, a chain of gold round his neck, a ring upon his hand, and a crown of gold upon his head. One night this great king had two very strange dreams. I will tell you what they were.

He thought he was standing by a river, and that seven fat cows came out of the river, and began to eat the grass that grew near. This was a pleasant sight; but soon after he saw seven very thin cows (more ugly than any cows he had ever seen) come out of the river; and they ate up the seven fat cows; and yet, after they had eaten them, they looked as thin as they did before. Then the king awoke.

But soon he fell asleep, and dreamt that he saw a stalk of corn with seven fine ears growing on it. While he was looking he saw another stalk, with seven very bad ears of corn on it, and these bad ears ate up the seven good ears.

These were Pharaoh's two dreams. He thought them very strange, and longed to know their meaning. In the morning he told the servants to find some people who said they could tell the meaning of dreams. A great many men came who pretended to be wise, but they could not tell the king the meaning of his dreams. The king was very unhappy, but what could he do?

At last the butler thought of Joseph! He had not thought of him for a long while, and now he felt sorry. He said to the king, "I do remember my faults this day. You know, O King, that you were once angry with me and with your baker, and you shut us up in prison, in the house of the captain Potiphar. While we were in prison, the baker and I each had a dream, and a young man, a servant, told us the meaning of our dreams, and said that the baker would be hanged and that I should be let out of prison, and so it was: the baker was hanged, and you sent for me to be your butler again, just as the young man had said." Then Pharaoh told his servants to fetch this young man out of prison.

So the servants came to the prison, and said to the keeper, "We have come to fetch Joseph; the king wants to speak to him."

When Joseph came into the king's fine house, and stood before him, the king said, "I hear that you can tell the meaning of dreams."

JACOB'S WELL.

(85)

"It is not I myself," said Joseph, "that can tell the meaning, but my God can; and I know that He will tell the meaning of your dreams." Then Pharaoh told Joseph his two dreams—the dream about the seven cows and the dream about the seven ears of corn.

When he had done speaking, Joseph answered, "Both your dreams have the same meaning. This is what is going to happen: The next seven years a great deal of corn will grow in the fields; but afterward hardly any corn will grow in the fields for seven years. The seven fat cows meant the seven years when much corn would grow; and the seven thin cows meant the seven years when very little corn would grow. God sent you these dreams, that you might know what is going to happen."

Now what could the king do? First, there would be a great deal of corn, then scarcely any. Could you, my little child, advise the king what to do? Joseph gave him some advice. He said, "Save up some of the corn when there is so much, that you may have some when there is none growing in the fields. You should look for a very wise man, who will save up the corn, and put it into large barns; or the people will die when no corn grows in the fields."

Then Pharaoh said to Joseph, "You are so very wise that you shall help me to manage all the people in the land. Every one shall mind you as they do me, and you shall be the greatest person next to me."

Then Pharaoh took the ring off his hand, and put it on Joseph's hand; and he gave him beautiful clothes like his own, and a gold chain to wear round his neck. He gave him a fine chariot to ride in, and desired people to bow down when they saw him.

So Joseph was made a great lord; but he would not be idle. He went about all the country in his chariot to buy corn, and he built large barns everywhere, and filled them with corn, and so he did for seven years.

He was very glad he was let out of prison, and he thanked God very much. He was not happy because he wore fine clothes; but he was glad to be able to do good to people, by saving up corn. He married a wife, and he had two little boys; yet still he thought of

THE DESTRUCTION OF PHARAOH'S ARMY.

his dear old father, and hoped that he should one day see him again; and he thought of little Benjamin, and hoped his brothers had not killed him, nor put him in a pit, and he hoped that his brothers were sorry for their wickedness. He did not feel angry with his brothers. Joseph knew that it was God who had allowed them to sell him for a slave, and that God had let them do it that he might save up corn in Egypt.

It is God who makes all things happen; and God has wise reasons for all that He does. If He lets us be sick, it is for some good reason. One day we shall know why God let us be sick, or let wicked people hurt us, or take away our things.

Joseph's Brothers Come to Egypt to Buy Corn.

You have heard, my dear children, how Joseph was made almost as great as the king. A great deal of corn grew in the fields next year and the year after, and for seven years after the king's dream. But then scarcely any corn grew. The poor people came to King Pharaoh and said, "We have nothing to eat, and we shall die." Then Pharaoh said, "Go to Joseph; he can help you." So the people went to Joseph, and he opened his large barns full of corn, and sold the corn to the people.

Among those who came, there were ten men from a far country. Each of them had an ass, and on the ass a sack, and in their hands they brought money. Who do you think these were? They were Joseph's brothers. When Joseph saw them he remembered them, though he had not seen them for twenty years. He knew those cruel brothers, who had sold him for twenty pieces of silver.

Now you shall hear how he behaved to them.

The brothers thought Joseph was a great lord, and they did not know that they had ever seen him before; for he wore fine clothes, and he was grown to be a man, and he had another name, which the king had given him.

So when the ten brothers saw him, they bowed down to the ground before him. Then Joseph remembered his dream about the sheaves bowing down to his sheaf, and he saw that God had made it come true.

Joseph felt ready to forgive his brothers; but he wished first to see whether they were sorry for their wickedness, and whether they loved their father and little Benjamin: so he did not tell them who he was. He even pretended to be unkind. He spoke in a rough voice and said, "Where do you come from?"

"From the land of Canaan," they said, "to buy food."

But Joseph said he did not believe they spoke the truth. "You came," he said, "to see what a bad land this is, with no corn growing in it, and you mean to bring some king with soldiers to fight us."

"No, indeed," said Joseph's brothers, "we do not. We are ten poor brothers, and we have come to buy food."

But Joseph said he would not believe what they said.

Joseph's brothers answered, "We are all brothers, and once there were twelve of us; but one is dead, and the youngest is with our father, who is an old man." They tried to make Joseph believe what they said, but he would not: that is, he pretended not to believe them.

At last, Joseph said, "I must see your youngest brother. I shall send one of you to fetch him, and I shall keep the rest in prison till he comes back with the youngest brother."

Joseph put them all in prison, and kept them shut up together for three days. While they were shut up they had time to think of their wickedness to Joseph. The brothers were very much frightened: they did not know what Joseph was going to do with them.

At last he came to them in prison and said, "This is what you must do, and then you shall live: for I fear God."

How much surprised the brothers must have been when they heard Joseph say that he feared God! for the other people in Egypt worshiped idols.

Joseph said, "I will only keep one of you shut up in the prison, and all the rest may go back, and take corn home with you: but when you come again you must bring your youngest brother with you, or I shall think that you have not spoken the truth: but if you do bring him, I will believe you."

Then Joseph took one of the brothers, called Simeon, and said that he would keep him in prison till the others brought their youngest brother with them. So he had Simeon bound with ropes, or chains, while the other brothers stood around.

Then they must have remembered how once Joseph had been bound, and sold for a slave.

Simeon was left alone in the prison, and did not know whether his brothers would ever come back, and whether he would ever be let out.

Before the brothers set off to go home, Joseph said to his servants, "When you fill those men's sacks with corn, put back into their sacks the money that they paid me for it, and give them something to eat by the way." Joseph wished his poor brothers to have some food by the way. And the servant did as Joseph told him; but Joseph's brethren did not know what the servant had done.

How glad these brothers were to get away from Egypt, and to come back to their father and to their little children, who had scarcely anything left to eat!

When they came home they told their father all that had happened. "There was a great lord," they said, "who sold corn to the people; and he spoke very roughly to us, and said that we were not come to buy corn, but that we only wanted to see the land, that we might bring men to fight the poor, hungry people that lived there. He called us 'spies.' We told him that we were not spies, but were twelve brothers:—that one was dead, and that one was with our father in the land of Canaan. But the lord would not believe us, and told us we must bring our youngest brother with us; and he took Simeon, and shut him up in prison, and said that he would not let him out till we came back with Benjamin."

Poor old Jacob was very sad when he heard all this. Then the brothers began to open their sacks of corn, and they were quite surprised to find their money at the top of their sacks; but they were not pleased, for they thought that some one had put the money there to get them into disgrace, and that when they went back to Egypt they should be punished for stealing; so they were much frightened.

They were more afraid than ever of going back to Egypt, and of seeing the great lord: yet they wished very much to go, for they had brought only a little corn, and they wanted more, and they knew that poor Simeon would remain in prison till they went back to Egypt.

How could they persuade Jacob to let Benjamin go? For Jacob said, "No, I cannot trust Benjamin with you, lest some harm should happen to him. You have taken away two of my children, Joseph and Simeon, and you would not bring Benjamin back if I were to let him go. If any evil were to happen to him, you would bring down my gray hairs with sorrow to the grave." Jacob felt that it would break his heart to lose Benjamin, he loved him so very much.

So the brothers were obliged to stay in Canaan; for they knew it would be of no use to go to Egypt, except Benjamin went with them. What trouble now they were in! God was punishing them for their wickedness.

Joseph Makes a Great Feast for His Brothers.

As the brothers could not persuade Jacob to let Benjamin go with them, they were obliged to stay in Canaan. Soon they had eaten up all their corn, and none grew in their fields, and what could they do for food?

Jacob saw how hungry they were, and at last he said, "Go again, buy us a little food."

Then they said, "We cannot go without Benjamin, for the man who sold the corn said we should not see him unless we brought our youngest brother. If you will let Benjamin come with us, then we will go."

Jacob was very unhappy when he heard this, and he said, "Why did you tell the man you had a brother? It was behaving very unkindly to me to tell him."

Then the brothers answered, "The man asked us so many questions. He said to us, 'Is your father alive? Have you another brother?' Could we think that he would say, 'Bring your youngest brother?'"

Still Jacob did not like to let Benjamin go.

One of the brothers (called Judah) said, "I will take care of Benjamin, if you will let him go. I promise to bring him back to you; and if I do not I will take all the blame. For we and our children shall die if you do not let him come."

Jacob saw it was of no use to refuse any more, or they would all die, and Benjamin too. So he gave Benjamin into the care of Judah.

But Jacob was afraid of the man being unkind to them, and that he would say they had stolen the money. So he said to them, "Bring the man a present."

"Besides," said Jacob, "take the money back that you found in your sacks; take more money in your hands to buy more corn, and take Benjamin, and go to the man."

Jacob's heart was full of pain when he said this.

Then he began to pray to God. "May God give you mercy before the man, and send home Simeon and Benjamin!"

When Jacob bade his dear Benjamin good-bye, he thought of how he once had parted with Joseph, the day he sent him to look for his brothers, when he put on his pretty coat and never returned.

So they parted from their old father, and their wives and their little children, and they set out on their journey.

They all felt very sad that day. The brothers were frightened. They were afraid they should be taken up as thieves when they got to Egypt.

As soon as Joseph saw his brothers, he called his chief servant, who managed his house, and said to him, "Take those ten men to my house, and get a great dinner ready, for they must dine with me to-day."

ON THE ROAD FROM CANAAN TO EGYPT.

The brothers did not hear what Joseph said to the servant. The servant came to them, and told them to come with him. So they came, and he brought them to Joseph's own house—a fine, large house. Yet the brothers were not pleased, but very much frightened.

"Ah!" said they to each other, "we are going to be put into prison; and we shall be kept in prison, and be ill-treated and made to work hard."

Then they thought of their poor father, and of what he would do.

When they got to the door of the house, they came to the servant, and said, "O sir, we came here once before to buy a little food, and we paid money for it; but when we got home we opened our sacks and found the money in them, and here we have brought it back: and we have brought more money to buy more corn. We cannot tell who put the money into our sacks."

The servant answered them kindly, and said, "Fear not, God is your Father—God gave you that money, and put the money into your sacks."

You see the servant knew about God. Who could have taught him about God? The people in Egypt worshiped idols. It must have been Joseph who had taught his servant.

While they were waiting, the servant went and brought poor Simeon out of prison. He had been shut up a long while. I hope, when he was in prison, that he thought of his having once put Joseph in the pit.

The servant told them that dinner would not be ready till twelve o'clock; and while they were waiting he brought them water to wash their feet, and he gave some food to their poor, tired and hungry beasts.

At last Joseph came in from selling the corn, and the brothers came into the house, and brought the present in their hand, and they bowed down upon the ground. The eleven brothers bowed down, as the eleven sheaves had done in the dream.

This time Joseph spoke very kindly to them. He asked them how they were; but most of all he wanted to know how his dear father was.

"Is your father well?" he asked. "You said you had an old father. Is he yet alive?"

They said, "Yes, our father is well, and he is alive;" and as they spoke they bowed down their heads to the ground.

Then Joseph looked for Benjamin, and when he saw him he longed to throw his arms round his neck, and kiss him, but he would not do it yet. He only said, "Is this your younger brother that you told me of?"

And when they said yes, he spoke kindly to Benjamin, saying, "God be gracious to thee, my son."

When Joseph had said this, he felt the tears coming into his eyes, and he could not help crying; so he went quickly out of the room, and shut himself up in his own room, and there he cried by himself. He was a very tender-hearted man, and he loved this young brother very much.

Now the dinner was ready: so Joseph would not stay in his room: but first he washed his face, that no one might see that he had been crying, and then he tried to look cheerful, and he said to his servants, "Put the dinner on the table."

In the room where they were to dine there were three tables. One was for Joseph's servants, another was for Joseph himself (for he always dined at a table by himself), and the other table was for the eleven brothers.

Now they all sat down to dinner. It was long since they had eaten such a dinner, and they had made a great journey, and were tired, and hungry, and thirsty. Joseph sent them nice things from his table; but he sent five times as much to Benjamin as to any of the others.

Were the brothers envious of Benjamin because Joseph sent him the most? No, they were not. Once they had been envious of Joseph—but now they were not. They ate and drank, and were merry.

Joseph could see them all—and it was a pleasant sight to him. Once they had eaten their dinner while he lay in the pit, and they had given him none. Yet he would not treat them so, but would return good for evil.

Joseph Makes Himself Known to His Brothers.

The brothers spent a happy day with Joseph. They did not go home that day, but waited to set out on the morrow.

You know that they had come to buy corn, and they had brought empty sacks with them. Joseph called his servant, and said to him secretly, "Fill the sacks of those eleven men with corn, and put their money that they have given me for the corn back into their sacks. And put my silver cup into the sack of the youngest."

The next morning as soon as it was light, the brothers rose up, took their asses and their sacks, and set off to return home to their father. How glad they were to get away safely—not one left behind!

But soon was all their joy turned into grief.

They had gone but a little way, when some one called them. It was Joseph's servant; he came running after them.

"What has made you," said he, "behave so ill to my lord, after all his kindness to you? Why have you stolen his silver cup, out of which he drinks?"

The brothers were much surprised to hear that the cup was stolen.

"Why should you think," said they, "that we have taken it? We would not do such a wicked thing. Did we not bring back the money when we thought it had been put in our sacks by mistake? And now, would we steal a silver cup out of your lord's house? None of us has taken it. If any one of us has taken it, let him die, and let all the rest be slaves to your lord."

"No," said the servant, "it shall not be so; the one who has taken the cup shall not be killed; he shall only be a slave to my lord, and the others shall not be slaves: they shall all go home."

Then the servant told them to open their sacks; so the eldest brother took down his sack: the servant looked in amongst the corn, but could find no cup. Then the second opened his sack, but there was no cup hid in it. The third showed his, and each brother showed his in turn. At last Benjamin showed his. How much were they all surprised when they found the silver cup in it!

The servant said to Benjamin, "You must come back with me to my lord." He pretended that he was going to take him for a slave, and never let him return home; but he said that his brothers might go home.

And would they go and leave Benjamin behind?

"No," said they, "we will go back with Benjamin."

You see that they loved Benjamin, and that they would not leave him alone in his distress.

They put their sacks again on their asses, and followed the servant to Joseph's house. Their hearts were bursting with grief, and they cried as they went.

When they saw Joseph they fell with their faces on the ground.

Joseph spoke to them as if he were angry, and said, "What is this wicked thing that you have done?"

Do you remember that Judah had promised to take care of Benjamin? So Judah began to beg Joseph to forgive Benjamin.

Judah knew that it would be of no use to say that Benjamin had not taken the cup, so he only begged Joseph to take pity on them.

"God is punishing us for our sins," said Judah, "and we can say nothing; we must all be your slaves."

"No," said Joseph, "not all; only he who has stolen the cup, he shall be my slave: let the others go back to their father."

Joseph wanted to see whether the brothers would go back and leave poor Benjamin to be a slave.

Judah then came nearer to Joseph, and began to beg for Benjamin with all his heart.

"Let me speak a word to my lord," said he, "and do not be angry with me, for I fear you as much as I do the king. When we first came to buy corn, you asked us if we had a father and a brother, and we said, Yes, we had on old father, and a little brother that he loved very much indeed; and then you said that we must bring our brother to show you. Then we said we could not, because our father would not part with him, but you said we must bring him. So when we went back to our father, we told him what you had said, but he would not let Benjamin go. 'No,' said he, 'I had a dear child that I think was eaten up by a lion or a bear. If I let Benjamin go, perhaps some harm will happen to him, and then I shall die of grief, and these gray hairs will go down with sorrow to the grave.'

"Then I promised my father that I would take care of Benjamin. I cannot go home without him. If I were to go back without Benjamin we should see our father die. Let me be your slave instead of Benjamin, and let him go home to his father; for I could not bear to see my father die of grief."

Now Joseph saw that Judah did indeed love Benjamin and his old father.

He felt ready to burst into tears, yet he did not go out of the room to weep, as he had done before; but he said to all his servants, "Go out of the room;" and Joseph was left alone with his brothers. He cried so loud, that all the servants heard him, though they were not in the room.

At last he said, "I am Joseph. Is my father yet alive?"

Joseph did not wish to frighten them; he longed to put his arms round them and kiss them.

"Do not grieve because you sold me;" said Joseph: "God let you do it that I might save corn to feed your children. I wish you all to come and live with me here. You must bring my old father with you, and your children, and I will feed you all. Look at me, and you will see that I am indeed your own brother Joseph. It is my mouth that speaks to you. Go tell my father what fine things I have in Egypt, and bring him here to live with me."

This was the loving way in which Joseph spoke. Then he threw his arms round Benjamin's neck, and wept as he kissed him; and Benjamin wept too upon Joseph's neck. Afterward Joseph kissed all his brothers, and wept as he kissed each; and then his brothers no more felt afraid of him, but began to talk to him. They saw Joseph had quite forgiven them, and that he loved them with all his heart. They could not have expected such kindness, and it made them the more sorry for their own wickedness.

Jacob and All His Family Remove to Egypt.

Before Joseph told his brothers who he was, he had sent the servants out of the room; yet he had sobbed so loud that the servants had heard, and soon they knew the reason why Joseph had sent them out. The servants were glad to hear that Joseph had found his brothers. Joseph had not told the people of Egypt of his brothers' wickedness.

Pharaoh, the king, heard of the brothers being found; and he, too, was glad, for he loved Joseph.

He called Joseph, and said to him, "Your brothers must come and live near you, and you must send for your old father, and for all the little children; and they shall have the best food in all the land to eat." Then Joseph got wagons, with some beasts to draw them, and he gave his brothers some food to eat as they traveled home. He also made them some handsome presents, for

JACOB AND HIS FAMILY REMOVE TO EGYPT.

Joseph was very rich. He gave them each two suits of clothes; but to Benjamin he gave five suits, besides a great deal of money. He sent a present to his father; ten asses that carried all kinds of good things; and ten asses more that carried a great deal of bread and other food for his father to eat by the way.

When all the things were ready, Joseph told his brothers to go to Canaan, and to come back quickly. He gave them one piece of advice before they went. "Take care," he said, "that you do not quarrel by the way."

They must have had a pleasant journey.

Old Jacob had been longing to see them, much fearing lest Benjamin should not come back safely. At last they came, and he saw that not one was missing.

They told him the joyful news, "Joseph is alive: and he is the great lord that sells corn in the land of Egypt."

Perhaps you think Jacob was delighted; but no—he would not believe them.

"No," said he, "my son has long been dead."

"But we have seen him," said they.

"It cannot be true," said Jacob.

Then the brothers told him what Joseph had said. "He desires us all to come and live with him, and he sends for you."

Still Jacob could not believe them.

"Only come and see the wagons he has sent, and then you will believe us," said they.

So they took old Jacob to see the wagons, and when he saw them he believed and was glad.

"It is enough," said old Jacob. "Joseph my son is yet alive; I will go and see him before I die."

And so they all came into the land of Egypt.

Long before they came to Joseph's house they saw a fine chariot coming toward them. It was Joseph's. It stopped, and Joseph got out of it.

Old Jacob stepped out of his wagon. His hair was gray, his legs were weak and he could hardly walk. Joseph was a fine and glorious lord. He ran to meet his father, threw his arms round his neck; and then he wept for a long while.

The last time Joseph had kissed his father was when he was a boy, dressed in his pretty coat, and was going to look for his brothers to see how they did. How many sad days had Jacob spent since that time, in thinking of him! And now, at last, he had found him again.

The brothers did not feel envious now when they saw Jacob and Joseph folded in each other's arms.

"Now," said old Jacob, "let me die, since I have seen your face once more."

Then Joseph said to his father and brothers, "I will go and tell Pharaoh that you have come."

So he went to Pharaoh the king, and said, "My father and brothers, and their flocks, and all that they have, are come."

And then he brought five of his brothers, and showed them to Pharaoh. And Pharaoh said to them, "What is your employment?"

"We are shepherds, but there is no grass in Canaan for our sheep. Will you give us some fields where we can feed them?"

Pharaoh said that he would give them a great many fields, and that they might live there all together, with their children and their flocks.

Joseph wished them to live all together, because the people in Egypt worshiped idols.

Joseph wished the king to see his dear old father, so he brought him to the king. The king treated him with great respect, because Jacob was a very old man. Even kings should pay respect to old men.

Should not children pay great respect to an old man? When they see a gray-headed old man, they should be ready to wait upon him, and to do what he bids them.

Old Jacob lifted up his hands over Pharaoh's head, and prayed God to show him kindness. This was called blessing him. Jacob blessed Pharaoh, because he had been very good to his dear Joseph.

Pharaoh said to Jacob, "How old are you?"

Jacob said, "I am one hundred and thirty years old, but I am not as old as my fathers were; and my life has been full of troubles."

Then Jacob blessed Pharaoh again, and went away to the place he had given him to live in. There he lived, with all his children around him. Joseph did not live with him, but he often came to see him.

Jacob at last fell sick, and knew that he soon should die. He sent for all his sons that he might bless them before he died.

DEATH OF JACOB.

And when Jacob had made an end of commanding his sons, he gathered up his feet into the bed, and yielded up the ghost, and was gathered unto his people.—GENESIS xlix: 33.

Jacob had been lame a long while, and now he was almost blind, and very weak, and sick.

When his sons came, he sat upon the bed, and called them one by one, that he might give a blessing to each. After he had blessed them he said, "I am soon going to die; bury me in the cave in Canaan where Abraham my grandfather is buried, and Isaac my father."

He said a great deal more, and at last he gathered up his feet into the bed, and died.

Joseph fell upon his father's face when he was dead, and wept upon him, and kissed him. Those gray hairs had not gone down in sorrow to the grave, for God had comforted Jacob before he died.

Joseph took his father's body to Canaan, to put it in the cave where Abraham and Isaac were. All the brothers went with Joseph, and a great many servants, and chariots, and horses. Afterward they came back to Egypt.

A very sad thought came into the minds of the brothers. They said to each other, "Perhaps Joseph has only been so kind to us to please his father; perhaps he has not really forgiven us; and now, perhaps, he will punish us." So they sent a servant to Joseph, and told the servant to say to Joseph, "Your father, before he died, told us to beg you to forgive us our great wickedness. So pray forgive us."

When Joseph heard this message he began to weep, because he was sorry that his brothers should think he could be so unkind to them. Soon his brothers came and fell down before him, and seemed much afraid. Joseph said, "Fear not: it was wrong of you to sell me, yet God made it turn out for good; because when I was in Egypt I saved the corn, and you were kept from dying of hunger. I still will feed you and your little children." He spoke very kindly to them and comforted them.

Joseph lived to be a very old man, and at last he died.

This is the history of Joseph. You have heard the history of Abraham, Isaac and Jacob. God loved them all. Abraham was the grandfather, Isaac the father, and Jacob the son.

The Story of Moses, and How He Was Found in the Bulrushes by the King's Daughter.

You have heard how Joseph and his brothers lived happily in Egypt for a long while. At last they grew old and died, but they left a great many children; and their children had a great many children; till at last there were hundreds and thousands of people. These people were the grandchildren of Jacob, and his great-grandchildren and their children.

Did you know that Jacob had two names?

His other name was Israel. It was a name that God had given him.

All the sons of Jacob were called the children of Israel, or the children of Jacob; and the grandchildren of Jacob were called by the same name, "children of Israel." There were some men, and some women, and some children, and all of them together were called "children of Israel."

They did not live in Canaan, you remember; they had left Canaan, because no corn grew there for a long while: they lived in Egypt, and took care of their sheep. While the good king Pharaoh lived they were very happy. At last he died, and there was another king of Egypt; he too was called Pharaoh. You shall hear what he did, and then you shall tell me whether you think he was good.

He knew that the children of Israel had come from a great way off, and he said, "There are so many of them, perhaps they may some day fight against me with swords, and kill me and my servants. I will make them work hard, and I will try to kill them with hard work."

So he desired that they should make a great many bricks, and build very high walls. He sent some of his men to make them work hard.

The children of Israel were used to taking care of sheep, which is a pleasant employment. Shepherds lead their flocks to the green fields, and by the side of the quiet waters, and they sit under the shade of a tree when the sun is hot. But now the children of Israel were obliged to dig up the clay, and to make bricks, and dry them in the sun; and if they did not make a great many bricks, the men whom Pharaoh had sent beat them. So now they were very unhappy; they often sighed, and groaned, and shed tears.

MY MOTHER'S BIBLE STORIES. 105

Yet all this hard work did not kill them; so the king thought of another plan. He said, "Let every boy-baby be thrown into the river." He did not order the girl-babies to be drowned, because they would not be able to fight with swords when they grew up.

Whenever the king heard that one of the children of Israel had a little boy-baby, he sent his men to throw it into the river.

There was a very good woman who had a little boy-baby; she was one of the children of Israel.

This woman knew that God would take care of her child, and she prayed to God to take care of it.

THE EGYPTIAN WELL.

"The weary traveler wandering that way
Therein did often quench his thirsty heat."

She hid her baby, so that Pharaoh's men could not find it. I do not know where she put it, but God taught her to hide it in a very safe place.

When the baby was three months old, she found that she could not hide him any more. What could she do with her baby?

HAGAR AND HER SON ISHMAEL,
Who is the father of the Arabs.

In Egypt there is a great river called the Nile. Close by the river there grew a great many reeds and bulrushes, which are like very high, thick grass. She took some bulrushes and made them into a large basket. She wished to make a basket into which the water could not come; so she got some pitch, and covered the basket with pitch. Then she put her little baby inside, and took the basket in her arms. No one could tell what was in the basket.

She went to the river-side, and laid the basket among the great rushes, close by the water; she knew that God would not let the child be killed, and so she left it, trusting in Him.

She had a little girl of ten years old. This little girl was the baby's sister.

THE PRINCESS FINDS MOSES.

She stood a great way off, to see what would become of her baby-brother. Soon she saw some ladies walking by the river-side. One of these ladies was King Pharaoh's daughter. She was a princess. The other ladies were her maids, and they were going with the princess to some place where she could bathe. The princess was looking at the rushes, when she saw something strange peeping out of them. She thought it looked like a baby-boy, so she said to one of her maids, "Go and see what that is." The maid went and found the basket. She took it up and brought it to the princess. The princess opened the basket, and saw a sweet babe. It was fair and lovely.

It began to weep. Poor infant! it was used to lie in its mother's arms, but now there was no one to feed it or to comfort it. The princess pitied the child. She had heard how her father had desired that every boy-baby should be thrown into the river, and she said, " I suppose this is the baby of one of the children of Israel." She did not wish it to be thrown into the river.

The baby's sister had come nearer, and had seen what the princess had done. She saw that the princess pitied it; so she said, "If you want a nurse, I can find you one who will nurse the child for you." The princess said, "Go."

Then she went and called her own and the baby's mother. When she had come, the princess said to her, " Take this child and nurse it for me, and I will give you wages."

How glad the mother was to take care of it! She saw that God had heard her prayers, and saved her child from being drowned.

The mother could teach it about God as soon as it could understand. But she was not allowed to keep the baby always. When he was grown to be a large boy, the princess sent for him to come and live with her, and she called him her son. She gave him a name. "I shall call him 'Moses,'" she said; which means "drawn out," for he was drawn out of the water.

The princess lived in a fine house, and had a great many servants. Moses had beautiful clothes, nice things to eat, and servants to wait upon him. He had no hard work to do; yet he was not idle, but learned a great many things. The princess told the wise men to teach him.

He knew the names of the stars, the names of beasts, and birds, and plants. He learned about all these things, and grew

A HOME IN BIBLE LAND

(109)

very wise. But one thing these wise men could not teach him, and that was about God; for they worshiped idols. Yet Moses did know about God, for his father and mother knew the true God, and when he was little Moses lived with them. Of all the things Moses knew, this was the best. He was wiser than all the men in Egypt, for he knew the true God.

He was brave as well as wise, and all the people in Egypt praised him, and paid him respect. But he was not happy, and I will tell you why in the next story.

How Moses Slew the Task-Master.

I have told you how very hard the poor children of Israel worked, in making bricks. When Moses had grown to be a man, this thought came into his mind: "I live in a fine house, and am as great as a prince. I have no work to do; but my poor cousins, the children of Israel, they are working like slaves. Cruel men are beating them? Cannot I help them?" This thought made him sad.

Do you remember the promise God made to Abraham about his great-great-grandchildren? These children of Israel were the great-great-grandchildren of Abraham.

I am now going to tell you about these descendants of Abraham, and Isaac, and Jacob, and about their children, and their children: and I shall always call them the "children of Israel."

What promise had God made to Abraham about them? He had said that they should live in the land of Canaan—that sweet land, full of hills and rivers, grass and flowers, sheep and cows, milk and honey. God had said to Abraham, "I will give this land to your children." Not to Isaac, but to his great-great-great-great-grandchildren, and to their children, and their children's children.

Moses had heard of this promise; perhaps his mother had told him of it. He had heard how he had been saved from being drowned when he was a little baby, and he believed that God would let him bring the children of Israel into Canaan. He wished to save them from being slaves among the wicked people of Egypt, and to make them happy in that pleasant land of Canaan.

Moses left the king's fine house, and all his fine things, and went to the place where the poor Israelites were working hard. (The children of Israel were sometimes called Israelites.)

He wished to see whether they remembered God's promise to Abraham, and whether they wished to go to Canaan.

When he came to the place in Egypt where the children of Israel were working, how sad was the sight he saw! There they were, laboring in the heat of the sun. They worked from morning till night. They dug up the clay to make bricks: that was hard work. Then they made the bricks; they put them in heaps to dry them in the sun. Then they carried them to build the great walls for Pharaoh.

Moses was very sorry to see how the poor children of Israel were treated.

One day he saw one of the task-masters (the cruel men were called task-masters) beating one of the children of Israel. Moses could not bear to see the poor slave treated so cruelly. He looked to see whether there were any more task-masters near; he saw no one. So he killed the task-master, and then dug a hole in the ground, and covered him over with the earth.

Moses had been sent by God to kill this wicked man, that he might show the poor Israelites that he was come from God to make them happy.

One of the Israelites saw him, and soon King Pharaoh heard of it; and Pharaoh was very angry, and tried to find Moses, that he might have him killed. So Moses was obliged to go into a country a great way off, where the king could not find him. I will tell you another time what happened to Moses in that country. God loved Moses, and He took care of him wherever he went.

Moses might have lived always in a fine house, and ridden in a chariot, and had many servants; but you see how much he loved the poor children of Israel.

He wished to please God more than to be called the son of Pharaoh's daughter; he knew that God loved the children of Israel, and he knew that God would one day help him to take them into Canaan.

Story of the Wonderful Burning Bush.

Moses was grieved to leave the poor children of Israel groaning in Egypt; but he was forced to hide himself from Pharaoh.

He took nothing with him on his journey;—no servant, no companion! But God was with him.

At last Moses came to a place where there was much grass, and a great many sheep. Here, also, there was a well, and he sat down by the side of it; for he had taken a long journey.

He had no house, no bed, and no friends. He was like Jesus, who had nowhere to lay His head. But God took care of him.

Soon there came seven girls to the well. They were sisters, and they took care of their father's sheep. They brought their sheep with them to give them water. First they let down some pails, or buckets, into the well, and then poured the water into some great troughs that stood near, and the sheep drank out of the troughs. While they were doing this, some shepherds came to the well and tried to drive them away, that their own sheep might drink water out of the troughs; but the poor girls had filled the troughs with water, and it would have been very unfair to take the water from their sheep. But the men were stronger than the girls, and had often behaved in this way to them.

Moses did not like to see weak people ill-treated; and he was very strong; so he stood up, and would not let the shepherds send the girls away, but helped them to draw water for their sheep.

The poor girls thought Moses was very kind, because he was only a stranger, and yet he had helped them.

When they came to their father, he said, "How is it that you have come home so soon to-day?" And they said, "A stranger was by the well, and he would not let the shepherds drive us away, and he drew water for our sheep." Then the father answered, "Where is the man? Call him, and ask him to come and eat bread with us." So the girls called Moses, and asked him to come to their house. It was God who put it into the man's heart to be kind to Moses.

The old father asked Moses to live with him and his daughters, and Moses said he would. He took care of the old father's sheep, and he married one of the seven girls. Then the old father was called Moses' father-in-law, because he was the father of his wife.

Moses had once been a fine prince, and had ridden in a chariot; but now he led his sheep to eat grass among the green hills.

There was one thing that must

MOSES AT THE HOME OF LABAN.

have made Moses sad. What was that? He knew that the children of Israel were still groaning at their hard work. Could he be happy while they were so miserable? You know that he could not, because Moses loved these poor people.

The children of Israel were indeed working hard. King Pharaoh had died; but there was another King Pharaoh, as wicked as he had been.

At last the children of Israel cried to God to help them, and God heard their prayers; and He remembered the promise made to Abraham, and He determined to save them. Now you shall hear what God did to help them.

One day Moses was with the old father's sheep, among the high hills. He was quite alone. He looked up, and saw a bush on fire. As he looked the bush continued to burn, but it was not more burnt away than at first. This surprised him very much, and he said, "I will go and look at the bush, and see why it is not burnt up."

He was just going up to it, when he heard some one speaking to him. The voice came out of the bush. Whose voice could it be?

It was the voice of God, who said to him, "Moses, Moses!"

He answered, "Here am I."

Then God said, "Come not near this place, for I am here. I have heard the children of Israel crying to Me in their trouble, and I remember that I promised Abraham that his children should live in Canaan, and I am going to send them to Canaan. Moses, you must go to Pharaoh, and tell him to let them go."

Was not this a hard thing for Moses to do? But God said, "I will be with you and help you."

Then Moses said, "But perhaps the children of Israel will not choose to come out of Egypt. They will say, 'We will not go with you, Moses; you are not speaking the truth; God has not really spoken to you.' What shall I do then?" said Moses.

Then God said that He would teach him to do wonderful things. God, said, "What do you hold in your hand?"

Now Moses had a long stick in his hand, called a rod. He used to help his sheep to get out of holes with his rod, and when he climbed high hills he leaned upon it. So when God said, "What do you hold in your hand?" Moses answered, "A rod."

TRAVELERS IN PALESTINE SHOWING HOW MOSES TRAVELED.

"Throw it upon the ground," said the Lord. And Moses did so, and it was turned into a serpent. Moses was afraid of the serpent, and began to run away from it. Then God said, "Take hold of it by the tail." So Moses took hold of it, and it was turned again into a rod. God said to Moses, "When you go to Egypt, do this wonderful thing before the children of Israel, to show them that I have sent you; but if they do not believe you, do this thing, too, that I will show you. Put your hand into your bosom." So Moses put in his hand, and then he drew it out, and it was leprous; that is, it was all covered over with white spots. What a frightful sight this was! Then God said, "Put your hand in again;" and he put it in and pulled it out again, and then it was as well as it was before. Then God said to Moses, "If the children of Israel will not believe that I have really spoken to you, let them see you do this wonder."

Moses went back to his father-in-law, and told him that he must go back to Egypt; and he took his wife and his two little sons with him upon an ass.

As Moses was going to Egypt he met his brother Aaron, and Aaron was glad to see him, and kissed him. Then Moses and Aaron went together to the land of Egypt.

They found the poor Israelites at their hard work, crying and groaning. Aaron said to them, "God has sent us to tell Pharaoh to let you go to the land of Canaan." Then Aaron did the wonders that God had shown Moses when He spoke to him from the bush. You know what wonders I mean.

Did the people of Israel believe what Aaron said? Did they wish to go to the land of Canaan? Yes, they did; and they thanked God for having heard their prayers.

A Description of Some of the Terrible Plagues that God Sent upon Egypt.

The next day Moses and Aaron, and some of the children of Israel with them, went in to speak to King Pharaoh. He was a proud and wicked man, and he worshiped idols.

It was Aaron who spoke to Pharaoh. He said, "The Lord God desires you to let the children of Israel go."

Do you think Pharaoh did let them go? No, he spoke proudly, and said, "Who is the Lord, that I should obey His voice? I know not the Lord, neither will I let Israel go." This was his proud answer.

He was now more unkind than before to the children of Israel, and ordered the taskmasters to make them work harder; so that the children of Israel cried still more bitterly.

As Moses and Aaron came out from King Pharaoh, they saw some of the children of Israel waiting for them. These men said to Moses and Aaron, "You have only done us harm

THE RODS TURNED TO SNAKES.

by asking Pharaoh to let us go. He makes us work harder than ever." It was ungrateful of the children of Israel to speak in this manner to Moses, who had tried to help them. Moses was very meek and gentle, and he did not answer angrily, but he went and prayed to God, and asked what he must do now. God told him to go in to King Pharaoh and to show him the wonder of the serpent. So Moses and Aaron went in. Moses said to Aaron, "Take this rod and throw it on the ground!" And Aaron threw it down, and it became a live serpent; then afterward it was turned into a rod again.

Would Pharaoh now say he would let Israel go? No, he would not; his heart was very hard and he cared for nothing.

So God told Moses to do another wonderful thing, and I will tell you what it was.

Moses and Aaron went early in the morning down to the side of the great river, and waited there till Pharaoh came; for he came there very often to bathe. Then they said to him, "Because you would not do as God desired, and let Israel go, now you shall see what God can do."

Then Aaron took the rod, and lifted it up over the water; and in a moment the water was turned into blood.

The people of Egypt had nothing to drink, for all the water in the ponds was turned into blood, and all the water in jugs, and basins, and cups, was turned into blood. The fish in the river died, and a very bad smell came from the river. The people dug holes in the ground to get water. The water was blood for a whole week.

As Pharaoh would not mind, God sent him another plague.

Aaron stretched out the rod, and frogs came running out of the river, and out of the ponds, hundreds and hundreds of frogs. They ran into the streets, and into the houses, and went into the bed-rooms, and into the beds; they went into the kitchens, and got among the food; they went even into Pharaoh's house, and into his bed.

Then Pharaoh called for Moses and Aaron, and said to them, "Pray to God to take away the frogs. I will let the children of Israel go."

Moses went and prayed to God, and God made all the frogs die, so that the people swept the dead frogs into heaps, and these heaps had a very bad smell. But still Pharaoh would not let the people go.

So God sent another plague.

Aaron stretched out the rod, and turned all the dust into filthy little insects, that crawled over the men and over the beasts; but Pharaoh would not mind this plague.

Then God sent swarms of flies, that came in at the windows, and spoiled everything, in-doors and out-of-doors. But no flies came near the children of Israel.

Then Pharaoh said, "I will let the children of Israel go, if God will take away the flies." Then Moses prayed to God, and God took all the flies away, and did not even leave one. Then Pharaoh said, "I will not let the people go."

So another plague was sent.

The beasts fell very sick—the horses and asses, the camels, the cows, and the sheep—and a great many of them died. Yet Pharaoh would not let the people go.

Afterward God made a great many boils come upon all the men, and women, and children, but not upon the children of Israel, only upon Pharaoh's people. They were so sick that they could not stand; yet Pharaoh would not mind, for his heart grew harder and harder.

Other Great Plagues that Fell upon the Egyptians.

One morning Moses and Aaron rose up very early and went to Pharaoh, and said to him, "To-morrow God is going to rain great hailstones from the sky—such hailstones as were never seen in Egypt before. They will kill all men and beasts that are out-of-doors. Therefore you must keep your cows and horses, and asses in the stables, or they will be killed."

The next day Moses stretched out his rod toward the sky, and God sent thunder, and hail, and fire, which ran along the ground. It was a most dreadful storm. Such a storm was never seen before. The noise of the hailstones and of the thunder must have made every one tremble who heard it. But how glad those must have been who were in their houses! Many beasts and men were killed, and grass and corn were burnt up by the fire, and the trees were broken. Yet there was no hail where the children of Israel were.

THE STORM OF FIRE AND HAIL.

This storm frightened Pharaoh, and he sent for Moses and Aaron, and said, "I have sinned: only pray the Lord to send no more thunder and hail, and I will let the children of Israel go."

Moses said, "I will go out of the city, and I will stretch out my hands to God, and He will not send any more thunder and hail; but still I know you will not obey God."

So Moses went out of the city, for he did not fear the storm. Then he stretched out his hands, and God made the hail and thunder stop, and He made the rain leave off. Did Pharaoh then let Israel go? No; when he saw that the storm was over he would not. All Pharaoh's servants were wicked, too; for they did not wish him to let the Israelites go.

Then Moses and Aaron went to King Pharaoh again and said, "God will now send locusts into your country."

Pharaoh and his servants were very angry when they heard that the locusts were coming, and they spoke roughly to Moses and Aaron, and drove them out of the house. Moses stretched out the rod, and God made the wind blow very hard, and next day the wind blew a great number of locusts into Egypt. The locusts made the sky look black as the wind blew them along; but they did not stay in the air; they perched on the trees, and ate up the fruit

THE PEST OF LOCUSTS.

that the hail had left: they covered the grass and ate it up, and they even came into the houses. Pharaoh and his servants thought that they should soon have nothing to eat, so he sent quickly for Moses and Aaron. "I have sinned," he said, "against the Lord, and against you. Only forgive me this once, and pray to God to take away the locusts, and I will let Israel go."

So Moses prayed to the Lord. God sent another wind, and it blew the locusts away, and they fell into the sea, and there was not one locust left in Egypt.

But Pharaoh still said, "I will not let Israel go."

The next time Moses did not tell Pharaoh what God was going to do. He stretched out his rod toward heaven, and in one moment God made it dark. It was darker than ever it is at night. There was not the least light, except where the children of Israel lived; there it was quite light.

The people of Egypt were very much frightened. They were doing their work, or eating, or walking, when all at once this darkness came on. They stopped and sat down in the place where they were; and never moved, night or day. Now they had time to think of all their wickedness.

EATING THE PASSOVER.

It was dark for three days and three nights, and then it grew light.

But was Pharaoh sorry for his wickedness? No; his heart was harder than ever. He said to Moses, "Get away! you shall never see my face again. If you come unto me any more, you shall die."

Then Moses said, "You shall see my face no more."

God spake to Moses again, and said, "I am going to send another plague. At night I shall come into every house in Egypt, and kill the first-born in every house. But this is what I desire the children of Israel to do: Let each man take a lamb, a lamb without spot, and kill it, and eat it that night with his family: and let them take the blood of

THE ANGEL OF DEATH PASSING OVER EGYPT.

the lamb, and put some blood outside the door; and when I pass I shall see the blood, and I will not kill the eldest son in that house. Let the people in the house stand round the table while they eat the lamb. Let them all be dressed ready for a journey." So all the children of Israel killed young lambs, roasted them, and ate them at night. They stood round their tables, with their sticks in their hands. They ate some bread with the lamb, and some bitter herbs. They did not forget to put some blood on the posts of the door, for then they knew they were safe.

THE CHILDREN OF ISRAEL PREPARING TO DEPART.

The men of Egypt went to bed that night as usual, but in the middle of the night the eldest son in each house died. No one saw God's angel enter in, but he did come. No bars or bolts could keep him out; but when he saw the blood on the door, then he passed over the house. What a dreadful cry the fathers and mothers made in Egypt when they found their eldest sons were dead! They rushed out of their houses weeping. "Our darling son is dead!" said one. "And so is mine!" said another. "And mine!" "And mine!" There never was such dreadful crying heard in Egypt before. Even Pharaoh's eldest son was killed, as well as the sons of the people. Pharaoh rose up at night, and called for Moses and Aaron; but it was dark, so that they did not see his face.

"Go," said Pharaoh, "and take the children of Israel with you: they may take their sheep and cows with them, and all that they have."

And all the men of Egypt begged the children of Israel to go away as fast as possible, for they were afraid that God would kill them all.

Then the Israelites said to the women of Egypt, "Do give us some gold and silver before we go."

And they said, "We will give you what you want: only go."

So the women of Egypt gave them a great many beautiful things to take with them.

The Israelites went away in a very great hurry. They took their things just as they were. They put bread in their bags; they drove their sheep, cows, camels and asses, before them, and so they set out in the night.

There was a great crowd of people. No little child could have counted them.

So at last they came out of Egypt, where they had been slaves so long. God had remembered His promise to Abraham, and Abraham's children were on their way to the land of Canaan.

God said to Moses, "They must never forget My kindness in bringing them out of Egypt. They must eat a lamb every year, as they have done to-night. Eating the lamb shall be called eating the Feast of the Passover."

Why was this supper called the Passover? Because God passed over the doors where the blood was seen.

Now count how many plagues God had sent upon Pharaoh and the people of Egypt—

1. Water turned into blood.
2. Frogs.
3. Small insects from the dust.

4. Flies.
5. Death of the beasts.
6. Boils.
7. Hail and thunder.
8. Locusts.
9. Darkness.
10. Death of the eldest sons.

I hope, dear children, that you will obey God and not make Him angry with you. Jesus is praying for us and God is waiting that we may repent.

How Moses and the Children of Israel Crossed the Red Sea.

The children of Israel had begun their journey to Canaan. But they had to travel a long way before they could reach that pleasant place. How could they find their way?

God Himself showed them the way. He went before them in a dark cloud. The cloud moved, and they moved after it. But a black cloud could not be seen at night, so at night God made the cloud shine like fire. In the day the cloud was a shade from the sun, and in the night the fire gave light to the Israelites. When the cloud or the fire stopped, then Moses desired all the people to set up their tents on the ground. This was called "encamping."

The children of Israel went very fast till they came to the sea-side. Then the cloud stopped, and they set up their tents close by the sea. The sea was called the Red Sea. Perhaps you think that the water of this sea was red like blood: but the water was like other water, though it was called the Red Sea.

They had not been long in their tents before they heard a great noise: it was a noise of wheels and a noise of horses. They looked, and saw, a great way off, Pharaoh and his army in chariots and on horses. Pharaoh had become sorry that he let them go, and he was coming after them to bring them back.

The Israelites were very much frightened. What could they do? They could not get over the sea, for they had no ships; yet,

PHARAOH'S ARMY PURSUING THE CHILDREN OF ISRAEL.

if they stayed where they were, Pharaoh and his men would soon overtake them and fight against them, and Pharaoh's men could fight far better than they could. What could they do? They cried to God to help them. This was right: but they did something else that was not right,—they began to speak angrily to Moses. "Why have you brought us up out of Egypt? We would rather have died there than come here: for we shall certainly be killed."

It was ungrateful to say this to Moses: but he answered them meekly. "Do not be afraid: God will fight for you, and you shall never see the faces of Pharaoh and his men again."

Then Moses went and prayed to God; for Moses knew that God would save the children of Israel.

Then God said to Moses, "Lift up your rod over the sea, and I will make a dry path for the Israelites to walk upon."

So Moses lifted up his rod, and the waters obeyed him; and part of the water was lifted up on one side, and part on the other, and seemed like two walls of water, while a dry path was seen between.

The Israelites walked in the path, and all their cattle with them. It was the evening when they began to cross the sea, and they were walking across all the night; yet it was not dark.

I will tell you why it was not dark. You know that the cloud in the sky shone brightly in the night, and gave light to the Israelites. But God did not choose that Pharaoh should see the light; so God made the black cloud move backward, and it stood in the sky between the Israelites and Pharaoh: the bright side was turned toward the Israelites, and the dark side toward Pharaoh, so the Israelites saw a bright light: but the armies of Pharaoh were in the dark, and they could not go fast because it was so dark; but the Israelites walked quickly along the dry path, and by the morning they got to the land that was on the other side of the sea. They had not yet got to Canaan, but they were over the sea, and they were on their journey to Canaan.

Now I will tell you whether Pharaoh and his men got over the sea or not. When they came to the edge of the sea, they saw

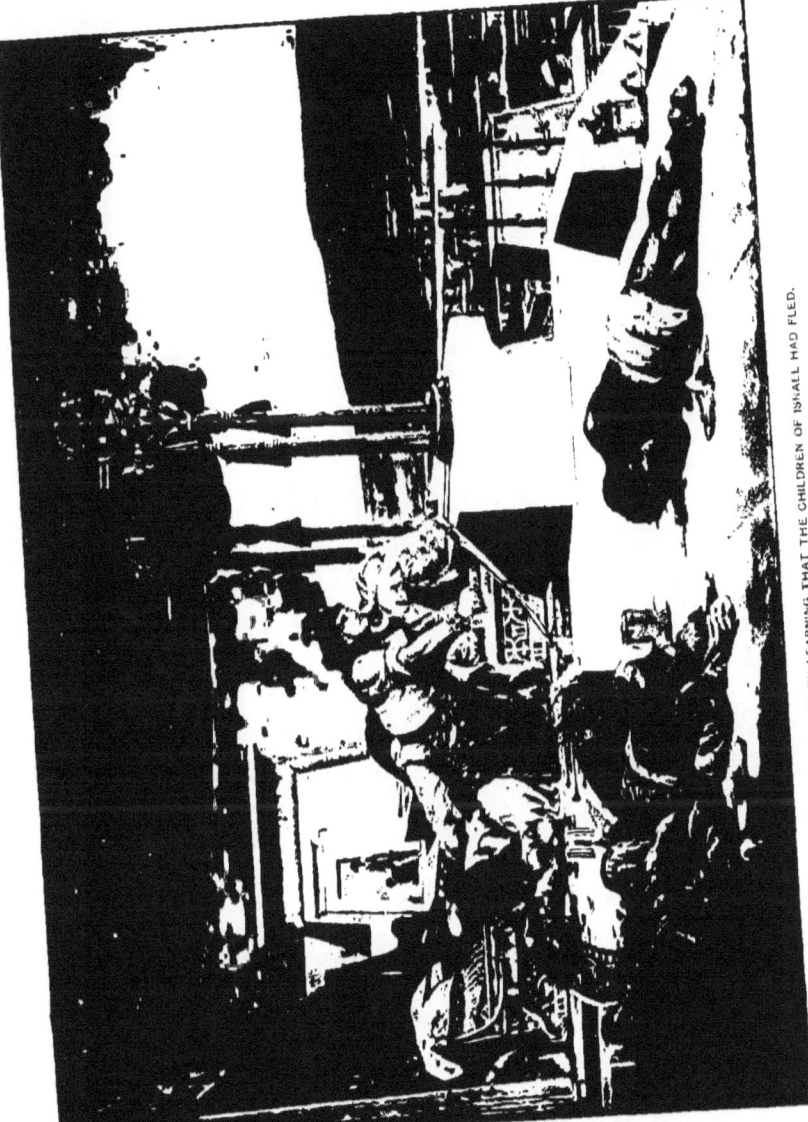

PHARAOH'S RAGE ON LEARNING THAT THE CHILDREN OF ISRAEL HAD FLED.

a dry path, and the wall of water on each side; so they went along the dry path. When they had gone about half way across the sea, and were hoping soon to overtake the Israelites, God looked at them through His cloud. Pharaoh and his men heard dreadful noises, and they were very much frightened. It was God who made them afraid.

They could not make their chariots go on, and they thought that God was going to help the Israelites to kill them; so they said to each other, "Let us turn back."

Ah! it was now too late: God was going to destroy those wicked men. They drove as fast as they could, that they might get out of the water, but it was too late; for the walls of water

THE SONG OF TRIUMPH.

fell down and covered them all, and they lay like stones at the bottom of the sea. This was the end of Pharaoh and of his wicked servants. Now the Israelites saw that the cruel men could hurt them no more: God had punished them for their wickedness, and had saved the poor children of Abraham as He had promised. This was a happy morning for the Israelites. They thanked God for His goodness in saving them, and they sang together a beautiful song of praise.

The song began with these words: "I will sing unto the Lord, for He hath triumphed gloriously: the horse and his rider hath He thrown into the sea."

How pleasant it must have been to see the poor Israelites singing and rejoicing! A little while before they had been working hard in the sun, they had been beaten by cruel men, and had cried and groaned: now they were slaves no more, but they were on their way to a sweet land, where they might live happily.

Story of the Manna and the Rock in the Desert.

The children of Israel were very glad that they had got away from their cruel masters. Now they had a kind master, even Moses. Ought they not to be good and happy?

There was such a number of people that they wanted a great deal of food to feed them. They had taken a little bread with them in their bags, when they left Egypt; but they ate it up very soon.

What ought they to do now? They ought to pray to God. He loved them, and would not let them starve. But these naughty Israelites began to grumble. They went to Moses and Aaron, and said, "We wish we had died in Egypt. At least we had bread and meat there, as much as we could eat; but now we shall be starved. You have only brought us out of Egypt to kill us."

How ungrateful they were to Moses and to God!

Yet Moses did not answer them roughly. He knew that God heard their wicked words; and God did hear them. God called to Moses, and said, "I have heard them, and I will feed them."

Did they deserve to be fed? Oh, no! How do you think God would feed them? He would rain down bread from heaven. Was not this kind?

Next morning the children of Israel, when they looked out at their tent doors, saw the ground was white. They looked to see what made the ground white, and they saw little round white things on the ground. They said to each other, "What can this be? We never saw anything like it before."

Then Moses said, "This is the bread that God hath sent you from heaven; gather it, and take it to your tents."

So all the men got jars and baskets, and gathered the manna for themselves, for their wives, and for their little children; and there was enough for them all: not too much, nor too little, but just enough. They tasted it and found it was as sweet as honey, and they called it "manna." Moses said to them, "Do not save any of the manna, for God will send you some every day. If it is all gone at night, do not be afraid; trust God. He will send you more."

GATHERING MANNA IN THE WILDERNESS.

But some of the people chose to save some of the manna. They were disobedient and ungrateful. They looked at their manna next morning, but it was full of worms. They could not eat it, but were obliged to throw it away. How foolish it is not to mind what God says!

Soon afterward the people had no water to drink. There was no river in the wilderness, and very few wells, or ponds. Do you think God would let them die of thirst?

These naughty Israelites thought God would. So they went to Moses, and spoke very angrily.

"Why did you bring us up out of Egypt? You mean to kill us, and our little children, and our cattle with thirst." They were so very angry that Moses thought they would soon throw great stones at him and kill him. Yet Moses did not answer, but began to pray to God. "What shall I do for these people?" said Moses. Then God said to Moses, "Take your rod, and go up a hill, and let some of the people go

WATER GUSHES FROM THE ROCK.

with you. Then, when you are come to a high place close by the rock, strike the rock, and the water shall come out."

So Moses took some people with him, and struck the rock, and the water came running out.

What a pleasant sight for the thirsty people! Their mouths were dry, and their tongues were stiff, their throats burning; but now they might stoop down and drink, or they might fill their jugs with water. The poor cows, and sheep, and asses, ran to the water to drink.

You see how kind God had been to the people in their distress. Ought they not to trust Him always, and to feel sure that He would help them?

The Terrors of Mount Sinai.

The Israelites went on traveling through the wilderness. The wilderness was very large, and it would be a long time before the people could get to Canaan.

They soon came to a very high mountain. It was called Mount Sinai. It was the same mountain where Moses had seen the bush on fire when he was keeping his sheep. Now he had brought the children of Israel to that very place where God had spoken to him first.

God told Moses to come up to the top of the mountain, for He had something to say to him. So Moses went up. Then God said to him, "You see how kind I have been to the children of Israel in bringing them out of Egypt; go down and ask them whether they will do what I desire them: for if they will, they shall always be My own people."

So Moses went down and asked them if they would obey God. And they said, "Yes, we will do all that the Lord tells us."

Then Moses went up to the top of the mountain again, and told God what the people had said.

Then God said, "I am going to let the people hear My voice, and they shall see Me speaking to you, Moses. Go down, and tell them to get ready."

So Moses went down and said, "In three days you will hear God's voice, and see Him in a cloud at the top of the mount. Get ready and wash your clothes."

So the people washed their clothes, that they might all stand in clean white clothes before the Lord. Moses desired men to put rails all round the mount, that no one might go up to it, or even touch it. Not even the sheep must eat the grass upon that mount, for it was the mount of God.

In three days, early in the morning, the people heard a loud voice, and they all trembled. Moses desired them to come out of their tents and to look upon God.

What a dreadful sight they saw! The mountain was shaking and moving up and down. On the top a great fire was seen, and a thick cloud, and such a smoke went up as filled the sky with blackness and darkness. There were thunders and lightnings, and a sound came out of the fire. It was like the sound of a trumpet, and every moment it grew louder and louder. Even Moses himself was frightened, and said, "I tremble, and am afraid."

The Lord said to Moses, "Come up to Me on the top of the mount." So Moses went up, and all the people saw him go. He went up on the shaking mount, and into the midst of the smoke.

When Moses came up, God said to him (but He did not speak very loud), "Go, tell the people not to come up after you, for they must not come up this mountain."

And Moses said, "I have put rails around the mount."

But still God said, "Go and tell them not to come near," for God knew how bold and disobedient the people were.

So Moses went down and said, "Do not dare to touch the mountain, or you will be killed."

Then God spake very loud indeed, so that all the people heard; and as they heard they trembled. Could you have seen that mountain, you would not wonder that they trembled as they stood round it.

What did God say in that loud voice? You have often heard the words at church. These are the words that God said: "I am the Lord thy God which have brought thee out of the land of Egypt, out of the house of bondage (or from the place where you were slaves).

I. Thou shalt have no other gods before Me.

II. Thou shalt not make images, and worship them. (Such images are called idols.)

III. Thou shalt not take the name of the Lord thy God in vain.

IV. Remember the Sabbath day to keep it holy, because in it God rested from His works.

V. Honor thy father and thy mother.

VI. Thou shalt not kill.

VII. Thou shalt not commit adultery (that is, a man must not take away another man's wife, nor must a woman go away from her husband and have another husband).

VIII. Thou shalt not steal.

MOSES BRINGS THE BOOK FROM MOUNT SINAI.

IX. Thou shalt not bear false witness against thy neighbor.

X Thou shalt not covet (or wish for other people's things).

This is what God said on the mount, and then He said no more.

Soon they came to Moses, and they said to him, "Ask God never to let us hear His voice again, it frightens us so much. We wish God to tell everything to you, Moses, and you can tell us what He says."

So Moses went up again to the dark cloud at the top of the mount, and told God what the people had said. "They do not wish to hear Thee speak to them again," said Moses.

And God said, "They have done well in not wishing to hear My voice. I shall speak to you, and you shall tell them; and oh, that they would obey Me, and that I might bless them always!"

You see that God wished the people to be good and happy; but He knew that they did not love Him in their hearts.

Moses did really love God. God talked to him a great deal. God told Moses to come up to Him quite alone, and to stay with Him at the top of the mountain; and so Moses stayed with God forty days and forty nights, and all that time he neither ate bread nor drank water; but God kept him alive, and talked to him out of the thick cloud.

At the end of the time God gave Moses a book. What kind of book? It was not made of paper, like the books you have seen. It was made of stone. It had only two leaves, and on those leaves very little writing. God had made this stone book, and God had written in it with His own finger.

You would like to know what was written in it. God had written in it all the words He had spoken in the loud voice from the cloud. The ten things God had told the Israelites are called the Ten Commandments.

He had written them down that Moses might read them to the children of Israel, so that they might never forget the commandments God had given to them.

The Building of the Tabernacle.

Whenever Moses talked with God his face shone for a long while afterward. When he had done talking he wore a thick veil over his face.

I hope, dear children, that your faces will one day shine bright in heaven. If you love God now, I am sure one day you will see Him in heaven, and then you will be like the angels.

Moses had been with God upon the mount a great many days. I have not told you what God was teaching him, but now you shall hear. God was showing him how to make a beautiful house.

Whose house was it to be? The house of God. God did not need a house, for His throne is in the sky; but He was so kind as to say that He would let the Israelites make Him a house in the wilderness.

When Moses came down from the mount he called all the people around him. He wanted to speak to them.

He said first, "God desires you to do no work on the Sabbath-day, but to worship Him, and He is going to have a beautiful house made, where you can come and pray to Him. Who will bring me things with which to make the house?"

THE GOLDEN CALF.

Had the children of Israel any beautiful things that they could bring to Moses?

You remember that the women of Egypt had given them a great deal of gold and silver, and cloth and linen. They had made a calf with some of their gold, but they had a great deal more beside.

But do you think they would give these things to God?—or would they say, "We cannot spare our things: we mean to make fine clothes, and to make our tents look pretty inside?" Do you think they would part with their pretty things? Yes, they would. They all went to their tents after Moses had spoken to them. They opened their boxes and their baskets, and they took out gold and silver rings and earrings, and they took out beautiful pieces of cloth; some were blue, some were purple, and some were scarlet: and a great deal of fine white linen, and skins of sheep and goats, and beautiful kinds of wood. They brought all these things to Moses. What a large heap there must have been!

Some of the rich men had beautiful shining stones, and sweet spices, and oil; and they brought them to Moses.

Moses was pleased to see that the people would give their things to God, and, most of all, he was glad that they liked to give them. They did not feel sorry when they gave them, but they were glad that they had something to give. If we feel sorry when we give things, God is not pleased.

Who was to make the beautiful house? It was very hard to make such a beautiful house as God would choose to have.

Moses called the children of Israel and said, "God has made two men very clever in cutting stones, in carving wood, and in making all kinds of curious things, and He has told me their names."

Then Moses called these two men, and he gave them all these beautiful things and said, "Now begin to make the house, and I will tell you what you shall make." And Moses called every one to help them: and he told these two clever men to teach the others.

It is God who makes people clever: so that when people can make beautiful things they should not be proud, but they should thank God.

So all these people began to work. The women spun blue, and purple, and scarlet thread, and worsted, the men made the thread into linen and cloth; they cut the wood with saws and hammers; they melted the gold and silver in the fire, and then made altars, and candlesticks, and shovels, and tongs, and basins, and many other things. They worked hard for many months, till all the things were finished.

I will now tell you what sort of a house God had told Moses to make.

It was not a house made of bricks or stone; because this house was to be moved from one place to another: so it was not fastened to the ground, but it was made like a tent, and it could be moved very easily.

THE CHILDREN OF ISRAEL DELIVER THEIR TREASURES TO MOSES.

You never saw so large a tent as this tent was. It was as big as a very large room. It was called "The Tabernacle."

There were a great many boards that were placed upright on the ground, and close together. These boards were the walls of the house: but there were no boards at the top; curtains were thrown over the house to cover the top. There was no door to the house, but a curtain hung down in front, and that curtain was instead of a door.

There was no floor to the house: green grass was the only floor. The house was very beautiful; for the boards were covered with gold, and the curtains were blue, purple and scarlet, and there were five posts of gold in front, over which a curtain hung down for the door, of which I told you before.

The house had two rooms inside. The first room was the largest. I will tell you about the beautiful things that were placed in them.

In the first room there were three very beautiful things.

1. In the middle, an altar of gold; but no lambs were burned upon it, only sweet spices, which made the tabernacle smell most sweet. The burning spices were called "incense."

2. On one side there was a golden table, and on the table

THE ALTAR OF INCENSE.

twelve loaves. They were called the shew-bread, or holy bread. There was fresh bread put there every Sabbath-day.

3. On the other side there was a golden candlestick with seven lamps. There was no window in the tabernacle, but these lamps made it light.

This room was very beautiful and sweet, but there was another room still more beautiful.

It was the inner room on the other side of the curtain. There was a curtain between the big room and the little room. This curtain was instead of a door. It was called "The Vail."

In the little room there was a golden box, with golden angels on the top. This box was called "The Ark." Inside the box the book of stone was placed. But what made this room so glorious was, that God used to come down in His cloud, and fill this little room with His brightness.

The cloud rested between the golden angels on the top of the box.

The top of the box was called the mercy-seat, because God sat there, and God is full of love and mercy. This little room was called "The Holy of Holies."

It had no window in it, and no candle, but yet it was light. The glory of God made it light! for God, you know is brighter than the sun. What a sweet place this little room must have been! It makes me think of heaven, for there God lives, and there He shines. But heaven is not a little place. It is a very large place, and it will hold all the people who have loved God on earth, besides all the angels.

I will not tell you any more about the tabernacle now; but I will write down the names of things in the tabernacle. Can you remember what they were?

In the first room—
    1. The golden altar.
    2. The table of shew-bread.
    3. The golden candlestick.
In the little room, or Holy of Holies—
    The Ark.

The Wonders and Beauties of the Tabernacle.

I have told you what kind of a place the tabernacle was. I am now going to tell you of some things that were placed outside of it.

THE BRASS ALTAR.

You know that houses often have a garden round them. The tabernacle had no garden round it, but there was a large piece of ground near it, called the court; and there were posts round the court. These posts were placed at a little distance from each other, and curtains were hung between the posts; so there was a wall of curtains round the tabernacle.

In this court there were two things of which I shall speak to you.

1. A brass altar. This altar was very large. It was not like the little altar of gold inside the tabernacle. This altar was not for the burning of spices, but for the burning of beasts, such as sheep, goats, bulls, and calves. This brass altar was for the sacrifices.

The lamb was to be killed, and its blood would flow all round the altar, and the smoke of the burning would go up to the sky.

2. A brass basin was placed in the court.

It was very large, and it was filled with water for the people to wash in. I shall soon tell you who washed in this basin.

God said that Aaron should be the "High Priest." Aaron was to offer the sacrifices, to burn the incense, and to light the lamps of the candlestick.

God said that Aaron might go into the little room, the Holy of Holies. God would not allow any person but Aaron to go in there, and He only allowed him to go in once every year. Aaron might lift up the vail, and see the cloud upon the mercy-seat. Moses might go in as well

THE BRASS BASIN FOR THE PEOPLE TO WASH IN.

as Aaron: and God promised to speak to him in that little room. God desired Moses to have some beautiful clothes made for Aaron to wear. The two clever men, of whom I told you before, knew how to make them.

1. He was to wear a white dress, with long sleeves.

2. A robe of blue. He was to wear this over the white dress. Little golden bells were hung round the edge of it: and they would sound sweetly as Aaron moved along.

3. An ephod made of white linen, worked all over with purple, scarlet, and gold. Aaron was to wear the ephod over the blue robe.

4. A band round his waist, called a girdle. It was made of white linen, and was worked with purple, scarlet thread, and with gold wire.

5. A breastplate. Aaron was to wear this in front. It was made of linen, covered with twelve shining stones. It was to be fastened to Aaron's shoulders by gold chains.

6. A mitre. Aaron was to wear a high white cap upon his head, called a mitre. A piece of gold was on the mitre, and on the gold was written, "Holiness to the Lord." Aaron ought to be holy, because he was to offer sacrifices to God.

He was to wear no shoes upon his feet: but he was often to wash his feet and his hands at the brass basin.

Aaron had four sons. God said that they should help him to offer sacrifices. His sons were to wear white clothes, but not the same beautiful clothes as Aaron. They were to be called "Priests," and Aaron was to be called "High Priest."

At last God desired Moses to set up the tabernacle.

Then Moses put upon Aaron his beautiful robes, and put the white clothes upon his sons, and anointed their heads with oil.

Then God came down in His cloud, and His brightness filled the whole place; and so God showed that He would have it for His house.

Was it not pleasant for the Israelites to think that God lived in a house in the midst of them? The cloud could be seen outside the tabernacle as well as inside, and in the night it shone like fire. How kind it was of God to let the people see some of His brightness! God wished them to be very good, and to obey all He said. God is very near us, too, though we cannot see Him; but we hope to see Him some day.

What place is more beautiful than the tabernacle was? Heaven. If we get to heaven, we shall be much more glorious than Aaron was, and we shall see God's face forever and ever, and so we shall be quite happy.

Story of the Twelve Spies.

Now the Israelites had a place in which to worship God and to offer sacrifices.

Every morning the priest offered up a lamb on the brass altar, and burned incense on the golden altar in the tabernacle. And every evening they offered another lamb, and burned some more incense.

The people went into the great court of the tabernacle to worship God, and to see the lamb killed and burned on the altar. Afterward they saw Aaron go into the tabernacle to burn incense. The people stood in the court while Aaron was in the tabernacle praying for them. They waited till he came out again to bless them. He lifted up his hands and said, "The Lord bless thee, and keep thee."

While the people had been making the tabernacle, they had stayed in one place near the great mount, Sinai; but soon after it was finished the cloud of God moved. Then the priests blew two silver trumpets, to tell the people that they were to move to another place.

Then the people packed up their tents and furniture, and put them on the backs of their camels and asses.

Then the priests went into the tabernacle, and covered all the things in it with blue cloths. No one might look while they were covering the things. Then they gave them to some men to carry upon their shoulders: but they covered the ark with the beautiful veil, and they carried it themselves. There were two long golden sticks fastened to it; the priests held the ends of the sticks, and so they carried it.

Then the priests desired some men to carry the curtains and the posts, and the boards of the tabernacle. The priests went first with the ark, and all the people followed them, and God in the cloud showed them the way.

146   MY MOTHER'S BIBLE STORIES.

When the cloud stopped, the priests and the people stopped, and set up the tabernacle and the tents.

In this manner the Israelites traveled all through the wilderness, until at last they came quite near the land of Canaan. So the Israelites came to Moses and said, "We wish to send some men to look at the land, and we wish them to come back and tell us what kind of a land it is."

Then Moses asked God if He would like for the men to go. Soon God said to Moses, "Send twelve men into Canaan to see the land." So Moses called twelve of the children of Israel, and said to them, "Go into Canaan, and walk up among the high mountains, and look at the land: see whether there are many people living in the land, and what kind of people they are; whether they are strong or weak: see whether there are many trees, and much corn and grass in the land; and bring back some fruit, to show us the kind of fruit that grows in the land."

AARON BLESSING THE PEOPLE.

JORDAN RIVER THAT BORDERS CANAAN.

So the twelve men set out on their journey. These men were called the twelve spies. They walked up and down the hills, and by the side of the water. They saw sweet gardens, and some fields covered with sheep, and some fields full of corn, and trees laden with fruit; and they saw holes in the trees, which the bees had filled with honey, so that honey dropped on the ground. They saw large towns with high walls round them, and they saw many strong men, and some of them were giants.

At last they came to a brook or pond. A vine grew by it, and on the vine there were ripe grapes; one of the bunches was very, very large. They said, "Let us bring it back to show to the children of Israel." One man could not carry this bunch by himself. So they took a staff, or stick, and fastened the bunch of grapes to the staff, and one man held one end of the staff, and another held the other. The rest of the men picked figs and other

THE RETURN OF THE SPIES.

fruit, and carried them back to the tents. The spies were forty days looking at the land of Canaan.

When they came back, the people saw the beautiful bunch of grapes. There were no such grapes in the wilderness. The spies then said, "The land of Canaan is a fine land, full of milk and honey; but we cannot get into it, for the people live in great towns with high walls; they are very strong, and some of them are giants, and when we saw them, we felt as if we were as little grasshoppers."

Then the children of Israel were very much frightened, and began to murmur and to weep.

"Ah!" said the people, "we shall be killed if we try to get in."

It was wicked to say this, because God had promised to help the Israelites to get into Canaan. It is wicked not to believe what God says.

Two of the spies were very good men; their names were Joshua and Caleb. They did not wish to frighten the people: and Caleb stood up and said, "Let us go into the land, for we can conquer the people that are in it."

But the ten other spies said, "No, we cannot, because the people of Canaan are stronger than we."

These ten spies were very wicked men, because they knew that God had promised to help the Israelites to conquer the men of Canaan, and they ought to have told the people to trust in God.

The Israelites cried all night long, and they were angry with Moses and Aaron for bringing them out of Egypt, and said, "Oh, that we had died in Egypt, or in the wilderness! The people of Canaan will kill us with their swords, and they will kill our wives and our little children!"

They spoke in this way all night long, instead of praying to God to help them.

At last they said, "Let us go back into Egypt."

They knew that Moses would not take them back. So they said, "We can make another man captain over us, and he will take us back to Egypt."

Moses and Aaron heard these wicked words; they were full of grief, and they fell down on the ground on their faces. They were grieved to see the people so wicked. Then Joshua and Caleb stood

THE PEOPLE THREATEN TO STONE CALEB AND JOSHUA.

up and said to the people, "We have seen the land, and it is a very beautiful land; and if we trust in God He will help us to fight: but the people of Canaan have no God to help them; therefore we ought not to be afraid of them."

The children of Israel would not listen to Joshua and Caleb, but were going to kill them with stones, when God shone brightly upon the tabernacle, so that the people saw that He was angry.

Moses was lying on his face on the ground, but God spake to him, and said, "How long will this people provoke Me? I will kill them with a plague." Then Moses prayed to God for the people.

"Oh, pardon this people," he said, "their great sin. Thou hast forgiven them many times, and Thy mercy is very great."

God heard Moses' prayer, and said, "I have pardoned them. I will not kill them all now, but they shall not come into Canaan: only their children shall come in. They shall stay in the wilderness forty years, and they shall all die in it; and when their children are grown up, they shall go into the land of Canaan. But there are two of the men who shall go into Canaan,—they are Caleb and Joshua."

The ten wicked spies soon fell sick and died, but Joshua and Caleb lived still.

The Story of Baalam.

In the land of the Midianites there dwelt a prophet named Baalam. But although Baalam was a prophet of the true God I am sorry to say he does not seem to have been a good man, for he would have cursed the children of Israel if God had permitted him to do so.

When the people came near to the borders of the Midianites their king, Balak, sent messengers to Baalam, asking him to come and curse the children of Israel, "for," said he, "I wot that he whom thou blessest is blessed, and he whom thou cursest is cursed."

Baalam asked the men whom Balak had sent to stay with him all night, and he would let them know in the morning what the Lord should speak to him during the night. When the men were asleep the Lord spoke to Baalam and told him that he should not go with them; "thou shalt not curse the people, for they are blessed."

So when the morning came Baalam told the men that the Lord would not permit him to go with them, and they returned to the king.

When Balak heard their report he sent other men, more distinguished than the first, and told them to say to Baalam that he must not let anything hinder him from coming, and that if he would curse the children of Israel he would promote him to very great honor.

Baalam answered the men and said, "If Balak would give me his house full of silver and gold I cannot go beyond the word of the Lord my God to do less or more." But he requested them to remain with him all night that he might know what the Lord would say to him.

In the night while they slept the Lord came to Baalam and told him he could go with the men, but he must speak only the words that would be told him.

God did this to try Baalam and see if his heart was right, for he did not intend that any harm should come to the children of Israel.

When morning came Baalam arose and saddled his ass and went with the men, and God's anger was kindled against him because of his perverseness. As they passed along the road an angel stood in the way with a drawn sword in his hand. Baalam could not see the angel, but the ass saw him and turned aside into the field. Then Baalam beat the ass and

BAALAM SEES THE ANGEL.

turned her back into the road; but they had gone only a little way when the angel appeared again in the path, between two vineyards, where there was a stone wall on either side, and the ass, being greatly frightened, thrust herself to one side against the wall and crushed Baalam's foot; whereupon Baalam beat her again and forced her to go on.

Soon they came to a narrow way, where there was no room to turn to either side, and here the angel appeared once more in the path with his drawn sword in his hand. Then the poor ass fell down and trembled with fright, and Baalam, being exceedingly angry, beat her with his staff. But the Lord opened the mouth of the ass and she said to Baalam, "What have I done unto thee that thou hast smitten me these three times." And Baalam replied in his anger, "Because thou hast mocked me. I would there were a sword in mine hand, for now would I kill thee." Then the poor ass said, "Am I not thine ass, upon which thou hast ridden ever since I was thine unto this day? Was I ever wont to do so unto thee?"

Then Baalam's eyes were opened and he saw the angel standing in the way with his sword drawn in his hand, and Baalam was so frightened that he fell down flat upon his face. The angel then asked him why he had been so cruel and wicked as to beat the unoffending ass three times, for, said he, if she had not turned aside he would have slain Baalam with his sword. On hearing this Baalam became very sorry for his wickedness and begged the angel to forgive him, and said he would return to his home if it was displeasing to the Lord for him to go with the men. But the angel told him to go, and commanded him that he should speak only the words that were told him.

So Baalam and the men proceeded on the way until they came to the city where Balak lived. Then Balak came out to meet them, and he made a great sacrifice, and told Baalam that he would bestow many honors upon him if he would curse the Israelites and drive them away. But Baalam told Balak that he could only speak the words that the Lord should put into his mouth.

Three times Balak offered sacrifices and sent Baalam up to the top of a high hill where he could see the children of Israel encamped on the plain, and told him to curse them; but each time the Lord put blessings into his mouth instead of curses.

Then Balak became very angry and sent Baalam back to his home, but soon afterward the soldiers that fought under Moses and Joshua overran the country of the Midianites and slew both Balak and Baalam.

The Sin of Moses and Aaron, and Aaron's Death.

The children of Israel lived in the wilderness a great many years. They moved about from place to place.

At last they came to a place where there was no water.

How do you think they behaved? Did they pray to God, or did they murmur?

They murmured against Moses and Aaron, as they always did when they were unhappy.

They said, "Oh that we had died before this time! Why did you bring us out of Egypt into this wilderness? Here there are no figs, no grapes, no nice fruit, and now there is no water to drink!"

Moses and Aaron were very much grieved to hear them murmur, and they went away from the people, and fell on their faces before the tabernacle; and soon God spoke to them.

He said, "Take the rod and call the people, and go to the rock and speak to it, and water shall come out of the rock, and then the people and the beasts shall drink."

So Moses took the rod, which was kept near the ark. Then Moses and Aaron called the people together, and told them to look at what they were going to do.

Moses and Aaron felt very angry with the people, and they said, "Hear now, ye rebels! must we fetch water for you out of this rock?"

Then Moses lifted up his hand and struck the rock twice with his rod; and the water came flowing out in streams, and the people and the cattle began to drink.

Do you think Moses and Aaron had behaved right? Had God told them to strike the rock?

God had said, "Speak to the rock."

Was it right to speak so impatiently, and to say, "Must we fetch water for you, ye rebels?"

Moses and Aaron had been in a passion. God was displeased with them.

Soon afterward, God said to Moses and Aaron, "Because you have done this, you shall not go into Canaan: you shall die in the wilderness."

What a great punishment this was! Moses had often longed to see that sweet land of Canaan; he had often wished to see the Israelites happy in their own houses and gardens; he had longed to see the

THE PEOPLE MURMUR AGAINST MOSES AND AARON.

place where Abraham had built altars and worshiped God; but now he must die in the wilderness. He prayed to God not to inflict this punishment upon him; but God would not grant his request. He said, "Ask me no more to do this." Then Moses knew that he must bear his punishment.

Moses was the meekest man in all the world. The Israelites had often spoken ungratefully to him, and he had made no answer. Yet at last he himself fell into a passion.

You see how much God hates passion. God wishes us to be very meek, like the Lord Jesus Christ, who never spoke an angry word.

Was it unkind of God to punish Moses and Aaron?

God cannot be unkind, but He will punish people for disobedience. God wished to show the Israelites that He would not allow any person to be disobedient— not even Moses.

At last the time came for Aaron to die, for God chose Aaron to die first. God said to Moses, "Go up to the top of the hill with Aaron, and take Aaron's eldest son with you, and Aaron will die on the top, and you must put his clothes upon

DEATH OF AARON.

his son." God chose Aaron's son to be high-priest instead of Aaron, so he was to wear Aaron's clothes.

So Aaron put on his beautiful high-priest's clothes; his blue robe with the golden bells, and his ephod over it, his shining breastplate, and his white mitre, with the golden writing upon it. Then Aaron walked with Moses and his son to the top of the hill, and all the people looked at them as they were walking up. Aaron knew that he should never walk down that hill, but still he obeyed God, and bore his punishment meekly.

When they were come to the top, Moses took the beautiful clothes off his brother Aaron, and put them on Aaron's son.

Moses parted from his brother Aaron on the top of the hill; for there Aaron died. Moses and his son left him dead upon the top, and came down the hill together. Then the people saw that Aaron was dead, and that there was another high-priest.

The Brazen Serpent.

The children of Israel traveled in the wilderness a great many years. Sometimes, when they were close to Canaan, the cloud moved the other way, and the Israelites were obliged to go on traveling in the wilderness. This made them very unhappy, for they longed very much to get into the sweet land of Canaan. If they had not behaved so ill in the wilderness, they would soon have got to Canaan; but God punished them by not letting them get in.

How do you think they bore their punishment? You know that they were always ready to murmur. They spoke against God and against Moses. They said, "Why have you brought us out of Egypt? We shall die in the wilderness. There is no bread here, nor any water, and we do not like this manna."

Was the manna nice food? It was fit for angels—spotless white, and sweet as honey; it came down from heaven, and did not grow out of the ground as corn does. Yet these ungrateful Israelites said that they hated it, and were tired of eating it.

God sent them a dreadful punishment this time. You know there were wild beasts and horrible serpents and scorpions in the wilderness, but God took care of the Israelites, so that they were not hurt by them; but now God sent serpents, whose mouths burned like fire. These serpents came rushing among the tents. The Israelites could not get away from them. If they climbed up a high place, the serpents could climb after them, and they could get through the smallest places.

THE BRAZEN SERPENT.

Many, many of the Israelites were bitten by these serpents. After they had been bitten they grew sick, and were full of pain, and got worse and worse, till at last they died. There was no medicine that could cure these bites; no plaster could make them well; every person who was bitten was sure to die.

The Israelites came to Moses, and said, "We have sinned; we have spoken against the Lord, and against you; pray to the

Lord that He take the serpents from us." For the serpents were still among the tents.

Did Moses pray to God for the people? or did he say, "You deserve to be punished, and I will not help you?" Moses was kind and forgiving, and he prayed for the people.

The Lord heard Moses' prayer, and He did more than Moses asked; for He not only called away the serpents, but He told him how to cure the people who were bitten by the serpents.

God said to Moses, "Take some brass, and make it into the image of a serpent, and put it on a pole, and tell the people who are bitten to look at it, and those who look shall be made well."

Was not this a strange way of making them well?

Moses believed God. He took some brass, and made it soft in the fire; and then made it like one of the fiery serpents and put it on a pole, and lifted it up, where every one could see it, and called to the sick people to look quickly at the serpent and be made well.

The people who were bitten could crawl to the door of their tents, and lift up their dying eyes toward the serpent. After they had looked their pain went away; they felt well and strong; they could walk and praise God.

The Death of Moses.

The time was almost come for Moses to die. The Israelites were very soon to go into Canaan, but Moses was not to go there with them.

Moses had written a great many books while he had been in the wilderness, and now he had almost finished them. Should you like to know what Moses had written about in these books?

He had written about how God made the world, how Adam ate the fruit, how Cain killed Abel. He had written about Noah, and Abraham, and Isaac, and Jacob; he had written about Joseph and his wicked brethren; he had written about himself, how he had been saved from the water when he was a baby. He had written about the ten plagues, and the ten commandments, and the tabernacle; he had written about his own sin. All I have told you Moses had written down in five books. They have all been copied in other books, and we can read all Moses wrote, for it is in the Bible.

But how did Moses know all these things? He was not born when God made the world. How could he write about things he never saw? Could anybody have told him how God made the world? No one was born when God made the world; no one but God could tell him, and God did tell him.

God spake to Moses by his Spirit; while Moses was writing with his pen, God was putting thoughts in his mind; so he always knew what to write.

Moses did not write in such books as you have seen. His paper was rolled up like a piece of cloth at the shop. He wrote five rolls, and those he called his books. If you had read in Moses' book, you must have unrolled it as you read it.

When Moses had done writing his books, he called the priests, and told them to take care of his books. Moses said to them, "You must read these books to all the Israelites, the men, the women, and the little children, that they may know how to please God."

Moses knew that he must soon leave the Israelites. He wished very much that some good man should take care of them after he was dead; for he loved them very much, though they had behaved so ill to him. So Moses begged God to give them to the care of some good man; and God heard his prayer and said to Moses, "I have found a man who will take care of the children of Israel after you are dead."

Who do you think this man was? It was Joshua, one of the good spies: he had helped Moses to do God's work for forty years; so that Moses had taught him a great deal. Moses was very glad that Joshua would take care of the Israelites when he was dead.

Moses called Joshua and said to him, "God will let you take the children of Israel into Canaan; you must be very brave, for you will have to fight against the wicked people; but God will help you: so do not be afraid. God never will leave you, nor forsake you."

Moses wished to speak to the people before he died, and advise them to be good; so he called all the people together, and told them he was going to die. "I am very old," said he; "I am a hundred and twenty years old this day. I offended God, and I must not go into the land of Canaan; but Joshua will take you there. Remember to obey God, and to love Him, and He will always bless you; but if you worship idols and are wicked, God will punish you."

God told Moses to teach the people a song, that they might sing it after he was dead. This song was about God's kindness to the children of Israel.

My dear children, you learn pretty songs or hymns about God. Do you know why you are taught to repeat them? It is to help you to think of God, that you may love Him. Some children repeat their hymns as soon as they wake in the morning.

MOSES BLESSES THE PEOPLE.

After Moses had taught the people the song, he blessed them, and then he left them for ever. God said to Moses, "Go up that high mountain alone: I cannot let you go into Canaan, but I will let you see that beautiful land of Canaan from the top of that mountain." Moses was glad that he might see Canaan, though he might not go in. So he went up the mountain quite alone. He was very old, yet he was not weak; he could walk as well as when he was young, and he could see as well; for his eyes were not dim; he read, and wrote, and saw things far off. God had not let him grow weak or blind.

BURIAL OF MOSES.

I think the Israelites must have felt very sad when they saw Moses go up that mountain all alone, and when they knew they should see him no more.

I hope they felt sorry for having behaved so ill to him, and for having so provoked him at the rock. What a kind friend Moses had been to them! When Moses was at the top of the hill, he looked and saw the land of Canaan a great way off. It was a beautiful land, and full of green hills, and rivers, of fields ripe with corn, and of trees laden with fruit. Moses was glad that the children of Israel would live in such a sweet land, where they might worship God.

When he had looked at the land, he died. No friend was near to close his eyes, or to hear his last sigh: no brother's hand was there to wrap him in his grave-clothes, or to cover him with the green earth.

Would God leave Moses' body to be eaten by the wild beasts, to be pecked by the birds of the air? No; God Himself buried Moses: not upon the top of the hill, but in some secret place under the hill. No one knows where Moses lies, but the angels, who carried his soul to God—they know; for they watch over God's dear children in the dust.

Thus Moses died. He was the only man to whom God talked as a friend: God spoke to Moses face to face, as friends talk to each other.

I shall tell you no more of Moses. You remember that he might have been a prince in the land of Egypt. King Pharaoh's daughter saved him from the water, and she gave him fine things, and called him her son. But Moses wished to help the poor children of Israel, and he did not choose to be a prince in Egypt.

Was it not much better that Moses should help the poor children of Israel, than that he should be rich and grand?

You see that God loved Moses, and made him His friend, and took him to heaven when he died.

Now, I hope all children will be like Moses. I hope that when you are grown up you will try to help poor people, and teach them to be kind to one another.

Joshua, the Great General.

The Israelites were now come close to the land of Canaan. They were sorry that Moses was dead; but Joshua was now to take care of them instead of Moses. Joshua was to tell them what to do. God would speak to him, and he would tell them what God said.

The Israelites would soon have to fight a great deal. Whom would they have to fight against? The wicked people who lived in

164   MY MOTHER'S BIBLE STORIES.

Canaan. God chose that they should be killed to punish them for their wickedness, and God chose that the Israelites should live in their land instead of them. There was a great river that rolled between the wilderness and Canaan. The Israelites would be obliged to cross the river before they could get into Canaan. They could see the green hills of Canaan on the other side of the river, and they saw a great town also with high walls all round it. This town was called Jericho. It was in Canaan, and wicked people lived in it. The Israelites knew that they would soon have to fight against the people who lived in this town. Joshua told two of the Israelites to go to the town and to look at it, and to come back and tell him about the town, and about the people who lived in it. These men were called "spies," because they went to spy or to look at the town. Joshua did not wish the people of Jericho to know when these two spies

JOSHUA, THE NEW LEADER OF THE ISRAELITES.

came into the town, lest the wicked people should kill them. So they went to the town when it was almost dark. The spies got over the river: there was one place in the river where the water was not very deep, and where people could get over. This was called a ford.

The gate of Jericho used to be shut when it was dark; but the spies came just before the gate was shut. They went to the house of a woman named Rahab, who kept an inn. Her house was built upon the wall of Jericho. The spies hoped that nobody had seen them come into Jericho; but some people had seen them, and these people went and told the king of Jericho that two Israelites were in Rahab's house. The king knew that the Israelites meant to come and fight against him, so he wanted to kill these two spies, and he sent some men to Rahab's house to bring them to him.

What could the poor spies do? Where could they go? But God took care of them. He put it into Rahab's heart to be kind to them. Rahab had taken the spies, when they first came, to the top of her house, to hide them. The roof of her house was flat, like the floor. On the roof of Rahab's house there were a great many stalks of flax. Flax is a plant which grows in large stalks, and the stalks are covered with a strong bark. This bark is peeled off, and is very fine and soft, and when woven in a loom it makes a beautiful white cloth, called linen. Rahab had spread the stalks of flax upon the roof of her house to dry them. When the spies had climbed up the stairs to the top of the house, she told them to lie down; and she covered them all over with stalks, so that nobody could see them.

The men who were come to bring the spies to the king of Jericho, could not find them in Rahab's house, so they went to look for them outside the city, among the hills, and by the river-side.

When the king of Jericho's men were gone, Rahab crept up the stairs to speak to the spies. It was night, so she could talk to them on the roof without being seen. The men came from under the heaps of flax. Rahab had been taught to worship idols; but you will see that she now believed in the true God, and not in idols. She had a great favor to ask of the spies. She was very much afraid lest, when the Israelites came over the river to fight against Jericho, they should kill her and her friends: so now she begged the spies to promise to save her, and those she loved. Poor Rahab said, "I know that God will let the people of Israel come and live in Canaan. Everybody is very much frightened lest you should kill them. We have heard how your God helped you to pass through the Red Sea. I know that your God is the only true God. Now promise, that when you come to this town you will not kill me, nor my father and mother, and brothers and sisters. I have been kind to you, and will you be kind to me?"

ESCAPE OF THE SPIES.

The spies said, "If you will not tell anybody about our having come here, we promise to save your life, and the lives of your father and mother, and brothers and sisters."

Then Rahab helped the spies to get out of the town. But it was night, and the gates were shut. If the spies waited till morning, the people of Jericho would see them going out, and would kill them. But Rahab found a way of letting the spies go.

Her house was built on the walls of Jericho. One of the windows looked toward the green hills outside of Jericho. The window was high; so Rahab took a rope, and tied it round one of the men, and let him down from the window; and then she tied it around the other man, and let him down.

When the men were standing on the ground outside the wall of Jericho, they called to Rahab, who was looking out of the window, and they said, "Take that red rope, and bind it to your window; bring your father and mother, and brothers and sisters, into your house. If they stay in it with you, we promise that they shall not be killed when the Israelites come to fight against this town; but if you, or any of your relations, are walking in the streets when we come, then, perhaps, you or they may be killed. Neither may you tell any other person about our having come here: you must keep it a secret." When the spies had said this they went away, and they hid themselves among the hills for three days, lest the men of Jericho should be watching by the river to kill them. At the end of three days they got over the river, and came back to Joshua, and told him all that had happened. Joshua was glad to hear that the people of Jericho were so much frightened, and he felt sure that God would help him to conquer all the people in Canaan.

The spies told Joshua about Rahab. They said, "You will know which house is Rahab's, because she has bound a red rope to the window." Joshua desired that nobody would kill the people in the house with the red rope on the window.

The Children of Israel Cross the River Jordan.

The people of Israel were now close to Canaan; but a deep river ran between the wilderness and Canaan. It was called the River Jordan. How were the Israelites to get over it?

Could they go over in boats?

How could wood be got to make boats for so many people?

Could they make a bridge? The people in Canaan would have shot arrows at the Israelites while they were making a bridge.

Could they swim over?

How could the children and the women swim? and how could they take their tents over?

God could help them to get over. How had they got over the Red Sea?

You shall hear what God told Joshua to do.

Joshua rose up early in the morning, and he said to the people, "Look and see where the priests take the ark, and do you follow them, but do not go too near."

Then Joshua said to the priests, "Take up the ark and go forward."

The ark (which was a golden box) was covered with a blue cloth, that none might see it, or see the golden angels on the top. Two long sticks were run through the rings joined to the ark, and the priests held the ends of the sticks.

The priests took up the ark when Joshua bade them. They went to the edge of the water, not knowing what they were to do. They were dressed in white, and their feet were bare.

Joshua called to them, and desired them to stand still. Then he spoke to all the people. "Now," he said, "you will see a great wonder that God is going to do; when the priests put their feet in the water a dry path shall be made."

All the people were coming out of their tents. They had got all their things ready for their journey and were looking at the priests.

Then Joshua desired the priests to put their feet into the water.

As soon as they touched it, the water stood up like a wall on one side, and there was a dry path made through the river. The priests walked along till they came to the middle of the river; then they stopped, and Joshua said to the people, "Now do you pass over Jordan."

MY MOTHER'S BIBLE STORIES. 169

While the people were crossing, the priests stood quite still in the middle of the dried-up river. At last, all the people had got over into the land of Canaan, except twelve men that Joshua had desired to stay on the other side.

Joshua said to these men, "See where the priests are standing; there are great stones lying near them; take up twelve great stones and bring them over with you into Canaan." These twelve men walked through the dry path: each took up a great stone in his arms and carried it to the other side. Then Joshua said to them, "Put the twelve stones by the side of the river in Canaan."

Why do you think the stones were to be put there? It was that

THE PRIESTS BEARING THE ARK.

people might never forget this great wonder of making a path in Jordan. God knew that, a long time afterward, little children would see the twelve stones, and would say to their fathers, "What are these stones for?"

Then their fathers would say, "These stones were once at the bottom of the water: but God made a path for us, and we have put the stones here to keep God's kindness in our minds."

God is pleased that children should wish to know the meaning of what they see. God wishes little children to know about His goodness, and the wonders He has done.

When the twelve men had carried the twelve stones to the opposite bank of the river, Joshua said to the priests, "Come up out of Jordan:" so the priests came up out of the river. As soon as they put their feet on the dry land in Canaan the water rolled along, and the river flowed on as it had done before.

How happy the Israelites must now have been! They had wandered forty years in the wilderness, but at last they had safely arrived in Canaan. God had been very good to them, and He would help them to fight against the wicked people of Canaan.

Why did God desire that the people in Canaan should be killed? Because they worshiped idols, and did a great many wicked things, so God chose to punish them.

The king of Jericho saw the Israelites come over the river. He could look at them over his high walls. He was very much frightened, and so were all the people in Jericho. Only Rahab was not frightened: she knew she was safe; she believed in the true God.

The priests put down the ark: all the Israelites set up their tents, and waited outside Jericho. Rahab's red cord could be seen upon her window on the wall.

So the Israelites knew which was her house, and Joshua told them not to hurt the people who were in it.

The gates of Jericho were kept fast shut, that the Israelites might not get in: no one in Jericho went out, and no one came in, but everybody kept inside the town.

Those wicked people would never again walk by the riverside: the day of their death was very near. Ah! why did they not turn to God before it was too late?

MY MOTHER'S BIBLE STORIES.   171

The Walls of Jericho Fall Down.

The children of Israel had placed their tents all round the city of Jericho, but they waited till God told them what to do. They could not get through the strong gates unless God helped them.

Joshua was the captain of the Israelites. He was a very brave man. He trusted in God to help him, and that made him brave.

I will now tell you a very wonderful thing that happened to Joshua while he was on the outside of Jericho.

One day he looked up, and he saw a man standing before him a little way off. The man looked as if he were a soldier, and he held a sword in his hand.

THE ANGEL APPEARING TO JOSHUA.

Joshua knew that this man was not one of the Israelites: but he could not tell who he was. Joshua went up to the man and said, "Are you come to help us to fight? or are you come to help the people of Jericho?" Then the man answered, "I am come as captain of the army of the Lord."

Then Joshua fell down with his face upon the ground, and worshiped Him, saying, "What will my Lord say to His servant?"

(Joshua called himself God's servant.)

Then the great captain of God's army said, "Take your shoes from off your feet, because this is holy ground."

Then Joshua took his shoes off, and waited to know what the Lord would say to him.

Why was the ground holy? Because God was there. You know the priests wore no shoes when they walked in God's house.

The Lord told Joshua how he was to fight against Jericho.

Such a way of fighting was never known before. You shall soon hear what the Lord told Joshua to do.

When the Lord had gone back to heaven, Joshua called the priests, and all the people of Israel, and showed them what they must do. Joshua told some of the priests to take up the ark.

Then he called seven more priests and said, "Each of you must take a ram's horn, and walk before the ark."

Then Joshua called all the soldiers, and told them to go before the priests, and he told the rest of the people that had not swords or spears to walk behind the priests.

He desired them to walk round the city of Jericho. The soldiers, with their swords and spears, went first; next came seven priests, dressed in their white clothes, blowing the rams' horns. Then came the priests carrying the ark, and behind them all the people, but with no swords or spears. You never saw such a great number of people walking along.

Before they set out, Joshua told them not to make any shoutings, but to wait until he said, "Shout!"

What is shouting? Calling out loud. Soldiers shout when they have conquered. The Israelites were not to shout till Joshua told them. They all walked once round Jericho.

The people of Jericho heard the trumpets blowing, and they saw the men with swords and spears.

I dare say they thought the Israelites were going to shoot their arrows over the walls, and try and beat down the walls. How much frightened they must have been! Rahab took care to keep in her house, with all her friends. The Israelites walked once round, and then Joshua brought them back to their tents.

Are you not surprised to hear this? What was the use of walking round? You will hear what happened in the end.

The next day Joshua made the people and the priests walk round once more, and then brought them home. Then, the next day after, they went round again: and the next day, and the next day. Six days, one after the other, they walked round Jericho, and came home to their tents again, without having fought.

DESTRUCTION OF JERICHO.

The Israelites behaved well in doing as Joshua told them, instead of asking why they must walk round without fighting.

Do you think that the people of Jericho began to laugh at the Israelites, and to think that they would never get into the city?

At last, after six days, Joshua told the Israelites to get up very early in the morning, as soon as it was light. He told them to walk all round as before; but when they had walked round, he did not tell them to go back to their tents, but to walk round again. That day they walked round seven times: they spent the whole day in walking round and round the city of Jericho.

When they had just finished walking round the seventh time, Joshua said to the people, "Now, when the priests blow again with the trumpets, you may shout: for God has given you the city. You will soon get in; you must kill all the people, except Rahab and her friends that are in her house. You will find many beautiful things in Jericho, but you must not keep anything for yourselves: but you must bring the cups of gold and silver, and brass and iron, to the Lord; and you must not keep anything for yourselves. Bring all you find to the house of the Lord; for God has cursed Jericho, and everything in it."

When Joshua had done speaking, the priests blew again with the trumpets, and the people gave a great shout. At the same moment, the walls of Jericho fell down. How horrible was the crash of those great walls! Now the men of Jericho saw that the day had come when they must die.

The two spies ran quickly to Rahab's house, and brought her out, and her father and mother, and brothers and sisters, and led them to a safe place near the tents of the Israelites. Rahab and her friends brought all their things with them out of the house: so they could make tents, and live together.

But what happened to the people of Jericho? They were all killed, the men, the women, and the children—even the sheep, and cows, and all the beasts were killed; not one was left alive. The Israelites killed them with their swords. Then they set fire to the houses, and burned them all up; but the cups and basins, made of gold and silver, and brass and iron, they brought to the priests for God's house.

All the other people in Canaan heard about Jericho, and they were more frightened than before. They said, "What a great captain Joshua is!"

But you know who was the Captain that fought for Joshua. Who was it threw down the walls? Was it not the man whom Joshua had seen? He was a captain over thousands of angels that filled the air, and obeyed all He said.

Conquest of Canaan and Death of Joshua.

You have heard what the Israelites did to Jericho. There were a great many other cities in Canaan, and the Israelites fought against them.

All the people of Canaan heard it, and were much afraid of Joshua; but still they took their swords and spears, and fought against him.

And who do you think conquered? God always helped the Israelites; so they always conquered. They went all through Canaan. First, they went to one city, and killed the people in it; then they went to another city, and killed the people there; so they went to hundreds of cities, till they had killed almost all the people in Canaan. God did not make the walls of the other cities fall down, like the walls of Jericho; but the Israelites were obliged to fight very hard before they could get in.

At last Joshua said to the children of Israel, "Now the people of Canaan are dead, I will give you places to live in." So he gave to each of the Israelites a house, full of nice and beautiful things, and a garden, and a field, and a well of water.

Now the Israelites rested. They sat down under the fig-trees and vines in their own gardens, and ate the figs and grapes that grew on them, and they drank water out of the wells in their gardens.

Did the Israelites build their own houses? No; they lived in the houses of the people of Canaan. The wicked people had built the houses, and they had dug the wells, and planted the trees in the

176   MY MOTHER'S BIBLE STORIES.

gardens; but God had taken them away from these wicked people, and had given them to the Israelites.

Might God give them to whom He pleased? Yes: God made everything, and everything belongs to God; and He may give things to whom He pleases. Sometimes He takes His things away from wicked people.

JOSHUA COMMANDING THE SUN AND MOON TO STAND STILL.

There was one thing which Joshua did not forget to do; that was, to place the tabernacle in Canaan. He set it up in the middle of Canaan, at a place called Shiloh. Now the Israelites would not be obliged to move it about any more.

Joshua told them all to come up and worship God in the tabernacle: but some lived so far off that they could not come often. So they came only now and then to the tabernacle. God desired the Israelites not to worship the idols that the wicked people in Canaan had made. The Israelites would find their idols in the fields and gardens; and some of these idols were made of silver and gold: but they were not to keep them, even if they were pretty images; they were not to take the idols into their houses: but they were to burn them in the fire; because God hated these idols.

At last Joshua grew very old, and he knew that he must die. So he called a great many of the Israelites together, that he might speak to them before he died.

He stood near a great oak-tree while he spoke. He said to the Israelites, "I am soon going to die. Whom will you worship after I am dead? Will you worship idols, or will you worship God who has been so kind to you?"

Now which do you think the Israelites would choose to worship? They all said, "We will worship God." Then Joshua said, "If you choose to worship God, you must not worship idols too."

Then they answered, "We will serve God."

DESTROYING IDOLS.

"Now," said Joshua, "you have promised to serve God only. You must keep your promise."

Then Joshua took a book and wrote down what the people had said. Afterward he took a great stone, and put it under the oak, and said, "See this stone; I have put it here to make you remember your promise always."

Then he told all the people to go home.

Very soon afterward Joshua died. He was more than a hundred years old at that time.

Did the Israelites keep their promise? Did they worship idols, or did they not?

At first they kept their promise. But at last they grew tired of serving God, and began to worship idols, and to do other wicked things, for which they were punished, as I will tell you in another part of this book.

Story of Samson, the Strong Man.

The Lord raised up many mighty men to deliver the children of Israel from their enemies. Jephthah was one of these. You may read the story of him in Judges, chapter xi.

After the death of Jephthah, other judges ruled; but they could not keep Israel from returning to their idols.

This time the Lord delivered Israel into the hand of the Philistines.

These Philistines lived in the land of Israel, and had strong cities of their own, with great lords to rule over them.

During forty years Israel groaned under these cruel tyrants, when the Lord again graciously gave them a deliverer. This time it was not a man—nor was it a woman that the Lord chose—but a babe.

As God had promised, Samson was born, and when he was grown he was very strong. One day a young lion met him and roared at him. Samson killed him, as he would a kid, and he had no sword, no spear—just his hands alone. Once he caught three hundred foxes, and tied firebrands or pieces of blazing wood to their tails, and let them loose, two by two, in the fields and vineyards of the Philistines. They set fire to the grain, and burned the olive trees and grape vines. The Philistines came up to take him. Samson was bound with new cords, but God gave him strength and they snapt like fine thread.

Samson killed a thousand men with the jawbone of an ass! and when he found the great city gates of Gaza shut against him, so that he could not get outside, he arose in the middle of the night, dragged up the two posts to which they were fastened, took the gates, the posts, and the bar which fastened them; put them all on his

SAMSON KILLS THE LION.

shoulders, and carried them to the top of a hill. A wicked woman named Delilah sent word to the Philistines that she had found out how to take away Samson's great strength. When he was asleep a man shaved the long hair from his head, and then they bound him with chains of brass; they put out his eyes, and threw him into prison, and made him grind corn with mill-stones. His strength was gone, for God had told him never to cut his hair.

SAMSON SLAYING THE PHILISTINES WITH THE JAWBONE OF AN ASS.

After a while his hair grew, and the Lord gave him his strength again. Now the Philistines made a great feast in honor of their idol, Dagon, and thousands of the people were gathered.

They sent for poor blind Samson to be brought to the feast, to "make sport" for them. A little boy led him to the great pillars of the house, for Samson had said, "Take me to the pillars that I may lean on them," and when Samson touched them he prayed, "O Lord, I pray Thee, give me strength only this once!" The Lord heard him, and gave him strength, and he pulled the pillars together, the great house fell down, and thousands of the wicked people were killed. And Samson died with them, and by his friends was buried in his father's sepulchre.

The Beautiful Story of Faithful Ruth.

I am now going to tell you what happened to a little family in Israel. There will be nothing about war and bloodshed, but a great deal about the joys and sorrows of home.

What I shall relate happened in the time of one of the judges, in the time of one of the *first* judges—perhaps in the time of Ehud, or of Barak, or of Gideon.

A little family lived in Bethlehem, among the green hills of the shepherds and the rich corn-fields of the valley.

They lived in plenty and comfort, until a great trouble came upon the land of Israel —one of those troubles which God sent to punish them for their sins

SAMSON THROWN INTO PRISON.

—a famine. Very little corn grew in the fields, and very little could be bought for money. What could be done? The father determined to do what Abraham once did—to go to another land.

So the father set out with his wife and his two little boys.

He traveled across the land till he came to the River Jordan. He crossed it, and came to the mountains of Moab, that country where Balak once tried to get Israel cursed. Though Balak had

SAMSON AND DELILAH.

long been dead, the land was still full of the enemies of Israel, and full of the idol gods, in whom they trusted.

Such a land, though beautiful and fruitful, was not a good land for bringing up the little boys.

After some time the father of the family died, and the mother was left alone with her sons.

She was now a widow. Her name was Naomi. She was a good woman, who feared the Lord: yet she was afraid to return to the land of Israel, lest there should not be corn enough for herself and her children. So she stayed in Moab, and her sons chose women of Moab for their wives. This was wrong: for the Lord had forbidden the men of Israel to marry heathen wives, lest their hearts should be turned to idols, through the love of their wives.

The two sons lived about ten years with their wives, and then they both died.

This was a sad trial for Naomi. She was a widow before, and now she had lost her children.

She had no one left but her sons' wives, they were her daughters-in-law, and she thought they would marry again and leave her.

At this time Naomi heard some one say that the Lord had made the corn grow abundantly in her own land.

Then Naomi made up her mind to return to Bethlehem all alone. But her daughters-in-law were very fond of her, and they wished to accompany her back.

Their names were Orpah and Ruth. These young widows had no children, but they had mothers living, with whom they might have stayed: yet they chose to set out with Naomi. When they had gone some way, Naomi stopped, and said to them both, "Go, return each of you to your mother's

SAMSON DESTROYS THE TEMPLE OF DAGON.

house. May the Lord be kind to you! for you have been very kind to my sons who are dead, and to me also. May the Lord give you each another husband and another home to rest in!" This kind woman thought more of her daughters-in-law than of her own trouble. No wonder they loved her so much.

ORPAH RETURNS HOME.

They cried again at the thought of parting; but at last Orpah gave Naomi the last kiss, and went home with a sorrowful heart.

But Ruth kept close to her dear mother-in-law, and determined never to leave her.

Then Naomi tried again to persuade her to go. "Behold," she said, " thy sister-in-law is gone back unto her people and to her gods; return thou after her." Then Ruth made this affectionate answer:

"Entreat me not to leave thee, or to return from following after thee: for whither thou goest, I will go; and where thou lodgest, I will lodge: thy people shall be my people, and thy God my God.

Where thou diest, will I die, and there will I be buried. Nothing but death shall part thee and me."

When Naomi saw how very anxious Ruth was to go with her, she left off persuading her to return home.

What a long journey these two poor widows had to make! more than a hundred miles. And they had to cross the River Jordan, and go over many steep hills. But they went on, day after day, till they came to Bethlehem.

Ruth had never before seen the beautiful land of Israel. It was early spring when they traveled; and the little white lambs were sporting on the green hills, the birds were singing in the thick woods, and the bees sipping the opening flowers. In Palestine, the flowers grow all over the hills and in the valleys, until, in some places, the ground is almost white with their blossoms, in others pink, and various hues and colors are blended together until the whole earth seems covered with a carpet of flowers, so beautiful that you cannot imagine how lovely it is. But the glory of the land was its God. There were some who sang His praises as they reaped the first ripe corn. Ruth had never heard such songs in the fields of Moab.

Ruth Gleans Corn in the Fields.

When Naomi arrived in Bethlehem, there were many people who remembered her.

As soon as they heard that she was returned they came crowding around her.

They looked to see whether she was much changed. It was about twenty years since she had gone away. Then she was happy with her husband and sons, but now she had lost them all. Besides, she had grown old, and sorrow had made her look older still.

But Naomi had one great blessing left. It was her faithful daughter-in-law—better to her than ever so many sons.

No one in that city had ever seen Ruth; but they heard from Naomi all about her faithful love in coming so far.

There lived at Bethlehem a very rich man, who had many corn-fields. His name was Boaz; and he was a relation of Naomi's dead husband. But Naomi did not go to his house, because she was very poor, and he was very rich, and so she thought it would seem bold to pay him a visit.

What could Naomi do for bread now? She had a faithful daughter, willing to glean for her in the fields. The Lord had made a law, that when men cut down the corn they should not gather it all, but leave some for the poor and the stranger.

Ruth was a poor stranger, and she said to Naomi, "Let me now go to the field and glean ears of corn. Some one may be kind to me, and let me have a good deal."

Naomi answered, "Go, my daughter."

Early one morning Ruth went out alone to glean. Her mother-in-law was too old and feeble to go with her.

It happened that Ruth went into a field that belonged to Boaz.

But it was God who let her go there, for He had a plan to do her good through going into that field.

Ruth was a timid, modest creature, and she was afraid of offending, by intruding, and taking too much corn; especially as she was not an Israelite, but a stranger from a heathen country. As soon as she came into the field she went up to the servants, and asked their leave to glean.

They allowed her to keep among the reapers, and to glean close to the sheaves.

The head servant was very kind, because he had heard how well she had behaved to her mother-in-law. When the sun was hot, he permitted her to sit with the reapers in a tent, to rest herself a little while; for he had observed how steadily she kept to her gleaning, without wasting her time in talking or loitering.

In the course of the day the master came into his field—even Boaz himself.

He was not a young man, nor was he very old. He had been well brought up by a pious mother. What was her name? It was a heathen name—Rahab. What! was she the woman of Jericho who hid the spies? Yes—she—even she was the mother of Boaz. After she had been saved from the city she had lived with the Israelites, among their tents: and she had married a chief man among them. His name was Salmon, and he was the son of the prince of Judah in the wilderness.

Salmon and Rahab were the parents of Boaz. Often must the mother have told her little son about the scarlet line that was hung out of the window.

When Boaz entered the field his first words to the reapers were, "The Lord be with you:" and the reapers replied, "The Lord bless thee."

These words were used instead of wishing good morning.

Boaz looked round on the people in the corn. And there were poor women and children gleaning the ears of corn scattered on the ground.

Among these gleaners was one that Boaz had never seen before. She was a sweet, modest young woman, with a sorrowful countenance;

RUTH BEFORE BOAZ.

speaking to no one, but busy at her gleaning. Boaz wanted to know who she was; so he asked his head servant, "To whom does that damsel belong?"

The head servant answered, "It is the young woman of Moab, who came back with Naomi." Then he told Boaz all about her kindness to her mother-in-law, and also about her quiet, humble behavior in the field. Boaz was much pleased with the account. He had not forgotten his own mother—once a heathen, like poor Ruth.

Boaz went first to the reapers, and desired them never to behave rudely to the poor stranger. And then he went to Ruth, and said, "Now, my daughter, hear what I am going to say. Never go to glean in any other fields, but stay in my fields with my maidens. I have desired every one to behave well to you. When you are thirsty, you may drink out of the same jars as the reapers."

When Ruth heard these kind words, she felt so grateful that she stooped down with her face to the ground, and said, "Why do you show me such favor, though I am only a stranger?"

You see how humble she was. She felt she was unworthy of the least notice.

Then Boaz answered, "I have been told of all your kindness to your mother-in-law, since the death of your husband; and how you have left your father and mother, and the land where you were born, to be with a people that you never knew before."

Then he blessed Ruth, and prayed God to bless her, because she was come to trust under His wings.

Boaz had before allowed her to drink with his reapers, but now he told her to eat with them also. "Come," he said, "at mealtime, and eat bread with the reapers, and dip your morsel in the vinegar." In many warm countries, like Palestine and ancient Rome, the people put a little vinegar in the water they drank, so it would not make them sick.

When the next meal was ready, Ruth went into the tent with the maidens, and sat with the reapers. Besides bread and vinegar, there was parched corn—that is, green corn dried by the fire. This was thought very excellent food. Boaz himself took a large quantity and gave it to Ruth. It was much more than she could eat herself, so she put by some, intending to bring it home.

After she had finished her meal, she went out again to glean. Boaz went out also, and gave more orders to his reapers about Ruth. "Let her," he said, "come close up to the place where you are binding up the sheaves, and do not find fault with her for coming there; and let some handfuls of corn fall on the ground, just on purpose for her to glean them, and do not find fault with her for taking them."

It was easy for Ruth to glean a great deal, when so much favor was shown her. In the evening she beat out the grain from the chaff, and measured the corn, and found it was a very large measure, called an ephah. That was enough to make sixteen of our large loaves—enough to last Ruth and Naomi for two months to come.

And now the day was over. It had been a day of peace and joy. Poor Ruth had been comforted and kindly treated. She felt the Lord was blessing her for having left her own land of idols, and for coming to live with the people of God, and with her own poor mother-in-law.

The Wedding of Ruth and Boaz.

In the evening the gleaners left the field, and returned to Bethlehem; but no gleaner had such a rich load to carry home as Ruth.

When she came back to Naomi in her little lodging, she showed her what a great quantity she had gleaned. Her mother-in-law was quite surprised.

"But that is not all," said Ruth. Then she took out from the folds of her dress a little nice food, part of her own dinner, that she had kept for Naomi.

Her mother-in-law saw that somebody had been very kind to her, and she said, "Where hast thou gleaned to-day? Blessed be the man who took so much notice of thee."

Then Ruth told her all about her gleaning, and about the care that was taken of her. "The name," she said, "of the man in whose field I gleaned was Boaz."

Naomi was indeed delighted when she heard that name. It was a name she knew well, and loved well too; for Boaz had been very kind to her husband and children before they left the land and went to Moab. Now, thought Naomi, he is kind to Ruth and me, as he used to be kind to my dead husband and sons; and she cried out, "Blessed be he of the Lord, who hath not left off showing kindness to the living, as he once showed kindness to those that are dead!"

Then said Naomi to Ruth, "This man is one of our near relations."

Ruth then told Naomi more of his kindness. "He bade me go on gleaning near his reapers, till all the fields were reaped."

Naomi was glad to hear this, and she said to Ruth:

"My daughter, keep with his maidens, and do not let any one see you gleaning in any other fields than his."

There was a law that God had made for Israel, and which Naomi thought of now. This was the law: If a man died and left a wife, but no children, then his brother was to marry the wife; or, if he had no brother, his uncle or his cousin was to marry her. Naomi knew that as Ruth's husband was dead, his nearest relation ought to marry her. And who was he? Was not Boaz the nearest relation? Naomi thought he was. But there was another man who was nearer still.

Boaz was very anxious indeed to have Ruth for his wife, but he had to go first and ask the nearest relation what he would do. He did not go to the man's house. He went to the gate of Bethlehem. There was a place with seats close to the gate, where the judges often came to judge the people.

Boaz sat down on a seat in the gate, and looked at the people who came by. A great many people were always coming and going, for the gate was the place where neighbors met to talk, and where country people brought their milk and vegetables to sell.

Boaz watched to see when the nearest relation would pass by. At last he saw him. He called him by his name, and said, "Ho, turn in here, and sit down." The man did not know why he was wanted, but he came in and sat down.

Boaz went on looking, and he called the chief men who passed, till he got as many as ten to sit down with him there. They were all wise, steady men, who could be trusted. A crowd of people came to look on, wondering what was going to be done.

Boaz spoke first to the kinsman (or relation). He said:

"Naomi, who went to Moab and came back, wishes to sell the land that belonged to her dead husband. So I sent for you that you might buy it, as it is your right to redeem it if you choose; but if you do not choose to redeem it,

BOAZ AND THE KINSMAN OF NAOMI.

then it is my right, as I am the next nearest relation." The man replied, "I will redeem it."

Thus he promised to buy the land for himself, and to give the money to Naomi.

But Boaz had something more to say: "One of Naomi's sons has left a widow, named Ruth. She is a Moabitess. On the day you redeem the land you must take her for your wife, according to the law."

When the kinsman heard this he answered, "Then I will not redeem the land, but you may redeem it instead."

When the kinsman refused to redeem the land, he gave a sign of refusing by drawing off his sandal (a kind of shoe bound round his foot). He took it off and gave it to Boaz, as much as to say, "You are to stand in my place, and do all I ought to do. Buy the land instead of me."

Then Boaz turned toward the ten men sitting as judges, and toward all the people crowding round, and said, "You are all witnesses that I have bought the land that belonged to Naomi's husband and sons. I have bought it of Naomi. I have also promised to make Ruth, the Moabitess, my wife, and I shall stand in the place of her dead husband, that his name may not be forgotten among his brethren. You are all witnesses of what I do."

The ten elders and the people answered, "We are witnesses."

Then they all joined in blessing Ruth.

This was a happy day for Boaz.

Very soon he married Ruth.

He looked upon Naomi as her own mother: and she counted Boaz as her own son.

After a while the Lord sent another blessing to this happy family.

Ruth had a little son.

Naomi reckoned him her own grandchild; as if he had been the child of her dead son.

The women who came to see the baby were pleased to find Naomi so happy; and they said to her, "Blessed be the Lord, which hath not left thee without a kinsman to make thy name remembered in Israel. And this child shall be a comfort to thy gray hairs: for he is the child of thy daughter-in-law, who loveth thee, and who is better to thee than seven sons."

And so, indeed, Ruth was better than seven, or seventy sons—she was the kindest of daughters.

And had not the Lord rewarded her?

She had become poor for Naomi's sake, and God had made her rich. She had left her home, and God had provided a better home, with the best of husbands. She had given up her father's idols, and God had become her God.

Naomi took the baby, and carried it in her arms, and hushed it, and fondled it, and loved it.

And what was his name?

It was not Boaz who gave it a name, because he counted the child to belong to Naomi's dead son.

So Naomi's friends gave it a name, and called it "Obed;" which means "serving."

Ruth's wish was granted. She had wished to live and die with Naomi—and she did so. But she had more than she wished for, and what she had never thought of—in her family the SON OF GOD at last was born. I will tell you how it was.

The little Obed grew to be a man, and had a son named Jesse. This Jesse had eight sons; and of these David was the youngest. So Obed was the grandfather of David.

The Story of Gideon.

And now I will tell you some wonderful things about Gideon, the son of Joash. The people had become very wicked and worshiped idols instead of the true God. So the Lord delivered them as a punishment into the hands of the Midianites for a period of seven years. These were a wicked, idolatrous people who lived near the children of Israel, and who were constantly fighting against them. They destroyed their grass and their corn, so that there was no food for their children or their cattle, and the Israelites fled to the mountains and hid themselves in caves and holes in the ground.

Here they began to be sorry for their wickedness, and they prayed to God to deliver them from the Midianites. Then an angel came and sat under an oak near the wine-press that belonged to Joash, where his son Gideon was threshing wheat, for he had to work in a secret place for fear of the Midianites.

THE ANGEL DEPARTING OUT OF GIDEON'S SIGHT.

The angel spoke to him and said, "The Lord is with thee, thou mighty man of valor." But Gideon remembered the sufferings of his people and he said to the angel, "If the Lord be with us, why then is all this befallen us?" But the angel told him that he should go in his might, that the Lord would be with him, and that he should conquer the Midianites and deliver the people out of their bondage. Then Gideon begged the angel not to depart until he should return, and he went and prepared some cakes and some meat and broth and brought them to the angel;

whereupon he told Gideon to lay the flesh and the cakes upon a rock and to pour out the broth; and when he had done so the angel put forth the end of the staff that was in his hand and touched the flesh and the cakes, and immediately a fire came out of the rock and consumed them. Then the angel departed out of Gideon's sight, and he was greatly frightened because he knew he had seen one of God's angels.

Not long after these strange things had occurred, the Midianites and the Amalekites gathered a great army together and came and encamped near the Israelites, intending to utterly destroy them. But Gideon blew his trumpet and sent messengers out to warn the people, and he soon collected an army of thirty-two thousand men. While this was being done Gideon prayed to God and asked for a sign, so that he might be sure God was on his side and would help him to fight the Midianites. He said, "I will put a fleece of wool on

GIDEON WRINGING THE WATER FROM THE FLEECE.

the floor, and if it is wet with dew in the morning, while the earth and the grass remain dry, then I will know that the Lord is on our side." So in the morning when he arose and took up his fleece he found it so wet with dew that he wrung a bowlful of water out of it. Still Gideon was not satisfied, and he prayed to the Lord not to be angry with him, but to give him another sign. This time he prayed that the fleece might remain dry while the ground should be covered with dew; and it came to pass just as he desired. Then Gideon knew that the Lord was on his side and would fight for the Israelites.

The Lord now told Gideon that the army was too large and he must send some of the people away, for if He delivered the Midianites into their hands they would claim all the glory for themselves and remain as wicked as they were before. So Gideon made a proclamation, and told the people that all who were afraid could return to their tents, and twenty-two thousand did so. They were a very cowardly people to run away from the enemy in such a manner.

But the Lord said they were still too many, and He told Gideon to take those who remained down to the water and let them drink, and that he should watch the men while they drank and select from among them only those who lapped the water with their tongues, like a dog. Accordingly Gideon did as he was directed, and when the men drank there were only three hundred who lapped the water with their tongues. These were marched away by themselves, and all the rest were sent back to their tents.

Gideon had now so small an army that he was afraid to attack the Midianites, but the Lord told him to go after dark with his servant down to the edge of the camp and he would hear something that would renew his courage. So when night came he took his servant and they went cautiously down near to the camp of the Midianites, and as they walked along they heard two men talking. One of the men was telling the other about a strange dream that he had dreamed. Said he, "I dreamed that a cake of barley tumbled into the camp of the Midianites and rolled along until it struck a tent, which it overthrew and stretched along the ground." The other man seemed greatly alarmed on hearing the dream, and said it meant that the Lord had delivered them into the hands of Gideon, who would come and destroy them with the sword.

Then Gideon knew that it would be as the man said; and he returned to his own camp and told his men that the Lord would deliver the Midianites into their hands. So he divided his three hundred men into three equal parties, and gave each man a trumpet and an empty pitcher, with a lamp in the pitcher. He directed them also to march to three different places near the camp of the Midianites, so that they would be on all sides of the enemy, and that when he gave the signal they should blow their trumpets, break the pitchers and shout, " The sword of the Lord and of Gideon."

Everything was done as he directed, and at the beginning of the middle watch of the night, all of the three hundred men having reached the positions assigned to them, Gideon gave the signal, and instantly all the pitchers were broken and there was a great flash of light from the three hundred lamps, while the trumpets sounded and a shout went up that struck terror into the hearts of the Midianites. They fled in all directions and were so frightened that each man's sword was set against his fellow, so that many thousands of them were slain by their own swords.

It was a great victory for Gideon and his men, and the Midianites were so frightened that they did not trouble the children of Israel again for forty years, or during the lifetime of Gideon.

The Story of Job.

And now I will tell you the story of Job, who was one of the best men that ever lived upon this earth. We do not know exactly when he lived, but we are almost sure that he lived before Moses—perhaps before Abraham.

We know where he lived, for it was in the land of Uz, a country near the great River Euphrates, and a great way from Canaan.

198 MY MOTHER'S BIBLE STORIES.

Job was the richest man in his country. Like Abraham, he had large flocks of sheep and herds of cattle. He had seven thousand sheep, three thousand camels, one thousand oxen, and five hundred asses. The oxen were used for ploughing, and two went in a yoke; so that he had five hundred yoke.

Job had a large family—seven sons and three daughters.

The sons had houses of their own, and they used to give feasts to each other; and they always invited their three sisters to come.

But at last trouble came upon Job—more troubles than ever came upon any other man. It was because of the hatred of Satan, who did not like to hear Job praised for his good-

ROBBERS ATTACKING THE SERVANTS OF JOB.

ness. God permitted these troubles, just to show Satan that Job would go on loving Him, even when he had lost everything. One calamity followed another, and one messenger after another came bringing bad news. One said that "robbers rushed upon the ploughmen in the field, killing them and stealing the oxen and asses; and I only am left." Another told him that "fire had fallen from heaven and burned the sheep and the shepherds; and I only am left." A third said that "the camels are taken and the servants are killed; and I only am left." The fourth brought the saddest news of all, "thy sons and thy daughters were all feasting in their eldest brother's house, when a great wind came and blew down the house, and it fell upon the young people, and I only am escaped."

Who ever heard such dreadful news as this? Ten children all killed at once! What could Job do? Did he curse God, as Satan said he would? Oh, no; instead of cursing, he blessed His holy name.

JOB'S ANGUISH WHEN TOLD OF THE DEATH OF HIS CHILDREN.

He showed his grief by tearing his cloak, shaving his head, and sitting upon the ground; and then he said, "I brought nothing into the world when I was born, and I shall carry nothing out of it when

I die. The Lord gave, and the Lord hath taken away; blessed be the name of the Lord."

But Satan tried Job in another way. He afflicted him with the most dreadful disease that could be sent, without killing him. He made very bad boils to break out all over his body. There was not a single spot without a boil upon it—even on his head there were boils—and on the soles of his feet.

While he was sitting suffering thus his wife came to him. Of course she was very unhappy, as well as himself, at having lost all her children. Yet she might now try to comfort Job. But she only made him more miserable. She gave him most wicked advice. She came to him in a mocking way and said, "Are you still faithful? Curse God and die."

Job gave her a most beautiful answer. He said, "Shall I receive good at the hand of the Lord, and shall I not receive evil?"

While Job was thus afflicted three of his friends came, for they felt they ought to go and see him in his trouble.

Did his friends begin to comfort him when they heard his sad words?

No; instead of comforting him, they began to find fault with him, and to accuse him.

The three friends were called El-i-phaz, Bildad and Zo-phar.

First, Eliphaz spoke, and Job answered him; then Bildad spoke, and Job answered him; then Zophar spoke, and Job answered him.

All the three friends said, that if Job had really been a good man such troubles would not have been sent.

Among the people who were listening to Job and his friends was a young man named Elihu. Elihu praised God very much: saying, "God is great; He makes small the drops of rain; He spreads the clouds in the sky; He fills it with light; He commands the thunder."

While Elihu was saying all this, a dreadful thunder-storm was heard; and in the midst of the tempest a voice was heard.

It was the voice of the Lord Himself.

The noise of the thunder had made the hearts of the hearers beat fast in their bosoms; but what did they all feel when God Himself uttered His voice! He spoke to Job. He asked him some questions very hard to answer.

The first question was, "Where wast thou when I made the earth, and when the morning stars sang together, and the sons of God shouted for joy?"

How could Job answer this question? for he was not born when God created the world.

Then God asked Job, "Who shut up the sea, so that it cannot get out of its place?

"Where does the light dwell, and where is the darkness kept?

"Didst thou give wings to the ostrich?

FIRE FALLS FROM HEAVEN AND CONSUMES THE SHEPHERDS.

"Didst thou make the horse strong?

"Will the eagle mount up in the air at thy command?"

All these questions, and many more, God asked, but none of them could Job answer.

Job now felt he had done wrong in boasting so much of his goodness, and he said, "Behold, I am vile! What shall I answer Thee? I will lay my hand upon my mouth. I have spoken; but I will speak no more."

This was a good and humble speech, and the Lord went on talking to Job.

When God had done speaking, Job spoke again, but not in his own praise. He felt himself to be a worm, and unworthy to utter a word. He cried out:

"I know that Thou canst do everything, I abhor myself, and repent in dust and ashes."

God liked these humble words: just as He liked the prayer of the publican, "God be merciful to me a sinner."

So God received Job into favor again, and gave him "twice as much as he had before."

The Story of Samuel and His Mother.

You have heard, my dear children, how the Israelites came into the land of Canaan. I shall now tell you some things which happened to them in Canaan.

Do you remember that the tabernacle was placed at Shiloh? The high priest lived in Shiloh, that he might offer sacrifices in the tabernacle.

I am now going to tell you of a high priest called Eli.

Eli was a very good old man.

A great many people used to come up every year to Shiloh to worship God at the tabernacle.

Among the people who came there was a good woman whose name was Hannah. She had a little son called Samuel.

When Samuel was about three or four years old, she took him up to Shiloh with her. Hannah did not mean to keep him always at home with her, though she loved him very much: for she wished the good old high priest Eli to bring him up, and to teach him. So she brought the child to Eli, and said to him, "I wish the child to be brought up to serve God."

Eli took the little boy to live with him. Hannah sang a beautiful song of praise to God for His goodness, and then she left her dear little Samuel, and went home again.

Do you think she ever came to see her child? Yes, every year; and she always brought him a present of a dress such as the people wore in those days. It was a linen dress down to his feet, and it had long sleeves. Samuel used to wear a linen ephod also, such as the priests wore, though he was not a priest himself. God had put His Spirit into Samuel's heart, so that he liked serving the Lord in the tabernacle, and seeing the sacrifices offered, and hearing the Lord praised by the priests and the people. As he grew older he pleased God more and more, and a great many people loved him. How glad Hannah must have been when she came to see him, to hear that he was a good child! It makes your parents, dear children, very happy to hear that you are good. I hope you will be like little Samuel, and be God's children while you are very young.

Eli and His Wicked Sons.

You have heard how Samuel lived with old Eli at Shiloh.

He did not live in the tabernacle, but in some tents very near it.

You would like to know whether Eli had any children of his own. He had two sons, who were grown-up men, and they were priests, and offered sacrifices at the altar.

I suppose you think that Eli's sons were good, because Eli was good; but I am sorry to tell you that they were very wicked men. They did not love God, they only cared for eating, and amusing themselves; and they did not wish to please God. Eli was good himself, but he did not punish his wicked sons; and that was very wrong of Eli.

The two sons went on in their wickedness. And now you shall hear something else that God said.

One evening old Eli was lying in bed; and little Samuel was lying in another bed a little way off. Samuel heard a voice calling him, "Samuel." Samuel thought that Eli called him, and he answered, "Here am I;" and then he got out of bed and ran to Eli, to know what he wanted. You see what a kind little child Samuel was, and how ready he was to wait upon Eli.

But Eli said to Samuel, "I did not call you;" then Samuel went and lay down again.

Soon afterward Samuel heard some one call again, "Samuel." So he went again to Eli, and said, "Here am I, for you did call me." But Eli said, "I did not call, my son; lie down again."

Then Samuel lay down, and he soon heard the voice again saying, "Samuel." Then he felt sure that it was Eli who called him, and he went to him and said, "Here am I, for you did call me."

Now Eli knew who it was who had called Samuel. So Eli told Samuel to lie down again, and when he heard the voice, to answer, "Speak, Lord, for Thy servant heareth." Samuel was to call himself God's servant.

So Samuel went and lay down again, and soon the Lord came and stood by him, and called as before, "Samuel, Samuel." Then Samuel answered, "Speak, for Thy servant heareth." God had never spoken to Samuel before. Samuel must have longed to know what the Lord had to say to him. It was something very sad and dreadful; it was about Eli.

God told Samuel that He should soon punish Eli's sons for their wickedness, and that he was displeased with Eli for not having punished them.

After God had done speaking, Samuel remained in his bed, and Eli did not call him. Samuel did not like to tell Eli that God was displeased with him.

So when the morning came, Samuel did not go to Eli, but began to open the doors round about the tabernacle; for it was Samuel's business to open the doors. Soon Eli called Samuel: for he wanted to know what God had said to him. Eli begged Samuel to tell everything to him, and to hide nothing from him.

Then little Samuel told Eli all that God had said.

How grieved Eli must have been when he heard that the Lord would punish his sons, and that the Lord was displeased with him; but he answered very meekly, and said, "Let the Lord do what He pleases." Eli really loved God, though he had done one wrong thing.

After this, God often spoke to Samuel, and told him how He would punish wicked people; and Samuel used to tell people what God had said, and all that Samuel told them came true. Samuel was a prophet: a prophet is a person to whom the Lord tells what He means to make happen.

The Israelites Ask Samuel to Give Them a King.

When Samuel had grown up to be a man, he was called a judge; but he was not a king. He used to tell the people what God wished them to do; and he used to punish bad people. Moses had once been the judge of Israel, and Joshua had been the judge, and Eli had been the judge. Now Samuel was called the judge. He did not sit on a throne, or wear a crown, as kings do; and he always asked God to tell him what the people ought to do, and then he told the people what God had said. The Israelites ought to have been very glad that God was their King. No other king was so good and so great as He was.

You will be sorry to hear that at last they grew tired of having God for their king. They said, "We should like to have a king that would go out to battle before us." They wanted to have a king that they could see. So they came to Samuel, and said, "Give us a king."

Samuel was very sorry to hear this, and he went and prayed to the Lord. Do you think that God would let the Israelites have a king? Yes, He would: He was displeased with them for wishing for a king, but as they wanted one, God said they should have one.

So Samuel called the Israelites together to speak to them, and then he said, "God will let you have a king, but this is the way in which the king will treat you:

"He will make your sons work for him; some of them will run before his chariots; and some will make swords and spears for him, and some will plough his ground, and reap his corn; and some of your daughters will bake, and cook, and make nice things for him to eat; and he will take away many of your fields, and gardens, and corn, and sheep from you, and give them to whom he pleases, and then you will be sorry that you wished for a king, and you will cry to God, and He will not hear you."

Did the Israelites still wish for a king? Yes, they would not mind what Samuel said; but they cried out, "We will have a king."

Then all the people went home.

God was to choose the king; and God would tell Samuel who was to be king.

I shall tell you about the man whom God chose to be the king of Israel.

Saul is Chosen King.

There was a young man whose father had some fields, and sheep, and cows, and asses. One day three asses were lost; so the young man went to look for them among the hills and fields. The young man's name was Saul. He took a servant with him, and he looked for the asses a long while, but he could not find them. At last he came near the city where Samuel lived.

The servant said to Saul, "I have heard that there is a man in that city who is a prophet; all he says comes true. Let us ask him where the asses are." Then Saul said to his servant, "Come, let us go." So Saul and the servant went into the city, and as they went along they met Samuel. Saul and the servant had never seen Samuel before; so they did not know who he was. Samuel was an old man by this time, and his hair was long, and he used to wear a cloak.

Saul spoke to this old man, and said, "Can you tell me where the prophet's house is?"

Samuel answered, "I am the prophet."

Did Samuel know who Saul was? Yes, he did; for though Samuel had never seen him before, God had told him that he would meet a man just at that time, who was to be the king of Israel. Samuel knew who Saul was, and he knew that Saul wanted to ask him where the asses were.

Before Saul had told him that he had lost some asses, Samuel said, "The asses that you lost three days ago are found." And Samuel told Saul that he had a great deal to say to him, and that he must come home with him that evening, and

SAMUEL ANOINTS SAUL.

that he would let him go away the next morning. So Saul and the servant went to Samuel's house, and Samuel took Saul to the top of his house, and talked to him alone; but I do not know what he said to him.

The next morning they all got up very early, as soon as it was light, and Samuel walked with Saul and the servant through the city. When they were come to the outside of the city, Samuel said to Saul, "Bid the servant to pass on before." So the servant passed on before; and Samuel and Saul stood still together quite alone.

Then Samuel took a bottle of oil, that he had brought with him, and poured it on Saul's head, and said to him, "God has chosen thee to be king over Israel."

Why did Samuel pour the oil upon Saul's head? It was as a sign that he was to be the king. Pouring oil upon a person is called "anointing."

"GOD SAVE THE KING."

After Samuel had anointed Saul, they parted from each other. Saul went on his way, and returned to his friends; but he did not tell any one that he was to be king of Israel. Soon afterward Samuel called all the Israelites together, to tell them who was to be the king.

He first told them that it was very wicked not to like to have God for their king, and then he showed them the man who was to be their king. When the people saw Saul they were very much pleased, for he was taller than any of the Israelites; no one else reached higher than his shoulder. The Israelites wished to have a king that would look very grand when he went out to battle.

The Israelites shouted when they saw him, and cried out, "God save the king!"

When the people had seen the king they went home to their houses.

You will soon hear what sort of a king Saul was, whether he loved God, or whether he did not.

Did the Israelites deserve to have a good king? No. How ungratefully they had behaved to God who had been so kind to them! How ungrateful they were to Samuel who had been their judge! But Samuel was not angry with them, he was only sorry that they were wicked.

King Saul Conquers the Amalekites.

I have told you how God made Saul the king of Israel. He sat upon a throne, and wore a crown, and went to battle in a chariot. He was a brave man, and could fight well against wicked soldiers who tried to hurt the Israelites.

Samuel used often to come and see him, and advise him to serve God. Samuel wished Saul to be good and he often prayed for him.

At last God chose to see whether Saul would do all He desired him to do. You remember how God once tried Abraham; and how Abraham did what God desired him, because he loved God.

There were some wicked people, who lived near the land of Canaan, called the Am-al-ek-ites. God was very angry with them, and He chose that they should all be killed.

One day Samuel came to Saul and said to him, "God desires you to go and fight against the Amalekites and kill them all,—men, women, and children, and oxen, and sheep, and camels, and asses."

210   MY MOTHER'S BIBLE STORIES.

Saul got a great army of Israelites, and went to the Amalekites, and he conquered them. Then Saul desired his soldiers to kill them with their swords, as God had told him. But he thought he should like to take the king of the Amalekites back to Canaan with him, so he would not let him be killed.

I think Saul wanted to bring the king home with him, because he thought it was a grand and fine thing to have a king shut up near him in Canaan.

Neither did Saul kill the fat and strong oxen and sheep; he only killed those that were thin and weak.

He wished to be rich, and to have a great deal of cattle.

That night God spoke to Samuel and told him that He was very angry with Saul. Samuel was grieved to hear this, and he prayed to God the rest of the night.

SAUL DEFEATS THE AMALEKITES.

God's Punishment of King Saul.

The next morning Samuel went to look for Saul, for God had told him many things that he must say to him. Saul did not know that Samuel knew of his wickedness; so he tried to make Samuel think that he had done all that God had told him.

When Saul saw Samuel he pretended to be glad to see him, and said, "I have done the commandment of the Lord." Then Samuel said, "What then is this bleating of sheep and lowing of oxen that I hear?"

Now Saul saw that Samuel knew what he had done. He saw it would be of no use to say that he had not saved the sheep and oxen, so he began to make excuses for himself.

RETURN OF SAUL'S ARMY WITH THE SHEEP AND OXEN.

Saul said, "It was the people who would not kill the fat sheep and oxen."

Was it the people who had saved the sheep and oxen? Had not Saul saved them too? and why did Saul let the people do wickedly? Was he not the king? Should he not have made them do what was right?

Would God like those sheep and oxen to be offered in sacrifice to Him? No; God would rather that Saul should obey Him than that he should offer sacrifices.

Then Samuel told Saul that God was very angry with him, and did not mean to let him be king much longer.

Saul was very much frightened when he heard that God would punish him, and he said to Samuel, "Stay and pray to God with me." But Saul was not really sorry: he was only afraid of being punished. Samuel knew that he was not sorry for having offended God, who had been so good to him, so Samuel would not stay with Saul. Then Saul took hold of Samuel's cloak, to hinder him from going away, and he tore the cloak.

SAMUEL DEPARTS FROM SAUL.

Samuel stopped and said to Saul, "God has torn the land of Canaan from you, and He has given it to a man that is better than you are. God has done it already, and He will not change His mind."

Saul begged Samuel very much to stay with him, and to pray to God with him, that the people might not know that God was angry with him. You see that Saul cared more about what people thought of him, than about God being pleased with him.

At last Samuel said that he would worship God with him.

Then Samuel left Saul, and he never came to see him any more; but he still was very sorry to think that he was so wicked.

I hope, my dear children, that when you offend God, you will feel sorry. If you love God, you will not like to grieve Him. Saul did not love God: he was only afraid of being punished.

The Story of David.

Samuel did not know whom God meant to be king instead of Saul. At last God said to him, "Fill a horn with oil, and go to Jesse, who lives in Bethlehem, for I have chosen one of his sons as the king."

Jesse was an old man, and he had a great many sons who were grown up to be men. Samuel found Jesse and his sons in Bethlehem. Then Samuel looked at the eldest of Jesse's sons, to see whether he was the man that God had chosen to be king.

Now this son was a very tall, fine-looking man, who seemed fit to be king, and Samuel thought to himself, "Surely this is the one that God will choose me to anoint."

But God told Samuel that He had not chosen him. God does not care how a person looks, but He cares for the heart. Now the heart of Jesse's eldest son did not please God, and this time God was going to choose a king who loved Him in his heart.

Then Samuel looked at Jesse's second son; but when he saw him he said that God had not chosen him. Then Samuel looked at the third son; but God had not chosen him. Then he looked at the fourth; neither had God chosen him. Then Samuel looked at the fifth, next at the sixth, and last of all at the seventh; and yet God had not chosen any of them.

So Samuel said to Jesse, "Have you any more children?"

And Jesse answered, "I have one more child, the youngest, and he is keeping the sheep." Then Samuel said, "Send and fetch him: I want to see him immediately."

So Jesse sent a person to desire this youngest son to come to him.

The name of this son was David. He was not a grown-up man, but only a boy. He had a beautiful color on his cheeks, and his eyes had a pleasant look.

When he came in, God said to Samuel, "Arise and anoint him; for this is he." So Samuel took the horn of oil, and anointed him while his seven brothers stood by.

Then Samuel went back to his own house.

You will hear a great deal about David. God did not mean him to be king for a long while; but David knew that he certainly should be king one day. He went on keeping his father's sheep. As he watched them, he played on his harp, and sang sweet songs of praise to God. His songs are called "Psalms."

Do you think that David wished to be king? I do not think that he wanted to sit on a throne, and to wear a crown, but I know that he would like to call people together to praise God. When David was king, he could have people taught about God; and he could be kind to poor people; and he could punish wicked people.

When Samuel poured the oil on David's head, God made His Spirit come on him, to make him very wise and brave, and fit to be a king; for it is God who makes people wise and brave.

David Plays the Harp Before King Saul.

Samuel did not tell Saul what he had done. Saul would have been very angry if he had known that David had been anointed; but he did not know it.

BETHLEHEM THE CITY OF DAVID.

Yet Saul was very unhappy.

Saul's servants saw that he had a wicked spirit in him, and they said to him, "Shall we look for a man who can play very sweetly on the harp? Perhaps, if you were to listen to sweet music, you might get well."

Then Saul answered his servants, "Look for such a man, and bring him to me."

Whom could the servants send for? One of the servants had heard of David, and he said to Saul, "I have seen one of the sons of Jesse, who lives at Bethlehem, and he can play beautifully on the harp; and, besides, he is a very brave young man, who can fight well; and he can speak very wisely, and he is very handsome; and God loves him: shall I send for him?"

Saul said that he would have this young man sent for. Some of Saul's servants went to Jesse, and said, "King Saul wishes to see your son David, who takes care of the sheep."

Jesse said that David might go; and he desired David to take a present to King Saul; some bread, a kid (which is a young goat), and a bottle of wine. David put all these things upon an ass, and brought them to Saul. When he saw David, he loved him very much. Perhaps Saul loved him because he had a sweet look, and could play well on the harp; but God loved him because he wished to please Him.

Saul liked David so much that he desired him to stay with him a long while, and to be always near him. So Saul sent a message to Jesse to say that he wished to keep him.

David very often played to Saul upon the harp, and when he played, Saul grew better, and at last grew quite well.

At last David went away from Saul, and fed his father's sheep as he used to do.

I think David liked taking care of the sheep better than living with Saul: for Saul was wicked, and many of his servants were wicked.

David was very happy when he was alone, thinking about God. Did you ever hear any of David's psalms? In one of these psalms he calls God his Shepherd. David took great care of his sheep, and led them to places where green fresh grass grew, and to smooth and clear water; and he made them lie down on the softest grass, in cool places by the river's side. While David was taking so much care of his sheep, he thought that God took still more care of him; and he said, "The Lord is my shepherd, I shall not want. He maketh me to lie down in green pastures, and beside the still waters."

Story of the Giant Goliath.

You remember who the Philistines were. They were wicked people who lived in some of the cities of Canaan. They often fought against the Israelites.

One day a great number of Philistines came and placed their tents on the top of a hill in Canaan. When Saul heard it he came with a great number of Israelites, and they placed their tents on another hill. The Philistines and the Israelites could see each other in their tents; and they intended to fight against each other; but they did not choose to fight immediately.

There was one man among the Philistines whose name was Goliath. He was called a giant, because he was very tall indeed. He was ten feet high.

He was very strong and big, and he could fight well. He wore armor. Armor is made of iron and brass, and worn outside of the clothes. People used to wear armor that arrows, and swords, and spears, might not hurt them easily.

He wore a cap of brass upon his head, and he wore a coat of iron; his legs were covered with brass. He held a great spear in his hand, and he had a great sword in a sheath by his side; and a man went before him with a shield, which is a great piece of iron, or brass, like a large tray, that men used to hold before their faces in battle to prevent the arrows from hurting them.

The giant Goliath thought that no one could kill him. Every day he used to call out with a loud voice, "Will one of the Israelites come and fight with me? If he be able to kill me, then all the Philistines will mind the king of Israel; but if I kill him, then the Israelites must mind the Philistines. Is there any man that will fight with me?"

When Saul heard the Philistine giant, he was frightened, and so were all the Israelites. They all thought they should be killed, if one of them fought with the giant.

While this was taking place David was feeding his father's sheep, but his three elder brothers were in the tents.

One day old Jesse said to David, "Go to the tents of Israel and see how your brethren are; and take with you some corn, and ten loaves, as a present for your brothers."

So David rose up very early, and left his sheep with another shepherd, and took the corn and bread with him, and went a long way till he came to the hill where the tents of the Israelites were. Then he ran to look for his brothers. As he was talking with them, he heard a man speaking in a very loud voice, saying, "Who is able to fight with me?" It was the giant Goliath. David had never heard the giant speak these words before, but the people who were near David told him about the giant, and they said, "King Saul has promised to give any man who kills the giant a great many things as a reward."

David was surprised that people should be afraid of fighting with the giant, because he knew that God could help an Israelite to conquer him, but he knew that the gods of the Philistines could not help them, because they were only idols; so David said, "Who is this Philistine, that he should speak in this manner to the people of God?" And David felt in his heart that he should not be afraid to fight with the giant.

One of David's brothers heard what David said, and he began to mock him, saying, "Why did you come here? Why did you not stay with your sheep?" But David answered his brother very meekly.

Very soon some one went and told Saul that there was a young man come to the tents, and that he said he would fight with the giant. So Saul desired the young man to be brought before him; and David came to Saul. Saul had seen David before; but he had forgotten him. He was surprised that David, who was so young, should wish to fight with the giant; and he said to him, "You are not able to fight against the Philistine. You are very young, and he has been used to fighting." Then David answered, "Once when I was keeping my father's sheep, a lion came, and took a lamb out of the flock, and I went after the lion, and met him, and took the lamb out of his mouth, and when the lion tried to kill me, I caught him by his hair, and killed him. And once a bear came, and I killed him too. I shall kill this Philistine as I killed the lion and the bear. It was God who delivered me from the paw of the lion and of the bear, and He will deliver me from the Philistine."

You see, my dear child, that David was not proud of his strength. He knew that it was God who had helped him to kill those beasts, and he felt sure that God would help him to kill the giant.

David's Battle with Goliath.

When Saul heard David speak these words, he told him to go and fight the giant. But David had no sword nor coat of iron, so Saul lent him his own armor, and his own sword; he put a cap of brass on David's head, and dressed him in a coat of iron. But David had not been used to wear armor; so he said to Saul, "I cannot wear this armor," and he took it off again; neither would he take a sword, nor a spear. He went to the brook and chose five smooth stones, and put them in a bag which he had, and took the bag with him, and a sling. You will hear what he did with the bag, and the stones, and the cloth. In the other hand he held a stick. Then David went to meet the giant.

The giant heard that one of the Israelites was ready to fight with him, and he came near to David; a man with a shield went before him.

When the giant looked and saw David, he was surprised; he had expected to see a great man like himself, dressed in armor, and holding a spear in his hand.

But David was very young, and his face was rosy like a child's, and he only wore a shepherd's dress, and held a stick in his hand.

DAVID SLAYS GOLIATH.

The Philistine giant was angry when he saw him, and cursed him, and used very wicked words. Then he began to laugh at David, and said, "Come to me, and I will give your flesh to the birds and to the beasts to eat."

But David was not afraid, and he said to the giant, "You have a sword, and a spear, and a shield; but God will fight for me; and He will help me to kill you, and take your head from you: and the beasts and the birds shall eat up the flesh of all the Philistines, and everybody shall see that the God of Israel is the true God, and that He can save whom He pleases."

Then the Philistine giant came still nearer to David, and David ran toward him quickly, and put his hand in his bag, and drew out a stone, and put it in the sling that he had: then holding one end of the cloth, he threw the stone out of it with all his strength, and the stone hit the giant in the forehead, and sank into it, and the giant fell upon the ground on his face.

Then David ran to the giant, and taking his sword out of its sheath, he cut off his head. When the Philistines saw what a great wonder God had done, they were frightened; and the Israelites shouted, for they saw that their God fought for them, and they ran after the Philistines, and the Philistines tried to run away; but the Israelites overtook a great many of them, and killed them. David showed the head of the Philistine to a great many of the Israelites, and he kept the armor that the Philistine had worn.

Then David sang praises to God for his victory, and played upon his harp. He did not wish people to praise him; he wished everybody to praise God. He wanted all the people to say, "How great God is! He helped the poor young shepherd to conquer the great giant."

Saul Tries to Kill David.

Saul was very glad that David had killed the giant Goliath. David was brought to him that Saul might speak to him. He came in with the giant's head in his hand. Then Saul said to David, "Whose son are you, young man?" And David answered, "I am the son of Jesse, who lives at Bethlehem."

While Saul was talking to David, there was a person standing near, whom you have not heard of before; it was the son of Saul. He was a grown-up man, very brave, and very good; his name was Jonathan: he was a prince, because he was a king's son, and the king's son is called a prince.

Jonathan began to love David very much, because he was so brave and good. David had also a very sweet look. Still it was God who made Jonathan love David so much. Jonathan told him that he loved him, and they both promised always to be kind to

222   MY MOTHER'S BIBLE STORIES.

each other. Jonathan gave his own clothes to David, and wore other clothes, and he also gave him his sword and his bow.

Saul told David that he must not go back to live with his father again, but that he must stay with him. So David and Jonathan saw each other very often. How much that must have pleased them, for friends like to be together.

Perhaps you think that David now was very happy. But there was one thing that soon happened to make him sad. I will tell you what it was.

DAVID FIGHTING THE PHILISTINES.

After the giant had been killed in the battle, the Israelites went back to their homes, and did not live in tents any more, and Saul, and Jonathan, and David, went to the place where the king lived. As they were going along they saw a great many women with harps in their hands, and these women played as they went, and sang, and danced. They were singing about David, and how he had killed the Philistines, and they said in their song that David had killed a great many more than Saul. These are the words they sang, "Saul has slain his thousands, and David his ten thousands."

Do you think that David liked to hear these songs? No. He did not wish to be praised. He desired that God should be praised. He would have liked to hear the women say that God had helped a poor shepherd to kill the giant.

But when Saul heard these songs he was very angry, for he wished to be praised, and he could not bear to hear David praised more than himself. "What," thought Saul, "do they say that David has killed more Philistines than I have, and that he is braver than I am?"

SAUL TRIES TO KILL DAVID.

How wicked Saul was! He was envious; he was like Joseph's brothers, and he was like Cain!

Then Saul thought, "Perhaps David is the man who is to be king instead of me?" He remembered that Samuel had told him that God had chosen a better man than he was, to be king. Then Saul hated David, and wished to kill him. He had these wicked thoughts in his mind when he came back to his own house. Instead of thanking God for His kindness in having helped the Israelites to conquer the Philistines, he was thinking how he could kill David.

SAUL AND THE WITCH OF ENDOR.

The next day after he was come home, David saw that Saul was ill and unhappy; so he took his harp, as he used to do, and began to play sweet music. Now Saul had a sharp thing in his hand, called a javelin; and he thought to himself, "I will throw this at David, and it shall go through his body." But David saw the javelin coming, and he slipped out of the way; so that Saul did not hurt him. Then Saul threw it at him again, but he could not hurt David, for God took care of him. Every one but Saul loved David, and this made Saul hate him still more.

David behaved so well, that Saul could not find any fault in him, for which he could punish him. Then he told David to take some men, and to go and fight against the Philistines. He hoped that the Philistines would kill him in battle. David went and killed a great many Philistines, but no one hurt him. Everybody praised him more, and called him brave. Saul grew more angry. At last he told all his servants to kill David, but they loved him, and would not kill him. Still Jonathan was afraid, lest some wicked person should mind Saul, and kill David; so he told him to hide himself, while he begged his father to forgive him. Then Jonathan said to his father, "Why do you wish to kill David? What has he done? Did he not once kill the giant? Then you were glad: why are you angry with him now?"

Saul promised that he would not have David killed. Then Jonathan called David and brought him to Saul, and David was with him as he used to be.

But soon Saul began to hate David again, and the evil spirit was on him still. Then David played on his harp to make him well. Saul had a javelin in his hand, and he threw it at David, but he slipped out of the way and the javelin stuck in the wall.

Now David was afraid of staying any more with Saul, and he ran away that night.

He did not go back to his father, for Saul would have looked for him there, and would have found him: but he hid himself in a great many places. You will hear of many sad things that will happen to poor David.

But God loved him and took care of him.

The Death of Saul.

At last David went to the land of the Philistines to hide himself from Saul. They were a wicked people, who worshiped idols, yet God made them kind to David, and to his men.

The time was now almost come when Saul must die, and I will tell you how it happened.

You know that the Philistines hated the people of Israel, and used to fight against them. One day the king of the Philistines called a great many of his soldiers together, and took them to a place in the land of Canaan, where they might fight with the Israelites. When Saul heard they were come, he took his soldiers, and went to fight against them. Saul's good son Jonathan went with his father to the battle.

The Philistines and the Israelites fought together upon some hills, and the Philistines conquered. God was angry with the Israelites, and he did not help them. The Israelites ran away from the Philistines; even Saul and Jonathan, though they were very brave, ran away; and the Philistines ran after them, and killed Jonathan. Some men with bows and arrows shot at Saul, and some of the arrows went into his body, so that he could not run any more; yet he was not killed by the arrows; he was only very much hurt.

DEATH OF SAUL.

When Saul found that he could not run away, he was very unhappy, for he was afraid that the Philistines would soon get him, and treat him very cruelly; so he wished very much to die before they overtook him. Then he said to one of his soldiers, "Take your sword and run it through my body."

But the soldier would not obey so wicked a command. Then Saul took his own sword, and fell upon the point of it; and it ran through his body and killed him. It is very wicked of people to kill themselves. People who love God wait till He takes away their breath.

When Saul was dead, the soldier who would not kill him when he had asked him, fell upon his own sword and died with him. It was Saul's wicked example that made him do so.

The Philistines went on running after the Israelites all that day, and they killed a great many.

David Becomes King.

David was in the land of the Philistines. He knew that Saul and Jonathan had been fighting a battle, and he longed to know who had conquered. At last a man who had been at the battle, came to David to tell him about it. The man bowed down before him, and David said, "Where do you come from?"

And the man said, "I come from the tents of Israel."

Then David said, "Pray tell me what has happened."

And the man said, "The Israelites have run away, and many are dead: and Saul and Jonathan, his son, are dead also."

The man thought that David would have been very glad to hear that Saul was dead, but he was deeply grieved, for he still loved Saul, and he was sorry that the Philistines should have conquered him. And David was very sorry for Jonathan, his friend. He would never see his face again in this world.

David sang a sweet song about Saul and Jonathan. He said that Saul and Jonathan had been like eagles and lions, they had been so brave; he said they had lived together, and had died together. And then he said in his song, "I am distressed for thee, my brother Jonathan; thy love to me was wonderful." He called Jonathan his brother, because he had been so very kind to him.

David did not speak of Saul's wickedness, he only spoke of his bravery: for he did not like to speak against the king.

Now the time was come when David was to be king. God put it into the hearts of the Israelites to ask David to be their king, and God had promised that he should be, and He kept his promise, and made him king.

Nathan Rebukes David.

David was a good man, and tried to please God, who put His spirit into his heart; yet still there was wickedness in David's heart, as well as goodness. Satan used to tempt him to do wicked things. Sometimes he did not pray to God to keep him from Satan, and then David used to mind what Satan said. Shall you not be very sorry to know that David committed a great sin? But God rebuked him for his sin and punished him.

One day, Nathan, who was a prophet, came to David. God had told Nathan what David had done.

Nathan said to David, "God has been very kind to you, and made you king. Why have you disobeyed His commandments? God will punish you for your wickedness. Your children shall fight each other, and kill each other, and behave very wickedly to you as long as you live."

David was very sorry when he heard that God was angry with what he had done, and he said, "I have sinned against the Lord."

Then Nathan said, "God has forgiven you; you shall not die."

David was really sorry for what he had done. He was not like Saul, who only cared for the punishment; he was most sorry because he had displeased God.

David played a very sad psalm on his harp, and he gave it to the singers to sing near the ark.

He asked God in his psalm to wash out his sins. These were some of David's words: "Wash me, and I shall be whiter than snow. Create in me a clean heart, O God; and renew a right spirit within me."

You see that David prayed to God to forgive him, and God did forgive him. But God had said that He would punish David

NATHAN REBUKING DAVID.

Wherefore hast thou despised the commandment of the Lord, to do evil in His sight? thou hast killed Uriah the Hittite with the sword, and hast taken his wife to be thy wife, and hast slain him with the sword of the children of Ammon. Now therefore the sword shall never depart from thine house.—II SAMUEL xii: 9, 10.

for his sin, even though He had forgiven him. David had a great many children, and some of them were very wicked when they grew up. I cannot tell you about all his bad children, but I will tell you of one called Absalom. He was a very proud young man: he was very handsome, and had beautiful hair, and he was very vain of his beauty: he also told lies, and he even killed one of his brothers who had offended him. When David heard how

Absalom had killed his brother, he was angry with him for a long time, and would not see him; but at last he let him come to his palace, and kissed him, and forgave him. David ought never to have allowed Absalom to come to Jerusalem again after he had killed his brother: but he was too fond of Absalom.

DAVID FLEEING FROM JERUSALEM

Yet Absalom did not love his father. He wished to be king instead of David, and so he behaved very kindly to all the people in Jerusalem, that they might love him better than they loved his father, and make him king. He used sometimes to kiss the poor people that he saw, and tell them that if he were king he would be very kind to them. This kind way of behaving made the people love Absalom, for they thought that he really cared for them. How very sly and deceitful he was? When Absalom saw that many of the people loved him, he asked David's leave to go from

Jerusalem into the country. And David gave him leave. David did not know what a wicked plan Absalom had made. This was the wicked plan.

Absalom had desired a great many men to wait till they heard the sound of a trumpet, and when they heard it—to cry out, "Absalom is king!" So when Absalom had left Jerusalem, and come into the country, he desired the trumpet to be blown, and a great many of the people called out, "Absalom is king!" and came to Absalom to be his soldiers.

Poor David was in Jerusalem, and a messenger came and told him that Absalom had made himself king. How grieved David was to hear this news! He could not bear to think that his son was so wicked as to make himself king. Then David thought of his own sin, and he felt that he deserved to be punished. He knew that it was God that let all these sad things happen to him.

He would not stay in Jerusalem, for he thought that Absalom would soon come there, and would perhaps kill him, and his servants. So the king left his palace on Mount Zion, to go a great way off. There were many people in Jerusalem who loved David, and they went with him.

First they crossed a little river that was outside Jerusalem, and as they went over all the people wept. They wept to think that their dear king was obliged to leave his house, and to wander about without a home.

Then David and his servants went up a high hill; and David wept as he went up, and he covered his head, and wore no shoes on his feet: he did these things to show he was unhappy: and all the people with him did the same, and wept as they went up. You see how much the people loved David.

And when David was come to the top of the hill he prayed to God. He knew that God would comfort him in his distress.

Then David and his men went on their sorrowful journey. At last they crossed over the river Jordan. On the other side there was a place called a wilderness.

Absalom is Found Hanging on an Oak Tree.

David and his men lived in a city in the wilderness. The city had walls and gates. Absalom soon heard where his father was, and he came after him with a great army. He crossed over the River Jordan, and desired his men to set up their tents near the city where David was.

DEATH OF ABSALOM.

Then David saw that his wicked son meant to fight against him. So one morning he desired his soldiers to go out of the city. David was going with them; but they begged him not to come, lest he should be killed in the battle. These people loved him very much. Then the king said, "I will do as you think best." He did not wish to go to this battle, for he did not like to fight against Absalom. David told the soldiers before they went to battle not to hurt Absalom: for he still loved his wicked son.

Absalom and his soldiers came out to fight against David's men.

Who do you think conquered? David's men, because God helped them; and Absalom's men tried to run away, and a great many of them were killed.

Now you shall hear what became of Absalom.

He rode upon a mule, and as he was riding he passed under a great oak-tree, and his long, beautiful hair was caught in the boughs, and the mule ran away and left him hanging by his head in the tree, with his feet lifted up from the earth.

One of David's soldiers saw him, and went to the captain, Joab, and said, "Behold, I saw Absalom hanging in an oak."

Then Joab said, "And why did you not kill him? If you had I would have given you a great deal of silver, and some clothes."

But the man answered, "If you would have given me a thousand pieces of silver, I would not have hurt Absalom, for I heard the king desire that no one should hurt him."

Then Joab went very quickly to the oak-tree, and found Absalom still hanging there. So he took three darts, and thrust them through Absalom's heart; and ten young men, that were with Joab, hurt him also with swords, or darts, and killed him.

Joab took his body down from the tree and cast it into a great pit in the wood, and laid a great heap of stones on the spot.

When Absalom was dead, Joab blew a trumpet to call back his soldiers from running after Absalom's soldiers: for now he was dead the Israelites might leave off fighting. Absalom's soldiers went back to their tents, and Joab took his soldiers back to the city where David was.

But before Joab and his men went back, two men ran very fast to tell David what had happened.

How much David longed to know whether Absalom was dead! He wished his men to conquer, and yet he did not want Absalom to be killed. No, he would rather die himself than that Absalom should be killed.

David's Grief for the Death of Absalom.

David was sitting near the gates of the city in the wilderness. A man stood upon the top of the wall near the gate, to watch and see whether any person was coming into the city. Soon the watchman saw a man running, and he cried out, "I see a man running alone." Then said David, "No doubt he brings some message." Soon afterward the watchman cried out, "I see another man running alone." Then David said, "He also brings a message."

The first man was a young priest. He ran up to David, and cried out, "All is well."

He said all was well, because David's men had

THE MESSENGERS TELL DAVID OF THE DEATH OF ABSALOM.

conquered. Then the priest fell down to the ground upon his face before the king, and he thanked God for having let David's men conquer.

Then the king said, "Is the young man Absalom safe?" The priest knew that Absalom was dead, but he did not like to grieve David by telling him this sad news all at once; so he said, "There was a great deal of noise and confusion when Joab sent me here." This young priest loved David so much that he did not like to tell him what the noise was about.

Soon the other man came running up to David, and he said, "God has punished the wicked people who fought against the king."

Then the king said, "Is the young man Absalom safe?"

And the messenger answered, "May all people who fight against the king be as Absalom now is!" The king knew that the man meant that Absalom was dead.

How very unhappy he was when he heard this! He went into a room that was near the gate, and he wept as he went up, and he said, "O my son Absalom! my son, my son Absalom! Would God I had died for thee, O Absalom, my son, my son!"

When David's soldiers were coming back into the city, they heard how much the king was grieved for Absalom, and they felt unhappy, too, because they loved the king. He did not come out to meet them, and to thank them for having fought for him, as he would have done if Absalom had not been killed; but he remained by himself, and he covered his face, and cried, "O my son Absalom, my son, my son!"

Did not Absalom come to a very dreadful end? He died in the midst of his wickedness.

How much David loved this wicked Absalom! He went on crying for him for some time. David knew why God had let him have such a wicked child. It was because of his sin; yet God had forgiven David.

Now Absalom was dead, David could return to Jerusalem. The people who had said that Absalom was king now wished David to be king again. So he went over the River Jordan on his way back to Jerusalem.

David's Farewell to His People.

God had promised David that one of his sons should be a good and a wise man, and that he should succeed him in the kingdom.

This son's name was Solomon. God told David that he was to be king after him. At last David grew very old and weak, and he knew that he should die. So he wished to make Solomon king before he died. He desired the high priest to pour oil upon his head; and so the high priest anointed Solomon to be king.

Then David desired his people to come together to a place in Jerusalem, that he might speak to them all before he died. When they were all come, the king stood up on his feet and said, "I once wished to build a house for the ark of God, but God would not let me build it, because I had shed so much blood in battle, but He said that my son should build it."

Then David spoke to Solomon, and said, "Solomon, my son, serve God, and He will bless you." Then David showed Solomon the things he had got ready for building the house; gold, and silver, and iron, and stones, and wood: and he asked the people whether they would give any of their things to build a house for God.

And the people gave a great many things: gold, and silver, and brass, and iron, and beautiful shining stones: and the people liked to give their things for God's house.

And David was pleased to see that they liked to give: for that was a sign that they loved God.

Then David prayed to God, and thanked Him for letting Solomon build Him a house, and for letting the people give their things to God. And David asked God to make Solomon love Him, and obey Him.

Story of Solomon the Wise Man.

Almost the first thing that Solomon did, when he was made king, was to offer sacrifices to God.

He did not offer these sacrifices on Mount Zion, where the ark was, but he went to the place where the old tabernacle was, that Moses had made, and where the great brass altar was, and there he offered a great many sacrifices to God. He offered the sacrifices in meekness and truth, to show that he loved God and wished to serve Him.

The night after Solomon had offered the sacrifices, God spoke to him while he was asleep, and said, "Ask what I shall give thee."

Now Solomon had just been made king, and he saw what a hard thing it was to be a good king: for he wished to judge the people righteously and kindly. People who quarreled with each other came to Solomon; and it is very hard when people quarrel, to find out who is in fault, and who ought to be punished.

He wished very much to judge the people well; and so he asked God to make him very wise.

He said to God that night, "Thou hast made me king over a great many people, and I am very young, and do not know what I ought to do. Make me very wise that I may judge the people well."

God was very much pleased with Solomon, and He said, "You did not ask Me to make you very rich, or make you live a long while, or make you conquer your enemies; but you asked for wisdom; therefore I will make you wiser than any man that ever lived; and I will make you very rich, so that no other king shall be as rich or as great as you: and if you love Me, and serve Me as David did, I will make you live a long while."

Then Solomon awoke. How pleased he must have been to think of the promise that God had made him! He went back to Jerusalem, and offered up more sacrifices near the ark on Mount Zion.

Story of the Two Women and the Dead Child.

One day there came two women to Solomon. They had quarreled with each other. Solomon was the judge, and the women stood before him.

One of these women held a dead baby in her arms, and the other held a living baby in her arms. Both the babies were very little creatures, only a few days old, so that the living baby was not old enough to sit up and to look about it, or to smile.

The woman who held the dead baby seemed very unhappy, and she said to the king, "This dead baby is not my own, the other baby is mine. I lived in the same house with that woman, and no one lived in the house beside us two; and one night that woman lay upon her baby in bed, and killed it, and so she got up, and put her dead baby in my bed while I was asleep, and took my living baby into hers: and when I awoke in the morning I was going to feed my baby, but I found only this dead one; but when I had looked at it, I saw it was not my own baby." Then the other woman said, "You do not speak truth: the living baby is mine, and the dead one is

SOLOMON AND THE TWO WOMEN.

yours." Then the other woman said again, "No, the living baby is mine, and the dead is yours."

Which of these women spoke the truth? How could Solomon find out? How could he tell which ought to have the living baby?

But God made Solomon very wise, and he thought of a way to find out who spoke the truth. So he called out, "Bring me a sword." And the servants brought a sword to the king. Then Solomon said, "Cut the living baby in two, and give half to one woman, and half to the other; because both the women say the child is theirs, so let them each have half."

Then one of the women cried out, "Oh, do not cut the child in half; but let that woman have it; only do not kill it."

But the other woman said, "Oh, let the child be cut in half, and let us each have half."

Now which do you think was the mother of the living baby? Was it not the one who said, "Do not let it be killed?"

How do you know that she was the mother? Because she loved the baby so much. Mothers would rather that any one should have their babies, than that they should be killed.

Solomon knew which was the mother, and he said to his servant, "Give her the living child, and do not kill it; she is its mother."

Solomon had not intended to kill the baby. He only wanted to see what the women would say, that he might find out which was the mother. Was not that a wise plan of Solomon? God had really made him as wise as He had promised He would.

Solomon Builds a Beautiful Temple.

Soon after Solomon became king he began to build the temple. He had a great many things to build it of: gold, and silver; iron, and brass; and stones, and wood; and he had a great many servants to build it. David, his father, had told him how to build it. God had told David, and he had written it down.

Solomon did not build the temple upon Mount Zion, but upon another high hill in Jerusalem.

He desired a great many large stones to be laid upon the ground for the beginning of the house; then he directed his servants to cut down a great many trees. He had some more wood which David had given to him. Solomon built the walls of wood, and he put wood at the top; and he covered the inside of the house with gold.

BUILDING THE TEMPLE.

How beautiful it must have been inside! How bright it must have shone when the candles were lighted; for Solomon made ten candlesticks of gold, to give light to the house. Solomon put other beautiful things in the temple, besides the ten candlesticks. He put ten tables for bread, and a golden altar to burn sweet spices in the midst. And Solomon made a court round the temple; with a stone wall round the court; and he put in the court ten large basins of brass, to wash the animals in before they were sacrificed; and he made one basin larger than the rest; and he made twelve oxen of brass, and put this large basin on the backs of the oxen; and he had the basin filled with water for the priests to wash in.

In the court, Solomon placed a very large brass altar that he had made. It was so large that a great many lambs, and bullocks, and goats, might be burned on it at the same time.

At last the temple was quite finished, and it was the most beautiful house in the world. It could not be moved about as the tabernacle had been in the wilderness: but Solomon never wished to move it from Jerusalem. It was a great deal larger than the tabernacle.

BRINGING THE ARK TO THE TEMPLE.

When it was finished, Solomon desired all people to come to the temple. The priests came, and they carried the ark into a little room in the temple called the Holy of Holies: and Solomon had made a great door to the little room: and he had placed a great curtain or vail over the door, and he had made two very large angels of wood, covered with gold, and placed them in the little room, besides the two golden angels that were on the top of the ark. The large angels stood upright, and each had two great wings stretched out all across the little room; the priests left the ark under the wings of the great angels, and no one could see into the little room because of the great door, and of the curtain or vail which was over the door.

The other part of the temple was filled with priests, and with singers all clothed in white, and holding harps and other musical instruments in their hands—and some of the priests blew trumpets; and these were the words the singers sang:—

"O give thanks unto the Lord; for He is good; for His mercy endureth for ever."

As soon as the priests had left the ark in the little room, and while they and the singers were praising the Lord in the temple, the Lord Himself came down in a cloud and filled the temple, so that the priests and singers were obliged to go out of the temple and stand in the court.

How glad Solomon was to see that the Lord was come into the house that he had built for Him!

Solomon had made a high place of brass, and he put it near the brazen altar in the court, and he stood upon the high place, so that all the people could see him.

He knelt down on this place, and spread wide his arms, and began to pray to God. His prayer was very long; but I will only tell you a little part of it. He asked God to hear all people who were unhappy, and who were sorry for their sins, and to forgive them.

When Solomon had ended his prayer, there came down fire from heaven, and burned up the beasts that had been killed and spread upon the altar. The fire did not hurt the people; it only burned the dead beasts on the altar. God sent the fire to show the people that He liked them to offer sacrifices to Him, and to pray to Him.

When the people saw the fire, and the glory of God all over the temple, they bowed themselves down to the ground, and praised the Lord, and said, "He is good; His mercy endureth forever."

At last the people went home to their own houses, but they very often came to offer sacrifices at the temple and to pray to God. Sweet psalms and sweet music might be heard at the temple both night and day.

Story of the Queen of Sheba.

After the temple was finished, God said to Solomon, "I have heard your prayer, and I will hear the people who pray to Me in the temple: and if you will obey Me as David did, I will bless you: but if you do wicked things and worship idols, then I shall be very angry, and this beautiful house that you have built shall be thrown down."

Solomon was very rich, and very wise, as God had promised. He built a great many ships, and he built a palace, and he built a great many towns; and he made a great throne with six steps all covered with gold, and images of two lions on each of the steps, a lion on each side; and a seat at the top for Solomon.

When he spoke, he said such wise things that people came from a great way off to hear him, and they brought him presents; some brought cups of gold or silver, and some brought him fine clothes, and some brought spices, and some brought horses and mules.

So Solomon grew very rich. He sent his ships to far countries over the sea, and they came back full of gold and silver, and ivory, and apes, and peacocks. He was the richest king in all the world. He was also very wise. He knew about all the plants, from the highest tree down to the least plant that grows; he knew about the beasts, and birds, and fishes, and worms, and insects: but he knew something much better than these things,—he knew about God, and how to please Him, and he gave people very wise advice.

Now there was a queen who lived a great way off, who heard of Solomon, and of how wise he was: and she wished very much to hear him talk, and to see the house that he had built. She had a great many questions to ask him; I believe that her questions were about God. She had not been taught about God in her own country and she wanted to know a great deal about Him. She was called the Queen of Sheba. It was right of the Queen of Sheba to wish to know about God. She was a very rich lady, so she brought a great many servants with her, and many camels with spices and gold, as presents to King Solomon.

Solomon was very kind to her, and answered all the questions that she asked him; and he showed her all the things that he had built. The queen was quite surprised at all she saw and heard, and she said to King Solomon, "How happy are your servants who are always standing near you, and who hear the wise

THE QUEEN OF SHEBA VISITS SOLOMON.

things you say! Blessed be the Lord your God, who made you king."

Then she gave a great deal of gold and silver to King Solomon, and he gave her all the things that she liked to have; and then the queen went back with her camels and her servants into her own country.

The Queen of Sheba brought back to her own home something better than her presents; she brought a great deal of wisdom in her mind, and I hope she left off worshiping idols, and loved the true God.

A great many of the wise things that Solomon said are written down in the Bible; they are called "The Proverbs." When you are older, you shall read them, that you may grow wise. I think even now you would understand some of them.

Solomon Forgets God and Worships Idols.

The first time God appeared to Solomon He promised to make him wise; and the next time He promised to bless him, if he served Him.

But did Solomon serve God? I must now tell you of the wicked things that he did when he was old.

He married a great many wives. This was wrong. People might then have two wives, or more; but God liked best that they should only have one. You remember that Jacob had two wives, named Rachel and Leah. If a man now was to have two wives, he would be punished; then he might have two; but not so many as Solomon had.

Solomon had seven hundred wives. I think he had grown proud, and that he wished to be a very grand king, and it was thought grand for a king to have many wives.

These wives were wicked; they worshiped idols. Solomon ought not to have married heathen women. At last his wives persuaded him to like their idols, and to build altars for them on the high places round Jerusalem. And Solomon did even worse than this: he worshiped some of the idols himself. You did not think that he could have been so wicked. Was he not very foolish to worship idols, which are only made of wood or stone? He knew what was right, but he did not do it.

How sad it must have been to see these women offering sacrifices, and burning incense to their idols, and Solomon bowing down to them! God was very angry with Solomon; and He said to him, "Because you have done this, one of your servants shall make himself king; he shall take away a great deal of the land of Canaan from your son, as soon as you are dead."

Do you know it is the rule, that when a king dies the king's son is king instead of his father? So when Solomon died, his son was king instead of him; but very soon one of Solomon's servants tried to make himself king. The servant's name was Jer-o-bo-am. This servant made himself the king over a great part of the land of Canaan; but Solomon's son was still king over the rest of the land.

What God had said came true; for He makes all He says come true. God had told Solomon that his son should only have a part of the land. This was the punishment that God gave Solomon. God will punish people who are disobedient.

I hope, my dear child, that you will not be like King Solomon, and love God only when you are young; but I hope that you will love God all your life, from the time you are a little creature, until your hair is gray, and your back is bent with age, should you live to be so old.

How Jeroboam Was Punished for His Wickedness.

Jerusalem was not in Jeroboam's part of Canaan; it was in the part that Solomon's son was king over. It was a good thing for Solomon's son that he had Jerusalem. You can tell me why it was a good thing—the temple was in Jerusalem, and God came down in the temple in a glorious cloud.

You know that God had desired all the people in Canaan to come to Jerusalem very often to worship Him. Jeroboam ought to have come to Jerusalem to worship God; but he would not. He was very wicked, and he told his people not to go to Jerusalem.

Why did he not like to go there? Because there was another king in Jerusalem. He did not like his people to go to a place where there was another king, lest they should like the other king best. You see how proud Jeroboam was. Then he did a very wicked thing: he made two golden calves, and set them up in his part of Canaan, one calf in one town, and the other calf in another town, that the people might worship them instead of God. He told his people to worship the golden calves. He said, "Do not go to Jerusalem, it is too far off: worship these golden calves." How wicked it was of Jeroboam to teach his poople to worship idols!

Jeroboam worshiped the calves himself. One day God sent a prophet to him, to tell him of his wickedness. Jeroboam was standing by an altar burning incense to a golden calf, when the prophet came, and told him how angry God was with the people who worshiped the golden calves, and how He would punish them. And the prophet said, "And this is the sign that God is angry: the altar shall be broken, and the ashes that are on it shall fall to the ground." When King Jeroboam heard this he was angry, and wished to punish the prophet: so he stretched out his hand, and said to his servants, "Lay hold on him." Now while Jeroboam's hand was stretched out, God made it grow dry and stiff, so that he could not pull it back again; and at the same time, the altar was broken, and the ashes fell upon the ground, as the prophet had said.

Do you not think that Jeroboam must have been frightened then? He knew that no one could make his hand well but God: so he said to the prophet, "Pray thou to the Lord thy God for me, that my hand may be made well."

Would the prophet pray to God for Jeroboam, who had been so unkind to him? Yes, he prayed to God, and God made the king's hand as well as it was before.

Story of Elijah and the Ravens.

You remember that Jeroboam was king over only part of the land of Canaan. Solomon had been king over all the land; but now Solomon's son was king over one part, and Jeroboam was king over the other part.

I will tell you what Jeroboam was called. He was called King of Israel; and Solomon's son was called King of Judah. Will you try to remember this?

At last Jeroboam died, and there was another king of Israel instead of him, and at last this king died, and then there was another king; and at last he died, and then there was another king: so there were a great many kings one after the other. I am sorry to say that they were all wicked, and that they all worshiped the golden calves that Jeroboam had made. I will not tell you the names of these kings; and my reason is, I am afraid that you will not remember so many. But I will tell you the name of one of them.

At last, after a great many kings had died, one after another, there was a king called Ahab.

He was more wicked than any of the other kings had been. One of the worst things he did was to marry a woman who worshiped idols. This woman was the daughter of the king of another country called Sidon. She had been brought up to worship idols, and she was very fond of them, and she did a great many wicked things. This woman's name was Jezebel. She was called the Queen of Israel, because she was married to Ahab, the king.

The name of Jezebel's favorite idol was Baal; and she persuaded Ahab to worship Baal, as well as the golden calves: and he built a temple for Baal in the town where he lived. There were a great many men who used to teach people to worship Baal; and these men were called the prophets of Baal; and Jezebel was very kind to them. For Jezebel was kind to the people who loved idols; but she tried to kill the people who loved God. There were some people in the land of Israel who would not worship Baal, and these people hid themselves in caves, lest Jezebel should kill them. God loved these poor people very much.

I will now tell you of a very good prophet that lived in the land of Israel. His name was Elijah: he would not worship idols, and he tried to persuade other people to love the true God. God often spoke to him, and told him what would happen, and Elijah prayed very often to God.

Ahab and Jezebel hated Elijah because he was good, and they wanted to kill him. Elijah was very sorry to see so many people in the land of Israel worshiping Baal, and he wished very much that they should be sorry for their wickedness. At last God sent the people a punishment. He sent no rain for a great many months, nor

JEZEBEL COMES FROM SIDON TO MEET AHAB.

did he let any dew come on the grass in the morning; so the hot sun scorched the grass, and the corn did not grow, and the trees did not bring forth fruit. And all the people of Israel were very unhappy; but God wished them to turn from their wickedness.

How did Elijah get food when there was no rain? God told him to go to a place where there was a pond or a brook, in a secret place, where he might hide himself from Ahab: and God promised to send some ravens to feed him.

So Elijah went to this brook, and he drank of the water of the brook; and in the morning some ravens flew to him and gave him some bread and meat; and in the evening they came again, and brought him some more bread and meat; and the next day they came again, both morning and evening: so Elijah had breakfast and supper every day; and he wanted nothing more.

God can do everything. Most ravens are fierce, but God made these gentle. How glad Elijah must have been when he saw them coming with the food! How he must have thanked God for sending them every day! God has promised to feed all hungry people who pray to Him. He does not send ravens to feed them; but He makes other people pity them and give them food.

Elijah lived quite alone by the brook: but he knew that God was with him. At last there was very little water in the brook; the sun dried up the water, and no rain came to fill it up. There was less water every day, and at last there was none left.

What could Elijah do now? God could have filled the brook with water, but He did not choose to do that. He told Elijah to leave the brook and go to another place.

I will tell you soon where Elijah went.

You see what care God took of Elijah: He will take the same care of you, if you love Him and pray to Him.

Story of the Widow and Her Son.

When the brook was dried up, God told Elijah to go a great way off to a place where a poor widow lived, who would give him food. This widow was very poor, for since there had been no rain, people could get very little food to eat, because so little corn grew in the fields.

JEZEBEL AND AHAB.

But Elijah went where God told him. He went all across the land of Canaan, till he came to Zerephath, just outside Canaan. Now the people who lived in this town were heathen people, and worshiped idols.

When Elijah was come to the gate of the town he saw a poor woman gathering sticks, and Elijah knew that she was the widow who was to give him food. Then he called to her, and said, "Fetch me, I pray thee, a little water in a cup, that I may drink."

I do not wonder that Elijah was thirsty, for he had walked a long way, and there was now very little water in the land of Canaan.

Now this widow was so kind that she was going to fetch the water for Elijah. Then Elijah called to her again, and said, "Bring me, I pray thee, a morsel of bread in thine hand."

Then the poor widow said, "I have no bread; I have only a handful of flour in a barrel, and a little oil in a jar; and I was just gathering some sticks, that I might make a fire, and make the flour and oil into a little cake, that I and my son might eat it; and as we have no more food, when we have eaten it, we must die."

Would Elijah take all the poor widow's food? God had told him what to say.

So he said to the widow, "Go and make a little cake for me first, and afterward make one for you and your son: for God has said that there shall always be some flour in your barrel, and some oil in your jar, till He send rain again upon the earth."

What a wonderful promise this was! Did the widow believe it? Yes, she made a fire, and mixed the flour and oil together, and made some bread for Elijah, and then she made some for herself and her son; and still there was flour in the barrel, and oil in the jar: and every day she found enough flour and oil to make bread for them all.

Elijah came and lived with this poor widow: he lived in a room upstairs near her house. The widow found it was a good thing to have such a man as Elijah in the house. Because God made the flour and oil last. Besides, Elijah could teach this poor woman about God: for you know that she had been brought up to worship idols.

Now, you shall hear of a very sad thing that happened to this poor woman. One day her child, who was a little boy, fell sick, and he was so very sick that he died. The poor widow was very unhappy. She knew that God had let him die, and she thought that God was angry with her: and she wished that Elijah had not come to her house; and she went to him, and spoke angrily to him. It was very ungrateful of her to behave in this manner. Then Elijah said, "Give me thy son."

Now, the widow was holding the dead child in her arms, and Elijah took the child in his own arms, and carried him to his room, and laid him on his bed. Then he began to pray to God. "O Lord, my God," he said, "hast Thou made this sad thing happen to this poor widow? Hast Thou killed her son?"

Then Elijah stretched himself upon the child as it lay dead; he did so three times, and he prayed to God, saying, "O Lord, my God, I pray Thee let this child's soul come into him again."

And the Lord heard Elijah's prayer; and He let the child's soul return to him, and then the little boy was alive again. Then Elijah took him in his arms, and brought him downstairs, and gave him to his mother again, and said to her, "See, thy son is alive."

"Now," said she, "I see that you are a man of God, and that all you tell me about God is true."

I hope the widow believed all that Elijah said, and I hope she loved the God who had been so very kind to her and given her food, and made her little boy alive again.

God still hears people when they pray.

Elijah Goes on a Long Journey to See King Ahab.

Elijah lived a long time with the poor widow. Ahab and Jezebel, the wicked king and queen, did not know where he was hid. They would have been glad to find him, that they might kill him. Ahab sent to all the countries round to look for him, but no one could find him.

The Israelites were very unhappy, because they had very little food; even King Ahab had not grass enough in his fields for his horses, so that a great many of them died.

Elijah was sorry for the poor Israelites, and he prayed to God to send rain, that more corn and grass might grow. God heard this prayer, and He told Elijah that He would soon send rain; but first He told Elijah to go and show himself to King Ahab.

Do you not think that Elijah would be afraid to go to King Ahab? But he did what God told him; for he knew that God could take care of him. So he left the poor widow and her son, and set out on a long journey to the place where Ahab lived. I think that the widow must have been sorry when Elijah went, for he had fed her and taught her about God: but God had promised to make her flour and oil last till He sent rain; and the rain had not come yet.

Now while Elijah was on his way to King Ahab, he met a very good servant of the king, whose name was Obadiah.

This servant was looking for some grass for King Ahab's horses. He knew Elijah when he saw him; and was very much surprised, for it was a long while since any one in Canaan had seen Elijah. This good servant fell on his face before Elijah, and said, "Art thou my lord Elijah?"

Then Elijah said, "I am; go tell your lord (King Ahab) that I am here."

Then the servant was afraid, for he thought that while he was gone to tell Ahab where Elijah was, God would take Elijah away to some other place, and then Ahab would be angry with his servant and kill him. Ahab was a cruel master, and his servant was afraid of making him angry.

But Elijah promised that he would stay in that place till King Ahab was come; so the servant believed Elijah's promise, and went to look for the king.

Ahab was in another place, looking for grass for his horses. His good servant told him that Elijah was waiting to see him. So Ahab came to the place.

When he saw Elijah, he spoke angrily to him, and said, "Are you the man that troubles the people of Israel?"

Ahab thought that it was Elijah who asked God not to let the rain come.

Then Elijah said to Ahab, "It is not I that trouble the people of Israel; it is you that have made these troubles come by your wickedness. You have not obeyed God, and you have worshiped Baal."

Then Elijah told Ahab what he wanted him to do. He told him to get all the prophets of Baal together, and send them to him to a very high hill or mountain.

Ahab promised to do as Elijah had bidden him, and in the next story I will tell you some very wonderful things that happened when the false prophets of Baal were gathered together on the top of the mountain.

Elijah and the Prophets of Baal.

One morning very early, Elijah was on the high mountain with Baal's wicked prophets, and a great many people were standing all round; and King Ahab was there, but Jezebel was not there.

Elijah wanted the people to see that his God was the true God: so he said to them, "Let Baal's prophets take a bullock and kill it, and lay it on an altar, and then let them ask Baal to send fire from heaven to burn up the bullock; and I will take another bullock and kill it, and lay it on the altar, and I will ask the Lord to send fire from heaven: and if Baal send fire, then you will know that he is the true God: but if my God send fire, then you will know that He is the true God."

The people liked what Elijah said, and they answered, "It is well spoken."

Then Elijah told Baal's prophets to take their bullock first. So they took it and killed it, and put it on an altar with some wood; but they put no fire to the wood. Then they began to pray to their god to send fire. They cried, "O Baal, hear us!" till twelve o'clock, and they jumped about the altar, as they used to do when they prayed to him. How tired they must have been after calling out so long, "O Baal, hear us!" Still the prophets of Baal went on praying for fire; and at last they cut themselves with knives, and made their blood flow, because they thought it would please Baal: they thought he was a cruel god, that liked their blood. So they went on till three o'clock in the afternoon; but no fire came from heaven.

KILLING THE PROPHETS OF BAAL.

Then Elijah said it was time to ask his God to send fire: so he built an altar with twelve stones, and he laid some wood on the altar, and on top of that a bullock: and then he desired the people to throw twelve barrels of water over the altar. There was a river just at the bottom of the hill, and a well also, whence the people could bring the water: Elijah made a ditch all around the altar, and this ditch was quite filled with water, and the altar was quite wet.

Then Elijah began to pray to God. All the people were standing round, while he prayed before the altar.

This is what he said: "Lord God of Abraham, of Isaac, and of Israel (or Jacob), let it be known this day that Thou art God, and that I am Thy servant. Hear me, O Lord, hear me."

Then all of a sudden fire came from heaven, and burnt up the bullock and the altar; and even the stones, and it licked up the water that was in the ditch.

How surprised the people were at this sight! They fell on their faces, and said, "The Lord, He is the God: the Lord, He is the God."

Now they saw that Baal was not the true God. So Elijah desired the people to take hold of the wicked prophets of Baal, and to bring them down to the river at the bottom of the hill, and to kill them with swords; and the blood of the false prophets was mingled with the water in the river. These prophets had taught the people to worship Baal, so God chose that they should die.

Did the people leave off worshiping Baal? Did they mind what Elijah said, and pray to his God? We shall soon hear what they did.

How much they wished that God would send rain! They must have felt sure that if God could send fire He could also send rain.

Story of the Little Cloud not Larger than a Man's Hand.

You have heard how the prophets of Baal were killed. Now Elijah knew that God would soon send rain: so he told Ahab that there would soon be rain, and that he might go, and eat, and drink. So Ahab ate and drank in some place near the high hill. But Elijah did not eat and drink. He went up to the top of the hill to pray to God. He threw himself down upon the earth, and bent down his head very low.

Then he told his servant to stand up while he himself was praying, and to look a great way off over the sea, and to tell him what he saw. Elijah wanted God to send clouds on the sky, that there might be rain. The servant went up and looked, and then said to Elijah, "There is nothing." Then Elijah told him to go and look, seven times. The seventh time the servant came and told Elijah, "I saw a little cloud a great way off, as big as a man's hand."

Then Elijah knew that God had heard his prayer, and that the cloud would grow larger, and that rain would soon be pouring down. So he told the servant to tell Ahab to get ready his chariot and his horses, and to drive as fast as he could to his own house, which was a great way off: for that there would soon be a great deal of rain. So Ahab rode in his chariot with his horses, and God made Elijah so strong that he ran faster than the horses, and he got first to the city where Ahab lived. While Ahab was driving and Elijah was running, there were a great many clouds in the sky, and soon there was a great rain.

ELIJAH AND THE ANGEL.

It poured down in great sheets, and filled the dried-up ponds, and refreshed the withered grass, and softened the hard ground. Now the people knew that more corn and grass would soon grow in the fields.

When Ahab got to his own city where he lived, he found the queen Jezebel there, and he told her all that had happened; he told her how Baal did not send fire from heaven, and how God did, and he told her how Elijah had killed the prophets of Baal.

On hearing this, Jezebel was very angry with Elijah, and she sent a man to tell him that she would kill him the next day.

I think she was afraid of the prophet, or she would have desired the man to kill him that same day; but perhaps she thought if she killed Elijah, there would be no more rain.

When Elijah heard that Jezebel wished to kill him, he was afraid, and he would not stay in the city where she lived, but went very quickly all through the land of Canaan till he came to a great wilderness. He did not take his servant with him, but he went there alone. In the wilderness there were trees and hills, but very few houses and people.

Elijah was quite alone in the wilderness. At last he sat down under a tree, and he prayed to God to let him die. Why was Elijah so unhappy? Was it because he was afraid of Jezebel killing him? He was more unhappy because Jezebel went on in her wickedness. Elijah saw that she would go on teaching people to worship idols, and he wished everybody to love God. After he had prayed, he lay down under the tree, and went to sleep. Soon some one touched him. Who was it? An angel. The angel said, "Arise and eat."

Then Elijah looked and saw a fire, and some bread near it, that had been just baked; and he saw a jug of water close to his head. Who could have got ready the bread and the water for Elijah? It must have been the angel. So you see that an angel was his servant. God sends His angels to wait upon people who love Him. The angels like to wait upon them; they fly down quickly from heaven when God tells them.

Elijah ate and drank the bread and water, and then he lay

down again, and slept. But soon the angel woke him again, and said, "Arise and eat, for you will soon walk a great way."

So Elijah ate and drank again, and afterward Elijah walked a great way in the wilderness: but the angel's food had made him strong: and he lived without eating and drinking for forty days. Was not that a great wonder? God can keep people alive without food, if he chooses to do so.

What Happened to Elijah in the Wilderness.

Elijah walked for forty days in the wilderness quite alone, till at last he came to a mountain. There he found a cave: and he went into the cave, and slept in it. While he was in the cave, God spoke to him, and asked him why he was come there.

You know, dear children, the reason why. You know that Elijah had left Canaan because of wicked Jezebel, and God knew this: but He chose that Elijah should tell him why.

Then Elijah said, "The people of Israel have thrown down God's altars, and killed God's prophets: and I am the only one left; and they try to kill me."

Then God told him to come out of the cave, and he came out and stood upon the mountain. And God made a very great wind to blow, that tore the mountain: then He made the mountain shake: and then God made a fire come. How dreadful it must have been to see and hear these things! But God wanted to show Elijah how strong he was; so that Elijah might know that God could take care of him, and could punish the wicked people who tried to hurt him. Then God spoke to Elijah in a very gentle voice, and when he heard this voice, he covered his face with his cloak, and went and stood inside the cave.

It was kind of God to speak to Elijah in such a gentle voice! God loved Elijah, and wished to comfort him. But Elijah remembered what a great God He was; so he hid his face. The angels who stand round God's throne in heaven. hide their faces between their wings.

God asked Elijah again why he came there, and then Elijah told the Lord that the people were wicked, and that they wanted to kill him. Then God told him that He would soon punish the wicked people for worshiping idols: but God said that all the people did not worship Baal; and that there were a great many in Israel who had never bowed their knees to Baal, nor kissed his image with their mouths.

After this God told Elijah to go and find a man called Elisha, and to anoint him to be a prophet.

Then Elijah left the cave, and went to look for Elisha. At last he came to a field where a man was ploughing. There were twenty-four oxen drawing the plough. They were

DOGS EAT THE BODY OF JEZEBEL.

harnessed two and two; and each two had a great piece of wood over their necks, called a yoke. A man was walking by the side of the two last of the oxen. This man's name was Elisha. Elijah came up to him, and taking off his own cloak, threw it over the man's shoulders. He meant in this way to show him that he was to come with him, and the man knew what Elijah meant, and he left his oxen, and ran after him, and said, "I will come with thee: only let me first go and kiss my father and mother."

Elijah allowed the man to go home for a little while.

Then he left his home and went after Elijah; and he was his servant.

Elijah is Taken Up to Heaven in a Chariot of Fire.

Do you remember, dear children, that Elijah once wished to die? But God chose that Elijah should never die, but should go up to heaven without dying. How pleased Elijah must have been, when he knew that God meant to do this! Should not you like, my dear child, to be caught up into heaven to see God, and to sing with the angels?

When Elijah knew that he was soon going up into heaven, he went to a great many places first, where his friends lived. These friends were some good young prophets who lived together, and learned about God.

Once Elijah had no friends; he had thought that no one loved God but himself: but now he had a great many friends. These young prophets knew that Elijah was soon going up to heaven. I think they must have felt sorry to part with him: only they knew that he was going to be happy.

Elisha wished very much to see Elijah go up to heaven. What do you think he determined to do?

To keep close to Elijah, and not to leave him. Elijah said to him, "Pray stay at this place, while I go to another, where the Lord has told me to go."

And Elisha said, "I will not leave thee."

Soon afterward Elijah said, "Stay at this place while I go on."

"No," said Elisha, "I will not leave thee."

Soon again Elijah said, "Stay at this place while I go on."

"No," said Elisha, "I will not leave thee."

So Elijah and Elisha walked a great way together from place to place. At last they came to the River Jordan. Then Elijah took off his cloak, and folded it up, and struck the waters with it; and God made a path through the waters, and Elijah and Elisha walked through the river on dry ground.

After they had gone over the river, Elijah said to Elisha, "Ask what I shall do for thee before I be taken away from thee."

For what did Elisha ask? He wished to be such a prophet as Elijah was, so he asked for a great deal of his spirit. He wished to be a great prophet, so he might teach people about God. He did not want people to praise him; he wanted them to praise God.

Elijah said, "You have asked a hard thing, but if you see me when I am taken from you, it shall be so: but if not, it shall not be so."

How much Elisha now hoped that he should see Elijah go up to heaven!

They still walked on, and talked to each other. What do you think they talked about? I am sure that they did not talk of foolish things. I think they talked of God and of heaven, and of what they could do to please God. How happy Elijah must have felt when he knew he was soon going to see the God he loved so much!

As they were talking, there came down from heaven a chariot and horses of fire, and Elijah was taken away from Elisha, and carried up into heaven: and Elisha saw him go up; and he cried out, "My father, my father!"

As Elijah was taken away his cloak fell from him, and Elisha picked it up; and when Elisha came back to the River Jordan, he struck the waters with it, as Elijah had done, and the waters went up on each side, and there was a dry path, and Elisha walked over alone.

Now Elisha saw that God had made him such a prophet as Elijah had been. Some of Elijah's friends were standing on the other side of the river, and they saw the wonder that Elisha had done, and they said, "The spirit of Elijah is in Elisha;" and they came and bowed themselves down to him.

The young prophets used to mind what Elijah said, and now they wished to mind Elisha.

Now Elisha went about from place to place, as Elijah had once done, and he taught people about God, and did many wonders, to show people that his God was the true God.

Story of the Bears and the Wicked Children.

Elisha was now growing old, and his hair had become thin, so that he was bald on the top of his head. One day he came near a town where a great many people lived who worshiped idols. One of the golden calves that Jeroboam made was in this town. A great many little children came out of it, and met Elisha as he was in the road; and they mocked him, and said, "Go up, thou bald head! go up, thou bald head!" They wanted Elisha to go up into heaven as Elijah had done, that they might not see him any more, nor hear what he said.

How did they dare to speak in this way to the prophet of the Lord? Elisha turned back, and looked on them, and told them that God would send them a dreadful punishment.

The children soon found that Elisha had spoken truth; for two bears came out of the wood, and tore forty-two of these children into pieces.

No doubt the children cried, and screamed, and tried to run away when they saw the bears coming; but it was of no use; they could not escape: the bears overtook them, and killed them. What must their parents have said when they heard what had happened to their dear children?

How sad it is to think of the children who were eaten up by the bears! Perhaps their parents had not taught them to love God. Never laugh at any person who is lame, or blind; but more than all, never laugh at people who pray to God.

Elisha Restores Life to a Little Boy who had Died.

Elisha used to go about from place to place to teach people about God. Those people who loved God were kind to Elisha and gave him food.

There was one very rich lady who used to ask him, whenever he passed by her house, to come in.

This kind woman wished that she had in her house a room for Elisha to sleep in, and she said to her husband, "Let us make ready a little room close to our house; and let us put in it a bed, a table, a stool, and a candlestick, that Elisha may sleep in it when he comes this way."

And the lady's husband allowed her to have such a little room for the prophet. Soon afterward Elisha came by that way, and he slept in this room. He must have liked it very much—he could sit there alone, and think of God: and he could write in it, because it contained a table, and when it was dark he could light the candle, and go on writing or reading.

This rich lady had a little child. One day, when the child was grown old enough to talk, he went out with his father into a field where men were reaping corn: for his father had a great many fields full of corn, which his servants reaped. It was the morning, yet the sun was getting hot, for the child soon cried out, "My head, my head!" The child felt such a pain in his head that he could not stay in the field.

So the father said to one of his servants, "Carry him to his mother." The servant carried him home to his mother, and he sat on her knees till twelve o'clock, and then he died.

Oh, how sad the mother was when she found her little boy was dead! I have often heard of little children dying quite suddenly, like this poor little boy. Every day we should think, "Am I ready to die, if I were to die to-day?"

Now you shall hear what the mother did with the dead child. She went into the room she had made for Elisha, and laid him on his bed, and shut the door, and went out. Elisha lived at a place a good way off, and the lady wished very much to go and see him. I need not tell you why she wished to see him. She asked her husband to allow her to have one of the servants to go with her, and one of the asses for her to ride upon, that she might go to Elisha and come again soon. And her husband said, "Why do you want to go to Elisha to-day? This is not the Sabbath-day;" because Elisha used to teach people about God on the Sabbath-day.

And the woman said, "It shall be well;" but she did not tell her husband why she wanted to go; I suppose she was afraid of grieving him. A servant went with the lady, and she said to the servant, "Go quickly and do not stop unless I tell you."

At last they came to the hill where Elisha was. He was with his servant Gehazi; and he saw the woman coming while she was still a great way off, and he wanted to know why she was coming to him so quickly, for he thought that something was the matter; so he said to Gehazi, "Run now to meet her and say, 'Is it well with thee? Is it well with thy husband? Is it well with the child?'"

So Gehazi ran, and asked the woman whether it was well with them. And she said, "It is well." Why did she say it was well? Was not her child dead? But she knew that it was well, or right, because God had made her child die, and she knew that all that God does is well. Yet the poor lady felt very unhappy. When she came up to Elisha she alighted and threw her arms round his feet, and Gehazi was going to thrust her away. Was not that very unkind? Elisha would not let him do so, but said, "Let her alone; she is very unhappy, and God has not told me what has happened to her;" because Elisha only knew those things that God had told him.

Elisha saw that her son was dead. So he gave his own staff, or stick, to Gehazi, and told him to go quickly, and not to stop to speak to any one by the way, and to lay the staff on the face of the child. But the woman would not go with Gehazi: she said to Elisha, "I will not leave thee." She liked better being with Elisha than with unkind Gehazi. She knew that Elisha loved God: Gehazi did not love God: he was wicked, but I am not sure whether the woman knew that he was wicked, for he pretended to be good.

Gehazi went on first, and laid the staff on the child's face; but the child did not hear his voice, nor did he speak. So Gehazi went back, and met Elisha coming along with the woman, and Gehazi said, "The child is not awaked."

At last Elisha came to the house. He went into his own little room, and found the child lying dead on the bed, and he shut the door, and he stayed in the room alone with the dead child. Then he prayed to God to make him alive again: and he lay upon the child, putting his mouth upon the child's mouth, and his eyes upon the child's eyes,

ELISHA RESTORES THE CHILD TO LIFE.

and his hands upon the child's hands, and he stretched himself upon him, and the child's flesh began to grow warm. Then he got up and walked up and down, and then he stretched himself again over the child; and the child sneezed seven times, and then he opened his eyes.

Then Elisha called Gehazi, and desired him to tell the woman to come. And when she was come into the room Elisha said, "Take up thy son," for the child was lying on the bed. Oh, how glad the mother was! How thankful to God and to Elisha! Before she took up the child she fell at Elisha's feet, and bowed herself to the ground, and then she took up her child, and went out of the room.

Was not this a great wonder that Elisha had done?

Elijah once made a widow's child alive again: and Elisha made a child alive again: for Elisha was such a prophet as Elijah had been, and could do wonders like him. God had promised that he should be like Elijah, if he saw him taken up to heaven: and God kept his promise. Ought not the people of Israel to have minded all that Elisha said, when

THE DEAD MAN RESTORED TO LIFE.

they heard of the wonders that he did? They might be quite sure that Elisha was a true prophet.

The power of God continued to abide with Elisha even after his death and burial, for it is related in II. Kings, chap. xiii. 21, that as some men were burying a man, they became alarmed at the approach of a band of Moabites, and being near Elisha's sepulchre, they threw the body therein and fled. A very wonderful thing now occurred. As soon as the body of the man touched the bones of Elisha he was restored to life and sat up. We are not told anything more about the history of this man, but we are sure his little children were very glad to have him return to them again alive and well. How wonderful are the works of God!

Story of Naaman the Leper.

There were a great many heathen people, who lived outside the land of Canaan. You know, my dear child, that people who worship idols are called "heathen." Some of these heathen people used often to come into Canaan and rob them and hurt them. Why did God let the people of Israel be robbed and hurt? Because they did not obey Him, or mind what Elisha taught them.

Once some of these heathen people came and took away a little girl out of the land of Israel: and they sold her for a slave to wait on a rich heathen lady, in a country a great way off. The lady's husband was called Naaman, and he was a great captain, and could fight well in battle.

But Naaman was very unhappy, for he had a dreadful disease, called the leprosy. He had very sore white places on his body. He could not find anybody who could cure him of the disease. No doctor could cure him; nor could any of the prophets of his idol save him. Now the little girl who waited on his wife had heard of the wonders that Elisha did, and she felt sure that he could cure her master, and she said, "Oh, that my master were with the prophet that is in my country, for he would cure his leprosy!"

Somebody heard what the little girl said, and told Naaman. He wished very much to be made well, and so he determined to go to the land of Israel, and to ask Elisha to make him well.

Now Elisha heard that he was coming, and he knew that God would help him to make Naaman well: and he hoped that when he was made well he would worship the true God, who could do such wonders: for Elisha did not wish people to praise him: he wished them to praise God.

Naaman came into Canaan in a fine chariot, with horses, and he brought a great many servants with him. He was very proud, and expected that Elisha would pay him a great deal of respect, because he was so rich and great. He drove up to Elisha's door; but the prophet did not come out to meet him: he only sent a messenger, who said to Naaman, "Go and wash in the River Jordan seven times, and your flesh shall be well."

Then Naaman was very angry, and he said, "I thought that the prophet would have come out to me, and would have stood, and called on the name of the Lord his God, and struck his hand over the sore place, and made me well." Besides being angry at this, Naaman did not like to wash in a river of the land of Canaan: he would rather have washed in one of the fine large rivers of his own country. He was so very angry, that he was going home to his own country without washing in Jordan: but his servants came to him to persuade him to do as Elisha had directed. They said, "If the prophet had desired you to do some very hard thing, would you not have done it, that you might have been made well? Now he tells you to do a very easy thing, only to wash in the River Jordan; and will you not do it?" It was kind of the servants to try and persuade Naaman to wash in Jordan.

Naaman listened to what they said: he went to Jordan, and he dipped in it seven times, and his flesh grew as soft and smooth as the flesh of a little child.

Now Naaman was very glad that he had done as Elisha had told him. I hope he was sorry for having been in such a passion at first.

Where do you think Naaman went, when he was well? Did he go home immediately to his own country again? Oh, no, that would have been very ungrateful. He went first to Elisha's house, and he brought all his servants with him.

He did not feel so proud as he had done before: he did not expect Elisha to come out to him; but he went in to Elisha; and he told him that he was sure Elisha's God was the true God, and he promised that he would never worship idols any more. How glad Elisha must have been to hear Naaman say that he would worship the true God!

Naaman wished to give Elisha some money and some beautiful things as a reward for having made him well: so he begged him to take some of the things he had brought with him. But Elisha would not take anything. He wished to show Naaman that he had not made him well that he might get money. You know, dear children, that Elisha had made him well that he might believe in the true God.

Naaman begged Elisha very much to take something: but he still said he would take nothing. You see that Elisha did not care for money.

Then Naaman set out in his chariot to go back to his own country.

You remember that Elisha had a servant called Gehazi: Gehazi heard his master say he would not take anything from Naaman, and Gehazi wished very much that he could get some of the beautiful things himself: so he thought of a way of getting them by telling lies.

Gehazi ran after Naaman's chariot: at last Naaman saw him running, and he stopped the chariot, and got out, for he was afraid that something was the matter. Naaman said, "Is all well?" And Gehazi said, "All is well; but there are two visitors, very good men, who are very poor, and my master wants some silver and two suits of clothes to give to them."

Was this true? Naaman did not know that Gehazi was telling lies; so he gave Gehazi twice as much silver as he asked for, and put it in two bags, and he gave him two suits of clothes, and he desired two of his servants to carry them for Gehazi: and Gehazi led the servants to a place with thick walls, where he used to keep things, and he desired the servants to put them there. Then the servants went back to Naaman, to go with him to their own land.

Then Gehazi went to Elisha's house to wait upon him. He little thought that Elisha knew of his wickedness. He thought that Elisha could never find him out, because Naaman was gone a great way, and could not tell Elisha that he had given some things to Gehazi. But there was One who saw him. God saw him, and God told Elisha what Gehazi had done. And God told Elisha what Gehazi meant to buy with the money.

He expected to buy vineyards, and fields, and sheep, and oxen, and slaves.

Now I will tell you what Elisha said to Gehazi when he came back. He said to him, "Where do you come from, Gehazi?" And Gehazi said, "I have not been anywhere." Was that true? You see that Gehazi told another lie to hide his wickedness. Then Elisha said, "Did not mine heart go with thee, when Naaman turned again from his chariot to meet thee? Let the leprosy of Naaman be upon thee for ever." Immediately sore white places came on Gehazi's skin, and he went out of Elisha's sight. Gehazi could not live with Elisha any more; for people who had the leprosy were obliged to live by themselves. I do not know whether he ever repented of his wickedness. You see, my dear children, how angry God is with liars, and what dreadful punishments He sends on them.

The Wonderful Story of Jonah.

God had many prophets in Israel and Judah, and one of these was Jonah, and God said to him: "Arise, go to Nineveh, that great city, and cry against it; for their wickedness is come up before Me."

Jonah would not go. He went away by sea intending to go to Tarshish.

But the Lord sent out a great wind into the sea, and there was a great tempest, so that there was danger of the ship being destroyed.

The sailors said to one another, "Let us cast lots, that we may know on whose account the storm has arisen."

They cast lots. There was one lot which, if a person drew, would show him to be the guilty one. This lot fell upon Jonah.

So they asked Jonah, "What shall we do unto thee, that the sea may be calm unto us?"

Jonah answered, "Take me up, and cast me forth into the sea; so shall the sea be calm unto you: for I know it is for my sake this great tempest is upon you." Then they took up Jonah and cast him into the sea. As soon as Jonah was in the sea it became calm.

Though the waters were now calm, yet he must soon have perished, had not God prepared a refuge for him. It was a fish— a very great fish—which swallowed Jonah. There was a place inside the fish where he could live, though it was dark and damp. Here Jonah thought upon his sins. He knew that he was now being punished for his disobedience. He prayed to God and vowed that if he were delivered he would sacrifice to the Lord, and give Him thanks.

The Lord heard Jonah's prayer, and on the third day he made the fish cast him out upon the seashore.

The word of the Lord came again to Jonah, "Arise, go unto Nineveh, that great city, and preach what I bid thee." This time Jonah obeyed and set out. The journey to Nineveh was five hundred miles.

At length he reached the city, with her walls a hundred feet high, and her towers of two hundred feet—the largest city in the world.

As soon as Jonah arrived he went into the midst of the city, and preached what God had told him, "Yet forty days, and Nineveh shall be overthrown."

The people listened, and feared and believed and repented. So God did not visit the city in judgment.

Was Jonah glad that God had spared Nineveh?

No—he was angry, for he thought he should be despised because his word did not come true. This was very selfish. He thought only of himself, and did not feel for those thousands of people in the great city.

God determined to show him his sin by something He was going to do.

God prepared a gourd—a climbing plant with large leaves. This gourd came up in one night over Jonah's booth.

In the morning Jonah was surprised to find this leafy shelter over his booth. He was now exceeding glad, because he had got something to please himself.

He enjoyed the cool shade for one day. The next day he found his gourd withered and dead, for God had prepared a worm to destroy the plant in the night.

Then God prepared another thing,—a fierce wind, that blew from the east, and was burning hot, and the sun beat upon Jonah's head till he fainted. Thus Jonah showed he could not bear heat himself; why did he wish the people of Nineveh to be burned up?

Again the selfish man wished to die, and said a second time, "It is better for me to die than to live." The Lord answered, "Doest thou well to be angry for the gourd?"

Then the Lord talked to him, and showed him his sin. And Jonah was ashamed and penitent.

Let us never fear to do what God commands; nor try to flee from God's presence.

The Story of King Hezekiah.

My dear children, I have told you a great deal about Elisha. You have heard what a great many wonders he did. Did the people of Israel mind what he said? or did they still go on in wickedness? They went on in their wickedness.

At last Elisha died. God did not take him up to heaven in a chariot of fire. He died in his bed, and his spirit went to heaven, but his body was buried in the ground. After he was dead, the people of Israel grew still more wicked. King Ahab had been a very wicked king, and Ahaziah, his son, who reigned after him, had been wicked, and when he died, there was another king, and he was wicked; and at last he died, and there was another king, and he was wicked: and there were a great many kings of Israel, one after the other, and they were all wicked. At last God determined to send a great punishment to all the people of Israel. You shall hear what it was. There was a king who

THE KING OF ASSYRIA AND HIS ARMY.

lived a great way off, in a country called Assyria, and he was called the King of Assyria. He was a heathen king and was very rich, and he had a great many soldiers who could fight well. The King of Assyria came with his soldiers into the land of

Canaan, and fought against the people, and conquered them; they got into all their towns, and took the people away to be their slaves. How unhappy the people of Israel were when they were taken away from their houses and gardens, and obliged to go a great way off, and work very hard!

This was the punishment God sent them at last, because they would worship idols, and do many wicked things. They never came into their own country again, but heathen people came and lived in it.

I am now going to speak to you about something I told you a long while ago. I shall be much pleased if I find that you have not forgotten it, for it is a thing hard to remember. Do you remember that God had been angry with King Solomon, and said that his son should be king over only part of Canaan? What God had said came true. Jeroboam took away a great deal of the land from Solomon's son. Jeroboam was called the King of Israel, and Solomon's son was called King of Judah. Now Solomon's son lived in Jerusalem, but Jeroboam lived in the other part of the land.

I have not told you about the kings of Judah. When Solomon's son died, his son was King of Judah, and when he died, his son was king—and so there were a great many kings one after another: some of the kings of Judah were good, and some were wicked. At last there was a good king, called Hez-e-ki-ah.

He lived at Jerusalem, and he liked to worship God in the temple, and he persuaded a great many people to come and worship God: for Hezekiah loved God.

Now you shall hear what care God took of Hezekiah. He had let the King of Assyria take away the people of Israel. Would God let him hurt the good King of Judah? Hear what God did!

The King of Assyria sent some of his soldiers to Jerusalem: and they brought their tents, and waited all round the city and tried to get in. The people shut the gates fast: still they were afraid lest the King of Assyria's soldiers should get in at last.

But Hezekiah knew that God could keep them from being hurt. The people of Assyria spoke very wicked words against God, while they were waiting outside Jerusalem: and one day the king wrote a letter, and sent it to Hezekiah.

It was a very wicked letter: this was what was written in it: "Your God cannot save you from the King of Assyria, who has conquered a great many countries: the gods of those people could not save them, neither can your God save you."

Some men brought this letter to King Hezekiah, and he read it. He could not bear to read such wicked words against God: so he took it into the temple, and spread the letter before God, and began to pray.

THE ANGEL OF THE LORD DESTROYING THE ASSYRIANS.

He said, "O God, Thou art the true God; Thou hast made heaven and earth. Other gods are only idols, made of wood and stone: they could not keep people from being hurt. Oh, save us from the King of Assyria, that everybody may know that Thou art the only God." God heard Hezekiah's prayer. Now I will tell you what He did that night. He sent His angel to kill a great many of the people of Assyria as they lay in their tents.

The angel did not kill them all, but the rest were very much frightened, when they found that so many had died in the night: and they went back to their own country, and they did not get into Jerusalem.

So God saved Hezekiah, King of Judah.

The King of Babylon Captures Jerusalem and Burns the Temple.

How kind God had been to Hezekiah, King of Judah!

God would not let the people of Assyria hurt him. At last Hezekiah died, and there was another king; and at last he died, and there was another king: and at last he died, and there was another king: and so there were a great many kings, one after another, and most of them were very wicked. Most of the people of Jerusalem were wicked, and worshiped idols. So God sent prophets to tell them that He would not keep them from being hurt any more, and that He would let some heathen king take them a great way off.

You remember that the people in the other part of Canaan (who were called the people of Israel) had been taken away by the King of Assyria: and God said that the people of Judah should be taken away by some other king.

At last there came a rich, proud king, called Nebuchadnezzar, to fight against the people in Jerusalem. This king came from a country called Babylon.

He had a great many soldiers, who placed their tents all round Jerusalem. They got into the city, and they broke down the wall, and they burnt a great many of the fine houses, and they even burnt the beautiful temple that Solomon had built, and they took away the golden things that he had put in it, the gold basins, and candlesticks, and altars, spoons, and cups, and shovels, and they took them to Babylon, to put them in the house of their idols.

There was a king in Jerusalem named Zedekiah. Nebuchadnezzar took this king and put out both his eyes, and brought him to Babylon, and kept him in prison till he died. Nebuchadnezzar killed a great many people, and he took a great many more to be slaves with him in Babylon!

How sorry the people were to leave their land, and go to Babylon!

They sat down by the rivers of Babylon and wept, and they would not sing psalms as they used to do, but they hanged their harps upon the willow-trees that grew by the water side.

Why did God let them be taken from the land of Canaan?

THE SOLDIERS OF BABYLON CAPTURE ZEDEKIAH.

Because they had sinned against Him by breaking His laws and hurting his prophets. At last He would punish them, as He had said He would.

Story of the Three Men Who Were Thrown into a Fiery Furnace.

Some of the people, who were taken to Babylon, loved God. I will tell you about three young men, who loved Him very much, and who would not worship idols.

Nebuchadnezzar once made a very large image of gold: it was higher than a very tall tree. This image was placed out of doors, and Nebuchadnezzar sent for all the judges and captains in his land, and for a great many rich people, to come and see this golden image. Now Nebuchadnezzar had made the three good young men judges; so that they were obliged to come and see the golden image.

When all these captains, and judges, and rich men were come, they stood round the image, and a man called out very loud, "O people, when the music begins to be played, then fall down and worship the golden image that Nebuchadnezzar has set up. Whoever does not fall down and worship, shall immediately be cast into a burning fiery furnace."

Do you know, dear children, what a furnace is? It is a place full of fire; it is like a very large oven. How horrible it must be to be put into a furnace! Would the three good young men worship the image, or would they not?

Very soon the music began to play, and the people fell down and worshiped the image.

Then some men came to Nebuchadnezzar, and said, "O king, live for ever. Did you not desire that every man should fall down and worship the golden image, when the music was played; and that if any one did not worship, he should be cast into a fiery furnace? There are three men who have not minded what you said: they never worshiped your gods, nor have they worshiped the golden image."

Then Nebuchadnezzar was in a rage, and he desired the men to be brought to him. Then these men were brought before the king. And Nebuchadnezzar said to them, "Is it true that you do not worship my gods, nor the golden image I have set up? Now, if the next time the music is played, you fall down and worship, it is well: but if not, you shall be cast into the furnace. And who is the God who can deliver you out of my hand?"

Then the young men answered the king, "O Nebuchadnezzar, our God is able to deliver us from the burning fiery furnace, and He will deliver us out of thine hand, O king. But, if not, we will not serve thy gods, nor worship the golden image thou hast set up."

Then Nebuchadnezzar was full of fury; and his face became dark and threatening, because he was in such a great passion.

He desired his servants to make the furnace seven times hotter than usual, and he ordered the strongest of his soldiers to throw the three young men into the furnace. First the young men were bound, so that they might not be able to move when they were in the fire; and their clothes were not taken off. Then the strong soldiers threw them into the furnace; and the flames were so great that the soldiers who put in the young men caught fire, and were burnt up. The three young men fell down in the midst of the furnace.

THE FIERY FURNACE.

Nebuchadnezzar stood near, and watched to see the young men burning. But how greatly surprised he was to see them walking about the furnace, and to see a man with them, who looked like the Son of God! Nebuchadnezzar cried out to his servants, "Did we not cast three men into the fire?" and they answered, "True, O king."

And Nebuchadnezzar said, "I see four men walking in the midst of the fire, and they are not hurt; and one of them is like the Son of God."

Nebuchadnezzar had never seen the Son of God; but he had never seen a man like him who was in the furnace: so he supposed that he must be a God.

Then Nebuchadnezzar went to the furnace, and called the three young men by their names, and said, "O servants of the Most High God, come forth, and come hither." And the three young men came out of the furnace. Then all the judges and captains came near and looked at the young men, and saw that they were not the least hurt; not a hair of their heads was singed, nor were their clothes scorched, nor did they even smell of fire. Then Nebuchadnezzar saw that there was a God who could deliver His servants from the burning flame; and he said, that if any person spoke against this God, he should be cut to pieces, and his house should be made a dunghill. And the king was very much pleased with the three young men.

Story of the Handwriting on the Wall.

At last Nebuchadnezzar, the proud King of Babylon, died, and there was another King of Babylon, called Belshazzar. He was the grandson of Nebuchadnezzar; and he was like his grandfather, for he was proud, and worshiped idols.

One day he made a great feast, and a great many rich men, called lords, came to his feast, and Belshazzar drank wine before them. Do you remember, my dear children, that Nebuchadnezzar had taken the gold and silver cups that were in the temple at Jerusalem, and had brought them to Babylon? Belshazzar desired that these cups might be brought for him, and his lords, and his wives, to drink wine out of them. So they were brought, and Belshazzar, and his lords, and his wives, drank wine in them: and while they drank, they praised their idols, which were made of gold, and silver, of brass, of iron, of wood, and of stone.

While they were drinking, the king saw the fingers of a man's hand writing on the wall of the palace, near where the candlestick stood. He did not see a man, only some fingers.

The king was very much frightened: he did not look merry any longer, but he trembled very much, and his knees knocked against each other.

Belshazzar wanted to know what was written on the wall: there were four words written there, but he could not read that kind of writing, so he sent for all the men in Babylon who were called wise and clever, and who said they could tell hard things

Belshazzar said, "Whoever will read that writing and tell the meaning of it, shall be clothed in scarlet (such as kings used to wear), and shall have a golden chain round his neck, and shall be made a great judge.

A great many people tried to read the writing, but they could not. Then Belshazzar was still more frightened, and looked very much terrified, and his lords were frightened also. They were afraid that something dreadful had been written on the wall: they thought something sad was going to happen. About this time the queen, Belshazzar's mother, having heard what had taken place, came into the room and said, "O king, live forever, Do not be frightened, there is a man in Babylon who is very wise indeed, and who can tell the meaning of things: his name is Daniel. Let him be called, and he will know the meaning of the writing."

THE HAND WRITING ON THE WALL.

Now this Daniel was one of the men whom Nebuchadnezzar had brought from Jerusalem: he was an Israelite. When he first came to Babylon he was quite young, but now he was old: he was very wise, and he loved God very much.

Belshazzar desired Daniel to come to him, and when he was come he said, "I hear that you can tell the meaning of hidden or mysterious things: if you can read the writing on the wall, and tell the meaning of it, you shall be clothed in scarlet, and wear a gold chain, and be made a great judge."

But Daniel said, "I do not want any reward, yet I will read the writing, and tell the meaning of it." Then Daniel told Belshazzar that the true God was very angry with him for being so proud, and for sending for the cups of His temple, and for drinking in them and praising idols; and for not worshiping God, though he had heard of Him. Daniel said that the writing on the wall meant that he should soon be king no more, but that some people would come and take his land from him.

THE SOLDIERS OF DARIUS KILL BELSHAZZAR.

Then Belshazzar desired that Daniel should be clothed in scarlet, and wear a golden chain about his neck, and that his people should obey him. That very night a king from another country came into Babylon, with a great many soldiers, and killed Belshazzar, and took his throne, and his crown, and all he had. So the words that God had written on the wall came true.

Daniel in the Lion's Den.

The name of the king that conquered Belshazzar was Da-ri-us. He was a proud man, and he worshiped idols; yet he liked Daniel very much: and he set him over all the other judges and lords, and told all the people to mind him. Daniel was a very wise man, and he was fit to be a judge. There were a great many rich men, who hated Daniel, because the king told them to mind him, and because the king liked Daniel better than them. These men were envious of Daniel. They were like Cain, who was envious of Abel; and like Joseph's brothers, who were envious of Joseph.

These wicked rich men wished to hurt Daniel, and to

A HUNGRY LION ATTACKING A TRAVELER.

get him into disgrace with King Darius: but they did not know how to get him into disgrace; they never saw Daniel do anything wrong. I suppose they were afraid of telling the king lies about him, lest they should be found out. But at last they thought of a way to get Daniel into disgrace.

They knew that he prayed very often to his God; so they went to the king and asked him to make a law, that no one should pray to any God or man, but to the king himself, for thirty days; and that if any one did pray to any one else, he should be cast into a den of lions. Now the king did not know why these men asked him to make this law: if the king had known that Daniel always prayed to his God, I do not think he would have made it, for the king loved Daniel.

But he was so foolish as to say that he would do as these men wished, because, you know, the king was a heathen, and he did not love the true God. So he wrote down the law, and promised not to change it.

Daniel heard of the law that the king had made.

He would have thought it very dreadful not to pray to God for thirty days. He wanted to praise God very often, and ask Him to bless him.

He used always to pray before the open window in his room. Perhaps you wonder why he did so. The reason was, he liked to look toward the place where he knew Jerusalem was. He could not see Jerusalem from his window, because it was so very far off; but still he knew which way it was, and he knew that God loved Jerusalem, and that God used to come down into the temple before it was burnt: so Daniel liked to look that way when he prayed.

He knelt down three times every day, and prayed, and thanked God for all his kindness to him.

The men who hated Daniel heard that he went on praying: so they went one day and watched him, that they might tell the king that they had seen him praying contrary to the law.

Then they asked the king, "Did you not make a law that if any one prayed to any god or man, excepting you, that he should be cast into a den of lions?"

And the king said, "Yes, it is true, and I cannot change the law."

Then the men said, "That Daniel, who was brought from Jerusalem to be a slave, does not mind you, nor your law, but prays three times a-day." Then the king was very sorry that he had made a law against praying, and tried to think of some way of not letting Daniel be killed: but he could think of no way. In the evening the men came to him and said, "You cannot alter the law that you have made, for in our country it is not permitted that the laws may be changed."

Then the king desired Daniel to be brought, and he was cast into a den of lions; the lions lived in a deep place underground. Lions are always very hungry in the evening, and roar for their food.

CASTING THE WICKED MEN AND THEIR FAMILIES INTO THE LIONS' DEN.

But Darius knew that Daniel's God was a very great God, and he said to Daniel, "Your God, whom you serve always, is able to deliver you." I think Darius must have heard how God once saved three men from being burnt in the furnace. A stone was brought, and laid upon the top of the den: and the king put his seal on it, that none might take away the stone; and he put on it also the seal of the men that hated Daniel.

Why did the king put his own seal on it? That he might find out if any one came and took Daniel away, for no one else had a seal like the king's: so if any one broke the seal, the king would find it out.

The king went to the palace that evening, but he was so unhappy that he could not eat, and he would not let his servants play music to him as usual, and when he went to bed he could not sleep.

He got up very early in the morning, and went to the den of lions. When he came to the den, he cried out in a very sad voice, "O Daniel, is thy God, whom thou servest always, able to deliver thee from the lions?"

The king longed to hear Daniel's voice—and he heard it.

Daniel said, "O king, live for ever. My God hath sent His angel, and hath shut the lions' mouths, that they have not hurt me: because I had done nothing wrong.

Then the king was very glad indeed, and he desired that Daniel should be taken up, and he was not the least hurt.

The king was very angry with those men who had asked him to put Daniel in the den, and he commanded them to be thrown down into the den, with their wives and their children. It was very cruel of the king to have the wives and children put into the den, but the wicked men deserved to be put there. The lions ate them up in a moment, and broke all their bones before they came to the bottom of the den.

So you see that the lions were very hungry, though they did not hurt Daniel.

Then King Darius wrote a letter, and sent it to all countries, and said that he had made a law that every one should fear the God of Daniel, because He was the true God, who could do wonders, and who had saved Daniel from the lions.

Story of Esther, the Beautiful Queen.

I am going to tell you a story of a great danger that befell all the Jews in all parts of the kingdom of Persia, and of the wonderful deliverance that God wrought for them.

The king who was now reigning in Persia was called Ahasuerus. He was a very strange, wilful man, as I think you will see when I tell you how he behaved.

He made a great feast in his beautiful palace at Shushan. It lasted six months. Great lords came from all countries; rich men from India, the land of elephants; black men from Africa; brave men from Arabia's sandy deserts. The court was hung with curtains, of white, and green, and blue, fastened with silver rings, to pillars of marble. The guests drank wine out of gold and silver cups, and they lay on couches of gold.

PEOPLE CAME FROM ALL PARTS OF THE WORLD TO THE FEAST.

The king's wife was Queen Vashti. She also gave a splendid feast to the women of Persia.

On the last day of these feasts, the king drank a great deal of wine. Much wine turns the head, and makes people foolish. A foolish wish came into the king's mind. So he said to his seven chief servants (called chamberlains), "Bring Vashti, the queen, with the crown upon her head."

The chamberlains went into the queen's palace, and gave the message to the queen.

But she refused to come.

Vashti felt that it would be bold and vain to come into the gardens, before all the people who were drinking wine. Therefore she told the chamberlains that she would not come.

When the king heard this refusal he was very angry. He was accustomed to be obeyed in whatever he said, and it provoked him to think that his own wife would not mind him.

He called the seven wise men of his kingdom, and asked their advice about Vashti. He said to them, "What shall we do to Queen Vashti for not having obeyed the king's commandments?" One of the seven wise men, whose name was Memucan, replied, "Let the king make a law (which cannot be altered) that Vashti come no more to see the king; but that another and better woman be made queen instead."

So the king sent letters to all countries, showing how Vashti was to be punished.

Then the king's servants said, "Let all the beautiful young girls in the kingdom be brought to Shushan, and let the king choose which he likes best, that he may make her queen instead of Vashti."

The king liked this plan, and he sent his chief servants to look for these beautiful maidens, and to bring them to his palace.

Among the servants at the palace was a Jew named Mordecai, who took his orphan cousin Esther to his own home as his daughter. She was taken with the young maidens to the king's palace, where the servants poured oil of myrrh and sweet perfumes over her, as was the custom in Persia, and at last after living a whole year in the palace, she was brought before the king. As soon as King Ahasuerus saw her, he thought he had never seen any one so beautiful. He loved her more than all the maidens before him: and set the royal crown upon her head. He made another great feast and called it Esther's feast. He set prisoners free and gave the servants gifts, and all the people rejoiced.

Queen Esther loved her people, the Jews, and Mordecai hoped more than anything else in the world, that God's chosen people should yet live in Jerusalem. Esther kept secret the fact that she was a Jewess, for Mordecai felt that she could better persuade the king to do his people good, if it were not known that she was one

ESTHER IS BROUGHT TO THE PALACE.

of them. Mordecai now sat among the king's servants, in the gate of the palace. While sitting there he was able to save the king's life in this way. Two of the servants who waited in the palace were angry with the king, their master, and made a plan to kill him.

These men had charge of the door of the palace, and might have pierced the king with a dagger as he went in and out. In some way or other, Mordecai found out the horrible crime these men meant to commit.

He sent a message to Queen Esther, begging her to let the king know of his danger. Esther told the king all about it, and she mentioned Mordecai as the man who had found out the deadly plot. The king sent his men to seize the two servants and to hang them on a tree; and it was written down in a book that Mordecai had saved the life of the king.

Story of the Wicked Haman.

There was a man in the kingdom named Haman. He belonged to the nation of Amalek, that nation of whom the Lord had said, in the days of Moses, it is cursed forever.

This Haman got into the king's favor, and at last he was made the first of all the princes of Persia. He was proud, and wished everybody to fall down before him and do him homage. This Mordecai would not do, for he was a Jew and believed it was wrong to worship any one but God. When Haman learned this he was very angry, and he formed a plot to have all the Jews destroyed. He went immediately to the king and spoke in a very sly, deceitful manner.

He said, "There is a people scattered over your kingdom who do not mind your laws. They will do your kingdom a great deal of harm. If it please the king, let a law be written to destroy them."

The king agreed to this, and took off his ring and gave it to Haman. On this ring was a seal; whoever had that seal could write what commands he pleased, for when people saw the king's seal on the writing they would obey what was commanded.

As soon as Haman got the king's ring he went to the king's writers (called scribes) and told them to write letters to all the rulers in the kingdom, and in these letters to say, "Let all the Jews be destroyed, whether young or old, whether women or babes." All these letters were sealed with the king's ring. Then they were given to men who rode on swift horses to take to the most distant places in the kingdom. The people in Shushan heard the dreadful decree sooner than any one else, and they were the first to be filled with sadness and fear.

When Mordecai heard what was done, he rent his clothes and put on sackcloth and ashes, to show how sad and wretched he felt.

The first that Esther heard of these troubles was from her seven maids and seven men-servants, or chamberlains. They told her that Mordecai was sitting in sackcloth, weeping and wailing.

Then Esther was very anxious to know what it was that had grieved him. There was one of her chamberlains, named Hatach, that she trusted more than the others, and she sent for him and told him to go and get Mordecai to tell him all about his grief.

So Hatach found Mordecai, and told him that Queen Esther wanted to know what grieved him. Then Mordecai told him all about the king's letters, and that Haman had promised the king a great sum of money. But lest Esther should not believe the sad history, he sent her a copy of the king's decree that the couriers were now taking into all countries.

Then Mordecai said to Hatach, "Now tell Queen Esther that I charge her to go to the king, and to entreat him to save her people."

But Esther felt she could not do this, and she told Hatach to go back to Mordecai, and say, "No one is allowed to go into the place where the king sits, unless sent for by the king; if any one does come in without being called, he is put to death—even a woman, if she comes in, is put to death, except the king holds out his golden sceptre to show that she may live; but as for me, the king has not called me for thirty days."

This message Hatach took to Mordecai, and he sent this reply:

"If you say nothing to the king about the Jews, they will be saved in some way, and you and your relations will be destroyed.

Who can tell but that you were made queen on purpose to help the Jews at this time?"

Mordecai was too brave to care for his own life. When he refused to bow down before Haman he knew that he risked his life, yet he was not afraid; but he could not bear that his people should be punished for his sake. He wanted Esther to be brave like himself.

And so she was, as we shall see.

When she heard Mordecai's last message, she determined to risk her life by entreating the king to spare the Jews. Again she sent a message to Mordecai. It was quite unlike the first one.

It was a command to Mordecai "Get together all the Jews that are in Shushan, and fast all of you for me, and neither eat nor drink for three days. I and my maids will fast also; and then I will go to the king without leave: if I perish, I perish."

Esther was now grown very brave. She was ready to die to save her people. But she knew that God would soften the king's heart, and so she wished Mordecai and all the Jews to pray for her while she prayed in the palace with her maids.

On the third day Esther dressed herself in all her royal robes, and went to see the king as he sat on the throne. He looked at her and loved her, and stretched out his golden sceptre toward her.

He said, "What is thy request, Queen Esther? It shall be given thee, to the half of my kingdom!" Esther said, "If it please the king, I want thee and Haman to come to my banquet." So they went to the banquet. Haman boasted to his friends that the king had set him above all other men, and that he would hang Mordecai on a gallows fifty cubits high.

At the feast the king asked Esther again what she wished. She replied by inviting the king and Haman to a feast again the next day.

Now Haman had built the gallows fifty cubits high, on which he was planning to hang Mordecai. But God was planning to save Mordecai and all the Jews.

God Saves the Jews, and Haman is Hanged on His Own Gallows.

That night the king could not sleep. He read over the books, giving accounts of things which had happened in his kingdom. He found that Mordecai had once saved his life, and he asked, "What reward has he received?" His servants said, "None."

Haman came into the court just then, and the king asked him, "What shall be done to the man the king delighteth to honor?"

Haman thought himself the man, so he said proudly—"Let him wear the king's robes and his crown, and let him ride upon the king's horse; let a noble prince lead the horse through the streets of the city, and cry to all the people—'Thus shall it be done to the man whom the king delighteth to honor.'" Then the king said, "Make haste and do as thou hast said to Mordecai, the Jew."

Haman was afraid to disobey the king, and he dressed Mordecai in the royal robes, and set him upon the king's horse, and led him through the streets, as the king had directed.

Then Haman went to his home mourning. That afternoon at the feast, he did not venture to say a word against Mordecai.

Little did he think what was going to be said about him. At last the king said to the queen, "What is thy request? and it shall be granted, even to the half of my kingdom."

The queen replied, "If I have found favor in thy sight, O king, and if it please the king, let my life be given me at my petition, and my people at my request; for we are sold, I and my people, to be slain."

"If we had been sold as slaves, I would have said nothing, although it would have done great harm to the king."

Esther knew that Haman had promised the king money to make up for his killing the Jews; therefore she said, "We are sold."

The king was very angry when he heard any one had tried to hurt the queen's people: for he knew now that she was a Jewess, and he cried out, "Who is he that was so daring as to think of such a thing?"

Then Esther said,—"The enemy is this wicked Haman."

Now Haman saw that he was found out, and he pleaded for his life.

But the king was determined to have him killed. One of the servants told the king of the high gallows; so the king said, "Hang Haman thereon." So Haman was hanged on the gallows he had built for Mordecai.

Queen Esther asked the king to save her life, and the lives of the Jews, her people. She asked with tears and very humbly. The king touched her with the golden sceptre, and granted her request.

Another writing was made and sealed with the king's ring and Mordecai sent copies, by messengers on camels, mules, dromedaries and horses, all over the kingdom. And when he came out from the palace, he was clothed in royal garments like the king; with a crown of gold on his head. The Jews were filled with joy, and gained the victory over their enemies. And Esther and Mordecai rejoiced that their God had delivered His people. They wrote letters, telling all the Jews to be sure and keep the feast of Purim every year for all time.

The book of Esther teaches us much about God. We learn in it how, when God's people are in the greatest difficulty and danger, He can deliver them; and we see how the hearts of kings are in His hands. He can incline their hearts and make them wish to take care of His people instead of hurting them.

Cyrus the Great King.

I told you how unhappy the poor Israelites were in Babylon. They wished very much to return to their own country, Canaan, but the kings of Babylon would not let them go back. However, God had made a promise, a long while before, that He would let them return some day.

Now, there was another king in Babylon besides Darius. This king's name was Cyrus. God put it in the heart of Cyrus to let the poor Israelites return to their own country. For God remembered His promise.

Cyrus had been taught to worship idols, yet he believed that Daniel's God was the true God: and he was ready to mind what the true God said.

So Cyrus told the Israelites that they might go back to their own country, and build the temple at Jerusalem.

Cyrus gave back to them all the gold and silver things that Nebuchadnezzar had taken out of the temple,—dishes, and basins, and cups of gold and silver.

Many of the people in Babylon gave the Israelites presents before they went away: horses, camels, and asses, to carry their things.

THE SHADOW OF THE CROSS.

How happy the poor Israelites were to leave such a wicked place as Babylon! But oh! when they had come to Jerusalem, how sad to see the walls broken down, and many of the houses burnt! but still the Israelites were very thankful to God for letting them come there again.

When they were come to Jerusalem they set up the altar, and offered a great many beasts on it, to show how grateful they were.

They wished to build the temple as soon as they could, and they got a great many carpenters and masons, and they sent for beautiful trees to help build it with.

At last they laid the first stone of the temple upon the high hill in Jerusalem. A great many Israelites came together to see the first stone laid. The priests stood near, dressed in white, with trumpets, and the singers played music, and sang psalms, saying, "The Lord is good, and His mercy endureth forever."

And when the first stone was laid, the priests blew the trumpets, and the singers sang psalms, and the people shouted for joy.

There were some old people there, who remembered having seen the temple before it was burnt, a long while ago, when they were little children; and when the other people shouted, these old people wept very loud, because the people had been wicked. Perhaps the old men were grieved because the people had been so ungrateful to God. The noise of the weeping and the shouting could be heard a great way off.

The people of Israel were a great many years building the temple. This temple was not so beautiful as the one Solomon had built, and God did not come down in a cloud, and fill it.

You will be glad to hear that the Israelites determined to worship idols no more. But though they did not worship idols, they did not love God with all their hearts; so they did a great many other wicked things. There were a few of them who really loved God.

The Israelites lived in Jerusalem and in the land of Canaan a great many years. They were now called Jews instead of Israelites. God sent them prophets sometimes to teach them, and to put them in mind of a promise that He had made to Abraham, that a Saviour should one day be born, who should be their King forever. God had made the same promise to David, and had said that this Saviour should be one of his descendants. Some of the Israelites, or Jews, thought very often of this promise, and longed for the Saviour to be born into the world. They knew that He would be born in Bethlehem, where David was born, because one of the prophets had said that He should be born in Bethlehem, and they knew that His mother would be some person of the family of David, because the prophets had said so; and they knew that He would be the King of the Jews, and of all people—for the prophets had said so.

REBUILDING JERUSALEM.

(300) OF SUCH IS THE KINGDOM OF HEAVEN.

PART TWO.

The New Testament.

Zacharias and His Wife Elisabeth.

And now I will tell you the wonderful story of Jesus, the Saviour, and how He came down from heaven and taught all people how to be good. I will also tell you how He loved little children, and was kind and gentle to them, and said that they should inherit His kingdom in heaven.

I will begin by telling you about a very good man named Zach-a-ri-as.

He was a priest.

He served God in His temple. He never went into the Holy of Holies, for he was not the High Priest. Sometimes he burnt incense on the golden altar inside the temple.

THE STAR OF BETHLEHEM.

There were a great many priests. Some of them lived in the country. These priests came up by turns to Jerusalem to stay a week, and serve in the temple.

Zacharias had a wife named E-lis-a-beth. Both Zacharias and Elisabeth were very old and very good. But they had no child. They had often prayed for a child, but God had never given them one.

The Jews thought it a disgrace to have no children. They thought it was a sign that God was displeased. But God was very much pleased with Zacharias and Elisabeth, though He had given them no little children.

Once Zacharias went up to Jerusalem to serve at the temple for a week.

Quite early in the morning he went to the temple. He drew lots with the other priests to know who was to burn incense that morning in the temple.

Zacharias drew the lot, and he went alone into the temple.

While the old priest was kneeling before the golden altar, he beheld a wonderful sight.

At the right side of the altar stood an angel, and Zacharias was greatly frightened when he saw him.

But the angel spoke kindly to him. "Fear not, Zacharias! Thy prayer is heard; and thy wife Elisabeth shall bear thee a son, and thou shalt call his name John; and many of the children of Israel shall he turn unto the Lord their God."

The child promised to Zacharias was to have a good heart and be a great teacher, and turn people's hearts to God. He would be like Elijah.

But Zacharias doubted what the angel had told him. Then the angel answered, "I am Gabriel. I stand in the presence of God. And because you have not believed my words, you shall be dumb, till what I have said has come to pass."

So Zacharias was struck dumb; and he was deaf also.

The angel went back to God; and Zacharias came out of the temple.

All the people were wondering what kept him so long. He could not tell them in words, but he made signs with his hands to show them that an angel had spoken to him, and that he was dumb.

At the end of the week he went back to his own house in the country. He lived amongst the hills near Hebron. He was able to tell his wife what had happened, for he could write an account of it for her to read. How he must have wished that he had believed at first.

Mary the Mother of Jesus.

Six months after Gabriel had spoken to Zacharias, God sent him to another person. She was the cousin of Elisabeth, and her name was Mary.

Mary lived a great way from Jerusalem. She lived in Naz-a-reth, a little town on the side of a pleasant, flowery hill.

She had promised to marry a very good man named Joseph; but she was not married when the angel came to her.

The angel said, "Hail" (or Be glad). "Thou art highly favored. The Lord is with thee. Blessed art thou among women!"

These were sweeter words than Gabriel had spoken to Zacharias. Was not Mary pleased to hear that God was going to make her very happy?

Mary was timid, and did not understand what the angel had said to her; so he told her over again.

Then he gave her his wonderful message.

He told her that a son should be born to her, and that she should call His name Jesus, and that He should be the Son of God and a great King.

Mary believed all the angel said.

Before Gabriel went away, he told her that a son would also be given to her cousin Elisabeth in her old age.

After the angel was gone away, Mary went hastily to visit her cousin Elisabeth. She had more than a hundred miles to go. I do not know who went with her. She was not yet married, or Joseph would have gone with her to take care of her.

Mary came at last to some beautiful green hills, among gardens of grapes, and dates, and figs. The hill country was near Hebron. She had traveled very quickly, for she was very anxious to see Elisabeth.

(304 BLESSING THE HOLY CHILD.

When she reached the house, she saw Elisabeth and spoke to her.

As soon as Elisabeth heard her voice, she began to speak, and the Holy Ghost taught her what to say.

"Blessed art thou among women! How is it that the mother of my Lord should come to me?"

Then Mary saw that Elisabeth knew about the babe that was promised to her, and she also spoke by the Holy Ghost the lovely song beginning—

"My soul doth magnify the Lord, and my spirit hath rejoiced in God my Saviour. For He hath regarded the low estate of His hand-maiden."

How humble Mary was! She spoke of herself as being low.

She did not think herself great or good, though she was to be the mother of the Son of God.

Birth of John the Baptist.

Mary paid a long visit to her cousin Elisabeth. She stayed three months in the house among the hills. All that time Zacharias could not speak a word to Mary, nor hear a word she said.

But Mary had many sweet conversations with Elisabeth.

Though one was young, and the other old, they dearly loved one another. Elisabeth knew that her babe would not be as glorious as Mary's.

John would be a sinner, though he would have the Holy Spirit: but Jesus would be without sin, the spotless Lamb of God.

At the end of three months Mary went back to her own home in Nazareth.

Soon afterward John was born, and all of Elisabeth's friends and relations were very glad when they heard of the birth of the child.

When the babe was eight days old, it was to be circumcised, according to the Jewish law. Circumcision was a ceremony similar in meaning to baptism.

This was also the time to give the child a name.

THE ANGEL APPEARS

The friends said, "Let him be called Zacharias, after his father."

"No," said Elisabeth, "he shall be called John," for she knew what the angel had said. The friends said, "Why should he be called John? None of your relations are called by that name." All this time Zacharias could neither hear nor speak. But the friends made signs to him to name the babe. So he called for a writing-book (or tablet).

Zacharias wrote these words, "His name is John." Every one was surprised at his choosing the name Elisabeth had mentioned.

But they were much more astonished when he began again to speak. All that the angel had said had now happened, and so Zacharias was no more dumb. He praised God for the Saviour who was soon to come, and all he said was by the Holy Ghost. He looked at his own little babe, and said, "Thou, child, shalt be called the prophet of the Highest."

Every one expected John to be a wonderful child; and so he was, for the Holy Spirit was in him, and God was with him to bless him and to teach him. When he grew older, he liked to wander alone in the wilderness, and to think of heavenly things.

Jesus is Born in Bethlehem in a Manger.

THE ANGELS AND THE SHEPHERDS.

Mary returned to Nazareth after visiting Elisabeth.

Soon she had to make another long journey.

Joseph and Mary set out together on this journey, for they were now married. They went to a city called Bethlehem.

They went there to have their names written down, for a great king, named Cæsar, had commanded all people to go to their fathers' cities to write down their names, that they might afterward pay him tax.

Joseph and Mary went to Bethlehem, because it had been the city of their father David, a long, long while ago. They were of the tribe of Judah. When they arrived at Bethlehem, they went to the inn, but there was no room for them in the inn, so they went into the stable, among the oxen. And in this humble place the little child was born.

Mary had clothes ready for it, and she wrapped her child in these long clothes.

But she had no cradle, and she laid him in the manger. No one in that stable knew what a glorious babe was laid in the manger.

Yet there were some shepherds in the fields near Bethlehem who knew that He was glorious.

While they were watching over their sheep that night an angel came.

A great light shone around them and they were much afraid.

The angel said, "Fear not, I bring you good news of great joy to all people."

A Saviour is born in Bethlehem.

The angel told the shepherds where the Saviour was: "He is wrapped in swaddling clothes and lying in a manger."

Soon the light grew brighter, for a multitude of angels were seen praising God in the sky.

This was their heavenly song:

> Glory to God in the highest,
> On earth Peace,
> Good-will toward men.

When the song was over, the angels went back to heaven, and the place was dark as before.

The shepherds said one to another, "Let us go to Bethlehem, and look for this babe."

They went quickly, and inquired for a babe in a manger, and they found it with Mary and Joseph close beside it.

With what love they looked at that babe. They knew He was the Son of God. They told Mary that angels had spoken to them in the field.

When they left the stable they told everybody what had happened in the night. Every one wondered when they heard

ANGELS APPEAR TO THE SHEPHERDS.

(309)

about the angels; but all did not remember what they heard. Mary went on thinking about these wonderful things as she held her dear little babe in her loving arms.

Simeon and Anna the Prophetess.

When the babe was nearly six weeks old, He was taken to Jerusalem, seven miles away, because God had made a law that every woman should bring her first born son to the temple, to present him to the Lord.

She also brought a sacrifice of two doves to offer with her babe. If she had been rich she would have brought a lamb as a sacrifice; but as she was very poor, she brought only two doves, as they cost very little money. In her arms she held a sweeter dove,—even her pure and spotless babe. He was her first-born child, and He was now presented to the Lord.

As Mary was standing with Joseph in the court of the temple, giving her offering to the priest, on old man came up to her. His name was Simeon. He was longing to see the Saviour. God had once promised him that he should see the Saviour before he died.

Just before he came in, the Spirit told him that Jesus was now in the temple.

Great was his joy when he beheld the babe. He took Him in his arms, and blessed God, and said, "Now Thou wilt let Thy servant depart in peace, since I have seen the Saviour."

Then he blessed Joseph and Mary.

He told Mary that grief would pierce her heart like a sword. She must have thought of this—long afterward—when she stood by the cross of her beloved Son.

Whilst Simeon was speaking, more people came in to see the babe. Amongst them was a very old woman named Anna. She must have been more than a hundred. She was a prophetess, and she knew that Jesus was the Saviour. She thanked God for having sent Him.

THE WISE MEN WORSHIP JESUS.

(311)

Story of the Wise Men of the East.

A very long way from Jerusalem some wise men lived. These men were not Jews. They were Gentiles. In their land people worshiped idols; but these wise men had turned to the true God.

These men often looked at the stars, and they knew the names of many of them.

One night they saw a strange star they had never seen before.

It was on the night that Jesus was born in the stable that they saw the star; but they knew nothing about the babe in the stable.

God told them that a king was born in the land of the Jews —just where the star was shining.

So these wise men set out on a long journey to that land. They were rich enough to have camels to ride upon. They took many precious things with them to give to the new-born King.

They traveled a long way. They could not see the star as they were going along, but they knew where they had once seen it, and they went toward the place.

They came at last to Jerusalem, the great city of the Jews. They did not know whether the babe was there, so they went about the streets asking, "Where is He who is born King of the Jews?"

There was an old king in Jerusalem called Herod. He was a very wicked man. He was proud, cruel, passionate and ungodly.

When he heard of the new king he was frightened, and so were all his great lords; for they thought the new-born child would make Himself king; and Herod decided to kill Him.

So he sent for the priests, and said to them, "Where will the King be born whom God will send?"

The priests said, "It is written in the Bible, he will be born in Bethlehem."

They showed him the place in the prophet Micah, v. 2: "O Bethlehem, out of thee shall He come forth who is to be Ruler in Israel."

The verse showed that Jesus, who was to be King, would be born in Bethlehem.

Herod could now tell the wise men where the King of the Jews was born. But he wanted to know when He was born. He thought the wise men could tell him when this king was to be born. So he sent for the wise men and asked them secretly, "When did you first see the star?"

They told him it was about a year ago.

Then Herod thought to himself, "The child is a year old."

Then he said to the wise men in a voice that seemed kind, "Go and look for Him in Bethlehem, and when you have found Him come back and tell me, that I may go and worship Him."

What a dreadful lie Herod spoke when he said this!

The wise men thought Herod loved this new King; and they meant to come back and tell him: for they did not know that Herod was a liar—as well as a murderer.

So the wise men went toward Bethlehem, about seven miles off, seeking the child.

But they had not to ask in the streets of Bethlehem where they should find Him, for they looked up and saw the star they had not seen for a long while.

Oh, how glad they were when they saw that star once more!

The star went before them to show them the way; and soon it stopped over a place in Bethlehem, not the stable, but another place.

What great joy they felt when they opened the door of Joseph's cottage, and saw the babe from heaven in His mother's arms! They bowed down before Him and worshiped Him.

Then they opened their packages, and took out their beautiful presents—precious gold and sweet-smelling myrrh and frankincense, and gave them to the child.

These presents showed the love they felt in their hearts for Jesus.

THE SHADOW OF THE CROSS.

(314)

Herod Sends His Soldiers to Kill the Little Boys who Lived in Bethlehem.

The wise men meant to return to Jerusalem and tell Herod they had found the child.

But they slept at Bethlehem; and in their sleep they had a dream. Probably each of them had the same dream.

In the dream they heard a voice saying: "Do not go back to Jerusalem to tell Herod you have found the child."

So the wise men went back by another way to their own country. They went back happy for ever, because they had seen the Saviour.

But Herod was very unhappy. He waited for the wise men to return to Jerusalem, until at last he heard that they were gone home to their own land—far away—where he could not reach them.

Then he was very angry. He did not know how to find which babe was the King; so he said he would kill all the babes in Bethlehem: then he thought he should be sure to kill the right one.

But God would not let him kill Jesus, so one night while Joseph was sleeping he saw an angel, and he heard him say, "Get up and take the young child and His mother, and go quickly into Egypt; and stay there till I tell you to come back, for Herod will try to kill the young child."

That moment Joseph got up, and though it was night, he took away Mary and her babe.

No one knew that Joseph had gone away, till the morning came, and then no one could find out where he had taken the child and His mother.

Soon afterward Herod's soldiers rushed into Bethlehem, snatching all the babies from their mothers' arms, and killing them with swords.

Oh, what screams of children were heard that day, and what shrieks of mothers!

But yet Jesus was not killed. He was safe in Egypt.

THE CHILDHOOD OF JESUS.

The cruel king died of a frightful disease soon after this murder of the innocent babes, and the worms ate his body.

When Herod was dead, Joseph had another dream in the land of Egypt, where he had taken Mary and the child.

An angel said to him, "Return into the land of Israel, for Herod is dead, and all the men that wished to kill the young child are dead also."

So Joseph set out on another long journey with the child and His mother. He must have been glad to leave Egypt, that land of idols. He wished to live near Jerusalem, where the temple of God was; but he heard that Herod's son was king, and this made him afraid.

DEATH OF HEROD.

Joseph did not know where to go till he had another dream; when an angel told him what to do.

Then he went with the child and His mother to live at Nazareth.

That was the place where Mary had lived before her marriage, and here the little child grew to be a man.

Joseph worked as a carpenter for his living; and Jesus must have often watched him at his work, and helped to saw the wood, and hammer the nails. Of wood His cross was to be made, and nails were to pierce His blessed hands and feet some day.

Jesus Talks With the Priests in the Temple.

When Jesus was twelve years old He went with Joseph and Mary to the feast of the Passover at Jerusalem.

The journey was long, for Nazareth was eighty miles from Jerusalem. A great many neighbors went up together. It must have been pleasant in the early spring to see the fresh green grass under the feet, and the blossoms on the trees, and the opening flowers; and to hear the singing of the birds and the cooing of the doves.

After staying seven days at Jerusalem, all the people returned to their homes.

Joseph and Mary set out; but Jesus was not with them. They thought He was with some of their friends who were going back to Nazareth; so they went on without looking for Him. But when evening came, they said, "Where can Jesus be?"

They went about inquiring among all their friends, saying, "Have you seen our son?" Every one said, "No, we have not seen Him to-day."

Then Joseph and Mary felt very uneasy. They could not go on their journey without Him, as He was their treasure and the light of their lives.

So they turned back.

They had to go twenty miles before they reached Jerusalem. Then they went about, looking for their beloved one.

At last they remembered that there was a great hall near the temple where children were taught by the priests. They went to the temple: they entered the great room; and there they saw their lost child sitting amongst other children, listening to the priests and answering their questions. Every one in the room was wondering at the wise answers He gave and the wise questions He asked.

Mary was surprised that He had stayed behind without telling her; for He was a very obedient child, and never did anything without leave. She said to Him: "Son, why have you behaved to

ON THE WAY TO JERUSALEM.
And when He was twelve years old, they went up to Jerusalem after the custom of the feast.—ST. LUKE ii: 42.

us in this way? Your father and I have been looking for you three days. We have been so worried!"

Jesus answered: "Why did you look for Me? Did you not know I must be about My Father's business?"

Jesus meant His Father in heaven, and not Joseph.

His mother did not know what He meant by His Father's business, nor did Joseph understand, but Mary never forgot what He had said.

He went back with Joseph and His mother, and continued to live with and obey them as He had always done. He lived at Nazareth till He grew to be a man.

He was so good and amiable that everybody loved Him. No one could see a fault in Him for He had no sin.

John the Baptist Preaches in the Desert.

John was six months older than Jesus, and he began to preach first.

He had walked much in the desert, and when he was thirty years old he began to preach there.

He was not like other men in his ways. He did not dress like them. He wore a garment of coarse cloth made of camel's hair, with a leathern band or girdle round his waist.

He did not eat as other men, but he ate the food he found in the desert, which was locusts and wild honey. Locusts are like grasshoppers, only a little larger.

They were about the size of your thumb. They lived upon the leaves and the grass, and people in that country used them for food. John could easily make a fire with sticks, and broil the locusts on the hot ashes.

Honey was very plentiful in the trees and rocks, and was very pure and sweet, for the bees made it from the flowers of the desert.

Many people heard of John's strange food and dress. They wanted to see him, and when they knew he preached, they came to hear him. Thousands of people came.

He preached repentence. His first word was "Repent!"

He wanted people to leave their sins, and to turn to God.

This is what the angel had said he would do.

And then he told them that the Saviour was coming.

Those that repented, John baptized in the Jordan. He washed them with water, as a sign that God would wash away their sins.

But what John longed for most, was to see the Son of God. He had been told by God that His Son would come to be baptized; and that when He did come, the Holy Spirit would rest upon Him.

At last Jesus came, but John felt that he was not good enough to baptize Him. He knew that Jesus was very good, and did not need to be washed from sin.

While Jesus was in the water, He prayed to His Father,—and then a wonderful thing happened.

The heavens were opened, and the Holy Spirit came down like a dove, and rested upon Jesus; and a voice was heard from heaven, saying,

"This is My beloved Son, in whom I am well pleased!"

Then John remembered what God had once told him; and he now was sure that Jesus was the Son of God.

Satan Tempts Jesus in the Wilderness.

When Jesus had been baptized, He left the River Jordan, and went into the wilderness to a different place from where John was preaching, to a place where He was quite alone. There were no living creatures with Him—but the wild beasts. Their howling might be heard in the night. But no lion, nor bear, nor wolf, was allowed to come near Him to hurt Him.

Jesus was in the wilderness forty days and nights, and during all this time he ate nothing. He did not eat locusts and wild

ALONE IN THE DESERT.

honey like John; but God, His Father, kept Him alive without eating.

After living without food for forty days, Jesus felt very hungry.

Then Satan came and said,—"If Thou be the Son of God, command that these stones be made bread."

But Jesus told Satan, that it was written in the Bible that man could live without bread, if God spoke the word.

Then Satan took Jesus to a very high place, on the top of the temple.

The temple was built on a very high, steep hill, and it was terrible to look down to the bottom.

Satan said to Jesus,—

"If Thou be the Son of God, throw Thyself down from this place; for God has promised to make His angels take care of Thee!"

THE ANGELS SERVE JESUS.

This was true; but Jesus knew that it would be tempting His Father if He threw Himself down from that high place.

So He answered,—

"It is written, Thou shalt not tempt the Lord thy God."

But Satan tried once more to make Jesus sin.

This time he took Him to the top of a very high mountain, and he showed Him all the grandest things in the world. We do not know what things he showed Him; but whatever we can think of that is grand, fine, or beautiful—these things Jesus saw. Thrones and crowns, ships and armies, palaces and temples, delicious feasts and glittering robes—such things Jesus saw.

Then he said to Jesus,—

"If Thou wilt fall down and worship me, I will give Thee all these things; for they are all mine!"

Was that true?

No. Everything belongs to God. Satan is a liar.

Jesus replied, "It is written, Thou shalt worship the Lord thy God, and Him only shalt thou serve."

Then Satan found it was of no use trying to make Jesus sin. So he left Him.

When he was gone, the angels brought food to Jesus.

Oh, how they must have hastened to feed Him! How dearly they loved Him! How glad they were to bring Him bread, or honey, or butter, or wine, or milk, or whatever food God pleased to send to His Son!

Those angels had served Him in heaven when He sat on His Father's glorious throne; and now they served Him on earth, when He was weak, and weary, and sorrowful.

The Disciples of Jesus.

John went on preaching in the wilderness. Some people thought that he was the Saviour that God had promised. They came to him one day and said, "Tell us plainly,—art thou the Christ?"

John said, "No, I am not. I am not worthy to stoop down and unloose the latchet of His shoe." Then John told them of the true Saviour, and of the Holy Spirit coming down on Him like a dove.

There were some men who always followed John that they might hear his words. These men were called his disciples.

One day John was standing in the wilderness with two of his disciples, and he saw Jesus walking a little way off. He showed Him to his disciples and said,

"Behold the Lamb of God!"

Why did he call Jesus a Lamb?

Because He was to be offered up as a sacrifice for our sins, just as lambs were offered up; only He was not to be burned, but crucified.

The two disciples, who heard John speak, went after Jesus, and walked behind Him.

Soon Jesus turned round and looked at them and said,—"What do you want?"

They answered, "Master, where do you live?"

Jesus replied, "Come and see."

Oh, how glad these men were to be invited to go home with Jesus.

One of them was named Andrew. The name of the other is not mentioned, but we believe it was John—the most beloved disciple.

Jesus had no house of His own; He had nothing of His own but His clothes. He lodged in a house.

The two men spent the evening with Jesus. It was four o'clock when they came to his lodging. They spent the whole evening with Him, and then they went away. What a delightful evening it must have been, for no one ever spoke so sweetly as Jesus did! These men never forgot that evening.

Andrew had a brother that he loved very much. His name was Simon.

Andrew and Simon were fishermen, and lived in a town near the great lake in Galilee.

Andrew went to look for his brother Simon, that he might tell him about Jesus.

He said to him, "We have found the Christ!"

Then he asked his brother to come with him to see Jesus. Simon went with Andrew.

JESUS AND HIS DISCIPLES.

Jesus saw him coming; and He said, "Thou art Simon, and thou shalt be called Peter."

Simon was quite surprised at Jesus knowing his name when he first saw him.

Why did Jesus give him this new name?

It was because the name Peter has a meaning. Peter means "Stone."

A stone is firm and strong. A large stone cannot be easily moved, or shaken, or broken. And Simon was to be faithful and firm and strong in loving Jesus. Jesus knew this, and gave him the new name of Peter.

How Nathanael Became a Disciple of Jesus.

The two brothers—Andrew and Simon, had come up all the way from Galilee. The great lake in which they fished was in Galilee.

There was another man who had come from the same place. His name was Philip.

He was not brought to Jesus by his friends; he was found by Jesus Himself.

The day after Jesus had seen Simon, He went to look for Philip. He said to him, "Follow Me."

That was enough for Philip. He went after Jesus immediately, with Simon and Andrew and John. He became a faithful disciple.

Philip had a friend named Nathanael. He went to look for him, and when he had found him, he said, "We have found the man about whom so much is written in the Bible. His name is Jesus of Nazareth. He is the son of Joseph."

Nathaniel knew that Nazareth was a wicked town; and he was surprised that any great prophet should come out of such a place.

He said, "Can any good thing come out of Nazareth?"

Philip replied, "Come and see."

So these two friends came together to Jesus, just as once the two brothers had come together.

Jesus saw them coming. He knew Nathanael, and spoke of him to the others.

He said, "Behold an Israelite who has no guile." Guile means deceit.

Jesus called Nathanael a man who had no deceit, a truthful, open, sincere man.

This was great praise.

Nathanael had never seen Jesus before, and he cried out, "How is it that you know me?"

Jesus said, "Before Philip called thee, when thou wast under the fig-tree, I saw thee."

Nathanael had been hidden under a fig-tree, where no eye could see him but God's eye.

He now felt sure that Jesus was God, or He could not have seen him under the fig tree; so he cried out,—

"Master, Thou art the Son of God! Thou art the King of Israel!"

Then Jesus told Nathanael that he should one day see the angels going up and coming down upon the Son of man.

Nathanael did see these angels a long while after, when Jesus went up to heaven. He saw angels go up and come down from heaven.

Jesus now had five disciples:—

Andrew and Simon, John, Philip, and Nathanael.

They all went with Him to Galilee, where they lived. They were poor men, who caught fish in the Sea of Galilee. They were happy to have Jesus for their Friend and Master.

The Miracle at the Wedding Feast.

When Jesus was in Galilee, near the great lake, He did His first miracle. He turned water into wine at a marriage feast.

He did this miracle at a place called Cana. That was the town that Nathanael came from.

Cana was very near Nazareth.

Jesus was invited to a marriage at Cana. His disciples went with Him, and when they saw Him turn water into wine, they believed on Him more than they had done before.

Afterward Jesus went up again to Jerusalem, to keep the Passover. In that city He did a great many miracles, and a great many people believed on Him.

It was the poor people who believed on Jesus.

Most rich people despised Him.

But there was one rich man who did not despise Jesus, and who wanted to hear Him speak.

His name was Nic-o-de-mus.

He did not like that people should see him go to Jesus; so he went in the night.

THE MIRACLE AT CANA OF GALILEE.

He thought that people would not see him go into the lodging where Jesus was.

He went in and found Jesus in a room.

He spoke to Him with great respect, saying, "Master, we

know that you are come from God, for no one could do such miracles as you do, except God were with him."

Nicodemus thought that Jesus was a great teacher, but he did not know that He was the Son of God.

Jesus answered,—

"Verily (or truly), except a man be born again he cannot see the kingdom of God."

Nicodemus was very much surprised, and said,—

"How can a man be born again? Can he be a little child once more?"

Then Jesus told him he must be born of the Spirit.

But Nicodemus did not understand what Jesus meant by being born of the Spirit. He could not see the Spirit, so he thought it never came into people's hearts. But when a man is born of the Spirit, then he feels it in his heart.

Do you know, my dear child, that you must be born of the Spirit?

The Spirit can come into your heart and make you a new child. Then you will love God for giving His Son to die for you.

Jesus told Nicodemus how God had sent Him to save sinners. He said,—

"God so loved the world, that He gave His only-begotten Son, that whosoever believeth in Him should not die, but have everlasting life."

Nicodemus soon believed, and was born of the Spirit, and then he felt it in his heart.

Then he loved Jesus, and he did not mind people seeing him come to Him.

Story of the Woman of Samaria.

Jesus soon left Jerusalem. He set out with His disciples to return to Galilee.

He passed through Samaria on his way.

One day He was very tired, and He sat by a well to rest. It

was twelve o'clock, and the sun was very hot. The disciples wanted food, and they went to buy some in the town of Sychar, about a mile off. While they were gone Jesus rested. He liked to be alone, for He loved to pray.

He was thirsty, but He could not get water from the well, because He had no bucket.

Soon a woman came with a can or jug to draw water. This woman was not a Jewess. She was a woman of Samaria. The people of Samaria, though they lived in God's land, were not His people. They had been put there by the King of Assyria. They were chiefly Assyrians, and they knew very little about the true God. They hated the Jews, and the Jews hated them. This was very wrong, indeed. This woman did not like Jesus when she saw Him at the well, because she saw He was a Jew. But Jesus loved her and longed to save her soul.

He spoke to her first, and asked her to give Him some water.

She was surprised, and answered, "How is it that you, who are a Jew, ask water of me, who am a woman of Samaria?"

Jesus was not angry at her unkind answer, but softly said,—

"If you had asked Me to give you water, I would have given you living water."

The woman could not think how He could get any water. "Sir," she said, "the well is deep, and you have nothing to get water with. How do you get this living water?"

The woman did not know what water Jesus meant by "living water," nor did He tell her. He meant the water of life.

This woman had been very wicked. But what did she feel when He told her that He Himself was the Christ, whom God had sent into the world?

The disciples then came back from the city, with food in their hands, such as bread, fruit, fish, or honey, and they wondered at seeing Jesus talking to the woman.

The woman left her can by the well, so the disciples could easily get water.

Jesus might now have had a comfortable dinner with His

disciples. But He would not eat, and when they said, "Master eat," He replied, "I have food to eat you do not know of."

They thought that some one had brought Him food, but He told them He was thinking of his Father's work—saving sinners, like this poor woman and her friends. This was the Father's work that was like food to Jesus.

The woman told the men of the city that Christ, whom God had sent, was sitting by the well. And the men went to the well and begged Jesus to come to their city.

So Jesus went to Sychar, and he stayed there two days teaching the poor Samaritans.

Many believed on Him, and said, "Now we believe; not because you told us, for we have heard Him ourselves, and know that this is indeed the Christ, the Saviour of the world."

The Men of Nazareth Try to Kill Jesus.

When Jesus returned to Nazareth He was not well treated as He had been at Sychar.

He had a long journey to go before reaching the home of His boyhood.

On the Sabbath day He went into the synagogue. A synagogue was a place where people met together to pray, and hear the word of God. It was not a fine, grand place, like the Temple at Jerusalem.

There was only one temple in the land; but there were many synagogues.

When Jesus went into the synagogue of Nazareth, He was looked at by everybody; for the people there had known Him when He was a little boy, and now they had heard of His great miracles, and they hoped He would do miracles in their city.

There were high seats for those who read the Scriptures.

Jesus was asked to read.

A man handed Him one of the books of the Bible. It was the book of Isaiah, written on a roll of paper, or parchment.

Jesus stood up, and opened the roll at the place where it is written, "The Spirit of the Lord is upon Me, because He hath anointed Me to preach the Gospel to the poor."

Then He rolled up the book and gave it again to the man who had the charge of the rolls.

He then sat down to preach.

Every one fixed his eyes upon Jesus, wondering what He would say.

He said, "This day the Scripture I have read has come to pass."

He meant that God had given Him the Spirit to preach the Gospel to the poor.

Every one admired the sweetness of His words, but some whispered together, "Is not this Joseph's son?"

Then Jesus told them that God had sometimes sent prophets to do miracles for people who were not Jews. It made the men of Nazareth angry to hear all this, for they wanted Jesus to do miracles in their own city.

They all rose up, and hunted Jesus out of the synagogue, and up the street to the edge of the hill, that they might cast Him headlong down the steep place, and that He might be dashed to pieces.

But God saved His Son out of the jaws of these men, fierce as wild beasts.

Jesus passed through the midst of them, and went to another city.

How different were these men from those of Sychar in Samaria!

The men of Nazareth had known Jesus from a child, and yet they hated Him.

The men of Sychar knew Him only for two days, and yet they believed in Him.

The Miraculous Draught of Fishes.

Jesus would not live at Nazareth any more. He lived in a city called Ca-per-na-um.

It was close by the great Sea of Galilee, or Lake of Gennesareth.

Many fishermen lived in this town—Peter lived there, and Jesus lived in the same house.

Peter and his brother Andrew had a boat, in which they fished upon the lake.

James and John, with their father, had another boat.

These four men shared the fishes they caught with each other, and so they were called partners.

Jesus sometimes preached on the beach, close by the water.

Once, while preaching there, He could hardly speak, because of the crowd that pressed Him on every side.

He saw the two boats, or little ships, in the water.

There was no one in them.

Jesus got into one of these ships. It belonged to Simon Peter. As soon as Simon saw his Master get in, he got in also.

The Lord asked him to push his ship a little way from the shore.

Then He sat down and preached to the people on the beach. He could speak freely now, for the crowd could not press upon Him.

When Jesus had done preaching, He said to Simon, "Push your ships further into the water, and let down your nets to draw fishes."

Simon would not do this at first, for he thought it would be of no use.

He said, "We have labored hard all night, and yet we have caught no fish; but if you tell me, I will let down the net."

This was right. Simon and Andrew let down the net; but when they tried to draw it up again they could not, for there were such numbers of fishes caught that the net began to break. They made signs to John and James in the other ship to come quickly and help them.

All four together were able to draw up the net and to fill both ships with fishes.

So heavy were the ships that they began to sink.

When Simon saw this miracle, he fell down at the knees of Jesus, and cried out, "Go away from me; for I am a sinful man, O Lord!"

Peter did not really want Jesus to go away, but he spoke in that manner because he was afraid.

JESUS AND THE SAMARITAN WOMAN.

(335)

He also felt he was unworthy of such kindness as Jesus had shown him.

But Jesus would not go away from Peter: He loved him too well to leave him.

He told Peter to follow Him always, and He made him a great promise,—

"One day thou shalt catch men."

He meant that Peter should save men from dying for ever and ever, by preaching to them about Jesus.

All the four fishermen were much astonished by the miracle, and when they had brought their ships to land, they left all they had and followed Jesus.

Jesus Heals a Man Who Was Insane.

I will tell you how Jesus spent one Sabbath day. You know that He lived at Capernaum, by the side of the lake. It was His custom to go to the synagogue, and to sit among the teachers, and to read the word of God to the people.

One day there was a man in the synagogue, who had a dreadful affliction. An evil spirit had entered into his heart, and greatly tormented the poor man.

Every one was listening to Jesus, and the wonderful things He said, when the evil spirit cried out with a loud voice,—

"Let us alone: what have we to do with Thee, Jesus of Nazareth? I know Thee who Thou art, the Holy One of God!"

At this Jesus cried out,—"Hold thy peace, and come out of him."

The evil spirit did not like to leave the man; but he was forced to obey Jesus.

He tormented the man as much as he could in coming out of him: for he threw him down in the midst of the synagogue, and tore him.

As soon as he was come out, the man felt no more pain, but was quiet and comfortable.

Every one was astonished at this miracle, and said, "Even the unclean spirits obey Him!" When Jesus left the synagogue, He went into the house where he lodged. It was the house of

JESUS CARETH FOR THE SICK.

Simon and Andrew. James and John came in with Jesus. They were all going to dine. But before they went to dinner, they told Jesus that there was some one in the house very sick. It was the mother of Peter's wife. She had a fever. Jesus went immediately into her room and found her lying on the bed, feeling very hot, and thirsty, and restless. He stood near her bed, and told the fever to go away; then He took her by the hand, and helped her to rise. The fever was gone, and the poor old woman felt quite well.

She dressed herself quickly and went into the dining-room, to wait upon Jesus at dinner. How much surprised her friends were to see her well so soon; for generally people are a long while getting well after having had a fever.

The Jews began their Sabbath on Friday evening and ended it on Saturday evening, when the sun had set.

It was now Saturday evening.

Numbers of people came to the house where Jesus was. They all crowded round the door. Some were sick, some were blind, some were dumb, some were tormented by devils. The devils cried out, "Thou art the Son of God!" But Jesus commanded them not to speak, and made them come out of the poor creatures.

Jesus had been doing good from morning till night. He must have been tired. He went to bed at last; but He did not lie there long. He rose up while it was still dark, and went quietly out to a place in the country where no one passed by. There He prayed to His Father.

Jesus Heals a Sick Man.

In the morning Peter could not find Jesus in the house, so he went to look for Him. A great many people came with him.

At last they found Him praying, in a lonely spot far away from the town.

They said to Him, "Every one is looking for you."

They wanted Him to come back with them.

But Jesus said that He must go and preach in other places.

So He went about preaching and healing sick people. Wherever He went, crowds of people brought their sick children and friends to be healed.

After some time He came back to Capernaum, where Peter lived. Jesus generally lived there too,—in Peter's house.

The people in the town were very glad to hear that Jesus was gone into the house. Numbers of people went to see Him, and soon the house was full, and those who could not get in stood around the door.

Among the people who came were some proud men called Pharisees.

These men thought they were very good, because they knew the words in the Bible, and because they made long prayers. But they hated Jesus and spoke against Him. They were in the house while Jesus was teaching.

Soon four men came to the door, and could not get in. These men were carrying a bed, or couch. A sick man lay upon it. He had the palsy and could not move his limbs. He was quite helpless, so his four friends carried him in a bed.

When they found they could not get in at the door, they thought of another way. There were stairs outside the house up to the roof—which was flat. They got up the stairs with the bed. It must have been hard work, but the men did not mind the trouble. When they got upon the flat roof, they took off some of the tiles and made a hole, and let down the bed with ropes from the top. Down came the bed through the roof to the floor, where Jesus was standing preaching.

When He saw this, He was much pleased; for He knew that the men believed He was able to cure their sick friend.

Jesus looked on the poor man and said, "Man, thy sins are forgiven thee."

Jesus knew the sick man was sorry for his sins.

But the proud men said, "How wicked Jesus is to say He can forgive sins! He speaks blasphemy."

Though the proud men did not say this out loud, Jesus knew what they were thinking, and He said,—

"Which is easier to say, Thy sins are forgiven thee; or to say, Rise up and walk?"

Then Jesus said to to the sick man, "Arise, take up thy bed, and go unto thine house."

And the man did so, praising God as he went.

Everybody who saw him was astonished; but the Pharisees went on hating Jesus all the same.

A Wonderful Thing That Happened at the Pool of Bethesda.

Sometimes Jesus left Capernaum and went up to Jerusalem.

He did many miracles there.

At Jerusalem there was a great pool. A very wonderful thing happened at that pool once a year. An angel came down and troubled the water, and the first sick person who stepped into the pool after this was done, was made well.

No one knew at what moment the angel would come; therefore many sick people came round the pool and waited there a long while.

They wanted some place to wait in, as a shelter from the cold at night and the heat by day. There were five sheds, called porches, in which they lay.

The place was called Beth-es-da, which means "House of Mercy."

One Sabbath-day Jesus came to the pool of Bethesda, and saw the poor creatures lying in the porches. There were crowds of other people who were not sick. They came to see the troubling of the water.

Jesus saw amongst the sick a poor man who was very weak, and only just able to creep along, but not able to go quickly. Many sick people had friends taking care of them, but this man had no one near him to help him. He was not like the man in Capernaum who had four faithful friends.

Jesus pitied this poor, lonesome, friendless man. He knew that he had been weak for a long time—even for thirty-eight years.

So He went up to him and spoke kindly to him, saying, "Would you like to be made well?"

CHRIST SOWS THE GOOD SEED IN EVERY HEART. (341)

The man answered, "I have no one to put me into the pool; but while I am coming, another steppeth down before me."

Jesus said, "Take up thy bed and walk."

The man rose, took up his bed, and walked along.

As soon as the man rose up, Jesus went away from the place, without any one seeing Him go.

The people standing near, saw the man carrying his bed, and they were astonished, for they remembered the weak man, who had often waited beside the pool.

Some of the proud men who hated Jesus were there: and when they saw the man carrying his bed, they began to blame him. They said, "It is wrong for you to carry your bed on the Sabbath-day."

The man answered, "He, who made me well, told me to take up my bed and walk."

Then they asked him, "Who was it said so?"

But the poor man could not tell them who had cured him, for he had never seen Jesus before.

But soon he knew who had cured him, for he went to the temple and there he saw Jesus.

When Jesus saw the poor man, He said, "Sin no more, lest a worse thing come upon thee."

The poor man had once done some very wicked thing, and he had been punished by a long sickness. Now Jesus commanded him to turn from his sins.

The man went back to the proud Jews and told them it was Jesus who had cured him. He did not know how much those wicked men hated Jesus.

They hated Him so much that they wanted to kill Him. Their real reason for hating Him was because He told them of their sins.

Jesus Chooses Twelve Apostles.

Jesus had a great many disciples. All who liked to hear Him, and all who loved Him were called His disciples. But they were not always with Him.

THE WINDS AND THE WAVES OBEYED CHRIST. (343)

Jesus wished to have twelve men always with Him, that He might teach them a great deal.

Before He chose them, He spent a whole night in prayer to His Father upon a mountain. He was quite alone that night.

As soon as it was light He called many of His disciples to come up the mountain.

When they were come up, He chose twelve and called them Apostles. He meant them to be always with Him, till He should send them out to preach.

The first I shall mention was Andrew, and then his brother Simon. This Simon had another name, which Jesus had given him. It was Peter, or "a stone." Andrew and Simon were fishermen. They were the sons of Jonas.

The next pair of brothers were James and John, the sons of Zebedee. They were fishermen, and they used to go out fishing with Simon and Andrew.

The next pair of brothers were James and Jude. A long while afterward they wrote two letters, which you will find in the Bible, called the Epistles of James and Jude.

So I have mentioned three pairs of brothers, which made six.

There were six more Apostles who were not brothers.

Matthew was an Apostle. His other name was Levi. Once, when he was sitting by the lake, at a little table taking money for taxes, he heard Jesus say, "Follow Me," and he followed Him; and now he was chosen to be an Apostle. A long while afterward he wrote the history of Jesus, called the Gospel of St. Matthew.

Thomas was chosen to be another Apostle,—afterward he was very slow to believe that Jesus had risen from the dead.

Philip also was slow to believe that Jesus could feed the multitude with five loaves.

Bartholomew was another Apostle—we think that his other name was Nathanael, and that he was Philip's friend,—and that he prayed under the fig-tree.

Simon had the same name as Peter; he was called the Canaanite, because he came from Cana, where Jesus turned water into wine.

There was one more Apostle, Judas Iscariot, who betrayed the Saviour at the last. He was always bad, and Jesus knew it. Yet He chose him to be an Apostle. It would have been better for Judas if he had never been born.

With these twelve Apostles Jesus came down from the mountain and stood in the plain. There He healed the diseases of the multitudes who came from all parts to ask for mercy.

No one can say how many disciples Jesus had, for all who loved Him were His disciples, but only twelve were called Apostles.

Something More About John the Baptist.

While Jesus was doing miracles in Galilee, John the Baptist was in prison.

Herod had put him there. Not that Herod who once killed the little children, for he was dead. This Herod was son of the other.

Why had Herod put John in prison?

I will tell you why, and you will see how wicked he was.

Though he was wicked, he liked to hear John preach, and he minded many things that he said. But there was one sin that he would not give up. He had taken away his brother Philip's wife. Her name was He-ro-di-as. She was very wicked to leave her husband and go and live with Herod. John the Baptist told Herod that he must not keep Herodias in his house any longer, but send her away.

Herod did not like to part with her, for he was fond of her. He told Herodias that John wanted him to send her away. Then Herodias was very angry, and said to Herod, "I want you to have John killed." But Herod would not do it, for he knew that the people thought John very good, and that they would be angry if he had him killed.

Though Herod was afraid of having John killed, he sent men to seize him and put him in prison.

The prison was in a great castle near the Dead Sea. John was cast into a dungeon, and his hands and feet were hurt with chains.

His voice was no more heard in the wilderness crying out,—

"Behold the Lamb of God which taketh away the sin of the world."

John Sends Messengers to Jesus.

While John the Baptist was in prison, his disciples often came to see him.

He had disciples as well as Jesus. They must have been very sad now their master was in prison.

One day they came and told him about the great miracles that Jesus had been doing. They told him how Jesus had brought to life the widow's son who was being carried to the grave.

John's disciples had not seen these miracles themselves, they had only heard of them. So John thought it would be best for them to go and see Jesus work his miracles; for he wanted them to believe that He was the Son of God.

John did not tell all of his disciples to make this long journey; he called two of them, and told them to go to Galilee, where Jesus was; and to ask him whether he was the true Saviour that God had promised to send.

It was a long way from the prison near the Dead Sea to the Sea of Gal-i-lee.

These two disciples came at last to the place. They found Jesus in the midst of sick, lame and blind people. They came up to Him, and said,—

"John Baptist hath sent us unto Thee, saying, Art Thou He that should come, or look we for another?"

Jesus answered not in words, but by doing miracles.

He cured all the people who were round Him, and cast out the evil spirits.

These disciples were greatly astonished at what they now saw. Then Jesus said to them, "Go your way, and tell John what

STREET LEADING TO HEROD'S PALACE.

things ye have seen and heard; how that the blind see, the lame walk, the lepers are cleansed, the deaf hear, the dead are raised, the gospel is preached to the poor."

So these disciples returned to their master in the prison, and told him all they had seen and heard. John was not surprised, for he knew well that Jesus was the Son of God, and could do everything; and he wished his disciples to believe on Jesus.

When the two disciples were gone away, Jesus began to praise John. He said,—

"No one that ever was born was a greater prophet than John the Baptist."

Yet though John was so great, wicked people said he had a devil.

And what did they say of Jesus? They called Him dreadful names,—a glutton, and a drunkard, and a friend of sinners.

The last is true; for though Jesus hates sin, He is indeed the Friend of sinners—the Friend who died for them—the Friend who lives to save them.

Herod Causes John to be Beheaded in Prison.

One day Herod gave a grand feast in his castle. It was on his birthday. Many great lords came to the feast.

Herodias did not come to the feast, for ladies were not invited; but she was in the castle at the time.

While the lords were eating their dainty dishes, and drinking their rich wines, a girl, gayly dressed, entered the dining-hall.

She was the daughter of Herodias. Her name was Sa-lo-me, and she was Herod's niece.

She danced beautifully before the lords, and Herod was greatly pleased.

Good men would have been grieved to see her dance; but the lords were delighted, and Herod was so much pleased that he asked what she would have as a reward.

"Ask what you will," said he, "and I will give it you,—even if it be the half of my kingdom."

He did not mean really to give her the half of his kingdom. That was only a way of speaking.

The little girl did not know what to ask for, so she ran to her mother for advice. That was right. But this poor child had a wicked mother who gave her bad advice. Salome told her mother all that Herod had said.

"My child," replied Herodias, "ask for the head of John the Baptist in a great dish." Salome, though so young, must have known that it was wicked to kill the holy prophet; yet she obeyed her mother (when she ought not), and ran back to the dining-hall, with the words on her lips, "John the Baptist's head in a great dish."

BEHEADING OF JOHN THE BAPTIST.

Herod was filled with grief by the child's request. He did not expect a child would ask for such a thing. He ought to have said "No," but he did not, because he feared the lords would laugh at him if he did not keep his promise.

But a wicked promise ought not to be kept.

Herod was more afraid of the laughter of his lords than of the anger of God.

So he sent for the executioner, whose horrible business it was to cut off heads, and he commanded him to cut off the head of John the Baptist immediately. So the man went into the dark dungeon, with a sword in his hand, and beheaded the holy prophet.

There were no gray hairs upon that head, for John was still young and strong. It was well for him to go to his God, and to wait above for the Lamb of God, soon to be crucified.

The executioner placed the bleeding head in a great dish, and gave it into the hands of Salome, and those young hands carried the cruel present to the fierce Herodias.

That wretched woman was glad with a joy like Satan's to behold the silent tongue, that could no more say to Herod, "Send her away."

But what did John's disciples feel when they heard of their master's death?

They were exceedingly grieved. There was one thing they desired to have. It was the headless body of their beloved teacher. Herod let them have it. The disciples bore it in their loving arms to the tomb which they had prepared.

Then they wanted to tell Jesus of their trouble.

They had a long journey to go, from the Dead Sea to Galilee. Two of them had lately made that journey, that they might see Jesus work miracles. Now they went to be comforted; and who can comfort as Jesus can?

He knew all—without their telling him; but He liked to hear them speak of their master's death. For Jesus loved John, as His faithful messenger and friend.

Jesus Restores Life to a Young Girl Who had Died.

A rich man came to Jesus, and fell down at His feet, and said "I have one little girl, and she is very sick; pray come and make her well."

Jesus went with the rich man.

When they were near the house, some servants came out and said, "The little girl is just dead; no one can make her well now."

But Jesus said, "Do not be afraid; I can make her well."

Jesus said to the father and mother of the little girl, "Come with me into the house. Peter, James and John, you may come in, but no one else."

So they went up to the room where the little girl was lying in bed. A great many people were in the room, playing sad music, and singing sad songs, and crying, because the child was dead. But Jesus said, "Leave off crying. The child is only sleeping: she is not dead." Jesus said she was asleep, because He knew that death only resembles sleep. He always spoke of death in that way. Those who die "fall asleep" for a little while and then they come to life again. But the people laughed at Jesus, and said, "She is dead;" and they would not believe that He could make her alive again.

Jesus said, "These people must be put out of the room." So He sent them out, and shut the door; but He let the father and mother, and Peter, and James, and John, stay in the room. He took the little girl's hand, and said, "Arise." At first she sat up, and then she rose up out of bed, and walked about the room. She was twelve years old. Jesus then said, "Bring her something to eat."

The father and mother were greatly astonished at what had happened.

Herod, on Hearing of Jesus, Supposed He was John the Baptist Come to Life Again.

Jesus went about from one place to another, and taught in all the synagogues, and cured all the sick people.

Herod had a fine house near the lake in Galilee. His servants came and told him about the miracles that Jesus did.

Then he remembered John the Baptist, whom he had so wickedly killed, and he felt afraid lest he had come to life again and was called Jesus; for though John had never done miracles, Herod thought that perhaps he could do miracles now that he was alive again.

So when his servants told him about Jesus, he answered, "It is John whom I beheaded."

Herod wished very much to see Jesus, that he might find out whether He was John the Baptist; but he was too proud to go to Him.

How unhappy he felt in his fine palace, thinking of the wicked things he had done long ago! yet he was not really sorry.

About this time Jesus sent out His Apostles to preach in all the towns and villages. He did not send each alone, but two together. He knew that it was a comfort to have a friend when any one goes to a new place. We do not know which two went together. Perhaps Peter went with his brother Andrew; perhaps he went with his friend John. Perhaps Philip went with his friend Nathanael (called Bartholomew). Who went with Judas Iscariot? No one would have liked to go with him if he had known how wicked he was; but they had not found him out.

Before they set out, Jesus gave them power to do miracles; even to cast out devils and to raise the dead. They took nothing with them but a staff each; they took no bag of bread with them, and no purse with money; for Jesus promised that kind people would give them all the food and clothes they wanted by the way.

So they went and preached, and did miracles.

When they had gone through a great many towns, they all returned to Jesus and began to tell Him what they had done. But they wanted to be quiet while they were talking, and there were so many people coming and going in that place that they desired to go to another place. Here they could not even sit down to a meal without being disturbed by some one. So Jesus said, "Let us go to a desert place, where we may rest awhile."

They were close by the sea, and they got into a ship and sailed a few miles along the lake till they came to a place where there were no houses.

SALOME DANCING BEFORE HEROD.

They meant to go without being seen. But some people who knew Jesus saw Him getting into the ship, and they told other people; and a great many ran along by the side of the lake, and got before the ship; so when Jesus got out of the ship with His disciples, He found thousands of people waiting for Him. How much disappointed the Apostles must have been to find that they could not talk alone with their Lord!

Jesus pitied these poor people, and began to teach them.

He went on teaching till the evening came. Then His Apostles hoped that the people would go home and leave them alone with their Master; but Jesus told the Apostles to feed them with five loaves and two fishes. Jesus made this small amount of food enough for five thousand men, besides women and children. The people even threw down little bits of bread and fish on the grass, because they could eat no more.

Jesus desired the Apostles to pick up the pieces, and when they had done so, they filled twelve baskets; which was more than enough for the suppers of all the Apostles.

Now the Apostles hoped they should be alone with their Master. But no; Jesus desired them to get into the ship and to go home by themselves, while He sent the people away. They were obliged to obey their Master, and they went away very unwillingly.

Jesus Walks on the Water.

When the Apostles were gone, Jesus remained to send the multitudes away. They were too far from home to get there that night, and they must have slept among the hills, or in the villages close by.

And where did Jesus sleep that night?

He did not sleep at all, but He went up on a mountain and prayed to His Father.

And how did the poor Apostles get on in the ship without their Master?

354 MY MOTHER'S BIBLE STORIES.

At first they went on very well; but when they were about half way across, the wind began to blow very hard. They had to take down the sails because the wind drove the ship back, and they tried with all their strength to get the ship on by rowing. But they were so much tossed by the waves that they were afraid they should all go down and be lost. Oh, how much they wished for their Master at this moment! But though they could not see

JESUS WALKING ON THE WATER.
And when the disciples saw Him walking on the sea, they were troubled, saying, It is a spirit; and they cried out for fear.—ST. MATTHEW xiv: 26.

Him, He saw them from the mountain-top, toiling at their oars, for the darkness and the distance could not hide them from His eyes.

In the darkest part of the night He came to them, not in a ship, for there was none, but walking upon the waves of the sea. Three or four miles He walked on the foaming roaring waters.

When He came near the ship, He did not go up to it, but seemed as if He was going to walk further.

His Apostles could just see a figure on the sea, but they could not tell who it was in the darkness, and they cried out in their fright, "It is a spirit!"

They thought it was a spirit without a body, as they knew that men with bodies would sink in the water.

Soon they heard a voice above the roaring of the sea, cry out,—

"Be of good cheer, it is I; be not afraid."

They knew that voice; and Peter called to Him:

"Lord, if it be Thou, bid me come unto Thee on the water."

Jesus answered, "Come."

Peter had the courage to spring out of the ship, and to walk upon the rough sea, for a little while, but when he came very near Jesus, he thought of the high and furious wind, and he felt afraid. Then he began to sink. In his fright, he called out,—

"Lord, save me!"

Immediately Jesus stretched out His hand, and caught him, as he was beginning to sink.

Jesus gently said: "O thou of little faith, why didst thou doubt?"

Then both Jesus and Peter got into the ship. That moment the wind ceased blowing, and the waves were stilled. The Apostles came around Jesus to worship Him, saying,

"Of a truth Thou art the Son of God!"

Jesus Preaches to the People.

It was morning when Jesus and His Apostles got out of the little ship and stood upon the shore. The people knew Him, and were glad to see Him; for Capernaum was close by where He lodged in Peter's house.

Those who saw Him land went and told others, and soon crowds of poor creatures were seen coming out of the city and from the country. Here were children leading their blind parents, and there were parents carrying their sick children. Every one who even touched the border of Christ's clothes was made well. But what had become of the people on the other side, whom Jesus had fed the night before?

They had slept near the place where they were fed; and they hoped to find Jesus when they woke next morning. But when morning came they could not find Him.

They could not think where He was. They thought He could not have crossed the lake, because there was no other ship, except the one in which the Apostles had gone away. They little knew that Jesus had walked on the sea in the night, and had overtaken his Apostles in the ship.

The people longed to get to Jesus. They thought He must have crossed over, though they could not tell how.

At last, some ships came from another place, and many of the people got into them, and sailed over into Capernaum.

They found Jesus on the shore healing the multitude. They ran up to Him and said,—

"Master, when did you come here?"

Jesus did not tell them how He had walked on the sea, but He said,—

"I know why you are come after Me; it is because you ate of the loaves and were filled."

That was the real reason why they had come after Jesus in such haste. They wanted to be fed every day, and to live without working for their bread. Jesus was displeased with them for caring more for their bodies than for the salvation of their souls.

He said, "Try and get that food which will make you live forever."

Then the people replied, "What wonder can you do? Our fathers ate manna in the wilderness."

They meant to remind Jesus how Moses gave manna to the Israelites, that He might do the same.

Jesus answered, "The bread of God comes down from heaven, and gives life unto the world."

Then they said, "Give us this bread always."

But they did not know what bread Jesus meant till He said, "I am the Bread of Life. All that the Father giveth Me shall come to Me; and him that cometh to Me, I will in no wise cast out."

But they did not yet know that Jesus was able to save their souls from endless death.

One day, when He was in the synagogue, He said,—

"I am the bread which came down from heaven."

When the chief men in the synagogue heard that, they murmured in whispers to each other, and said,—

"He did not come down from heaven. We know His father and mother."

Jesus knew what the Jews were whispering, and He said, "The bread which I will give is My flesh, which I will give for the life of the world; he that eateth of this bread shall live forever."

Jesus meant He was going to die for us, and that if any one believed in Him he should live forever.

But the Jews did not understand Him, and they said, "How can this man give us His flesh to eat?" And a great many who had believed in Him were displeased with this saying, and would not follow Him any more.

One day, Jesus said to His Apostles, "Will you also go away?"

Peter was the first to answer, "Lord, to whom shall we go? Thou hast the words of eternal life, and we believe and are sure that Thou art that Christ, the Son of the living God."

Jesus answered, "Have not I chosen you twelve, and one of you is a devil?"

He spoke of Judas Iscariot, for Jesus knew he would betray Him at last.

It is terrible to think that a man may be as wicked as a devil. Judas never believed in Jesus, and in the end he was lost.

Jesus is willing to save all that come to Him, for He has said,—

"Him that cometh to Me, I will in no wise cast out."

Glories of the Mount of Transfiguration.

At this time Jesus began to talk to His disciples about a very sorrowful thing. It was His own death. He told them He must soon go to Jerusalem to be killed.

The disciples did not like to hear this, for they hoped that He would go to Jerusalem to be made a king. They felt very sad when they heard Jesus say,—

"I shall be ill-treated by the priests and the great men, and I shall be killed."

Jesus went on to say, "I shall be raised again in three days."

But the disciples were not glad to hear this, for they did not know what Jesus meant by being raised again.

A week afterward a very wonderful thing happened.

One evening Jesus went up a mountain with His three favorite disciples, Peter, John and James.

On the mountain-top Jesus began to pray. As he was praying, His disciples observed a change in His face.

His face grew bright as the sun and His clothing became whiter than snow.

Two glorious men came from heaven and talked with Jesus. They were Moses and Elijah.

Moses had once died and been buried. But he had risen again.

Elijah had been taken to heaven without dying. These glorious men talked to Jesus about His death at Jerusalem, which was soon to occur.

The three disciples were delighted with what they saw and heard; and Peter said to Jesus,—

"Lord, it is good for us to be here. Let us make three tabernacles, one for Thee, and one for Moses, and one for Elijah."

But could Jesus live there in glory? Was He not soon to be killed? Peter had forgotten what Jesus had told him about being killed. He was so much afraid, he knew not what he said.

Suddenly a bright cloud came over Jesus and His glorious friends, and hid them from the disciples' eyes. A voice came out of the cloud, saying,—

"This is My beloved Son, in whom I am well pleased."

It was the Father's voice, heard once before at the baptism of Jesus. The voice made the disciples still more afraid. They fell on

JESUS TALKING WITH HIS DISCIPLES.
While He yet spake, behold, a bright cloud overshadowed them; and behold a voice out of the cloud, which said, This is my beloved Son, in whom I am well pleased: hear ye Him.—ST. MATTHEW xvii: 5.

their faces, nor did they lift them up again till they felt a gentle touch, and heard a well-known voice, saying,—

"Arise, and be not afraid."

When they looked up, they saw no one but Jesus; the glorious men from heaven were gone away. All these things had happened in the night.

When it was morning they came down the mountain with Jesus.

As they were going down, Jesus said, "Tell no man what you have seen—till the Son of man be risen from the dead."

Though they did not know what rising from the dead meant, the disciples obeyed their Master and never told any one what they had seen, till after Jesus had risen from the grave.

Jesus told them again that He should be cruelly treated at Jerusalem.

It was a comfort to the disciples to think of the glorious scene upon the mountain.

One day Jesus will come again in such glory as the disciples saw, and all His people will be bright and beautiful like their Lord.

Jesus Teaches Humility.

Jesus went about from village to village doing miracles; and everywhere He went a multitude followed Him, and pressed upon Him.

When He was alone with His Apostles He told them that He should soon be killed, and that He should rise the third day.

They were very sorry to hear He would be killed; but still they hoped that He would soon be a glorious king and reign in Jerusalem.

One day as they walked near Him they disputed with each other; but they did not wish their Lord to hear them. Yet Jesus always knew what they were saying, and even what they were thinking.

They came soon to Capernaum, where Jesus lived in Peter's house.

They all went into the house.

As soon as they were come in, Jesus asked them this question, "What were you disputing about as you went along?"

They were ashamed to answer Him; for they had been disputing which of them should be the greatest when Jesus was king.

They knew it was wrong to wish to be the greatest; yet they had proud selfish hearts, and often said what they knew to be wrong.

Jesus sat down in the house and called all His Apostles around Him. Then He said,

"If any man desire to be first, the same shall be last of all, and servant of all."

Then he called a little child and set him in the midst of them, that all the Apostles might see him, and He said,—

"Whosoever shall be humble like this little child, he shall be greatest in the kingdom of heaven."

Then in His kindness He took the little child in His arms.

JESUS LOVES LITTLE CHILDREN.

You see how much Jesus loves children. He wishes every one to be humble like them, for little children never wish to be great. They care not whether their mother is a queen or a poor woman, they love her all the same. When they grow older they grow less humble, unless they have the Holy Spirit, and then they grow more humble still.

But no one was ever so humble as Jesus; He left a throne of glory to be a poor man in this world. He is the gentle Shepherd, and children are His little lambs.

The Story of Mary and Martha, Who Loved Jesus.

The people in Jerusalem were very anxious to see Jesus again.

The poor people wanted to see Him do more miracles; but the proud people wanted to kill Him.

At last He came up to Jerusalem.

He taught in the temple, and many came to hear Him and to see His miracles. The poor people praised Him very much. This made the Pharisees and the priests more angry than before; and they sent men to seize Him while He was teaching, and to bring Him to them.

But when these men came to Jesus they heard Him speak these beautiful words, "If any man thirst, let him come unto Me and drink." Jesus meant He would give the Holy Spirit to those who believed on Him.

The men who were sent to take Him went back without bringing Jesus. The priests and Pharisees were provoked, and said to the men, "Why have you not brought Him?"

They replied, "Never spake man like this man."

Another time when Jesus was teaching, the Pharisees said to him, "Thou hast a devil." Was it not dreadful to speak so to the Son of God?

Jesus answered meekly, "I have not a devil."

Soon afterward He said, "If a man keep My saying, he shall never see death."

What saying did Christ mean?

The saying He meant was, "I am the Son of God."

If any man believed that saying he would live forever; Jesus would give him everlasting life. To keep that saying was to believe in Jesus.

Then the Jews mocked Him and took up stones to kill Him; but he passed through the crowd without any one seeing Him, for His time to die was not yet come.

But though Jesus had many cruel enemies, He had a few loving friends.

There was a little village near Jerusalem, called Bethany. It was a pretty place shaded by palm-trees, just below Mount Olivet.

In this little village a little family lived. There were two sisters, named Martha and Mary, and a brother, named Lazarus. They all loved Jesus and begged Him to come often to their house.

When Jesus came and sat down in the house Mary always sat at His feet, to listen to His words. But Martha went to the kitchen to prepare a fine dinner for her Lord.

She was not pleased with Mary for leaving her to do all the work alone, and she came to Jesus to complain of her sister.

JESUS AT THE HOME OF MARY AND MARTHA.

She said to Him, "Dost thou not care that my sister hath left me to serve alone? Bid her, therefore, that she help me."

It was very wrong of Martha to tell the Lord what He ought to say.

But she was angry and said what she was afterward sorry for. She thought Jesus would praise her; but He blamed her and praised her sister. He told her that she cared too much for the things of this world; but He said of her sister, "Mary hath chosen that good part which shall not be taken away from her."

What good part had Mary chosen?

To listen to the words of Jesus; and Martha could not take her away from sitting at His feet.

Jesus did not care for eating or drinking. He cared most about teaching men how to be saved.

If Martha had known how to please Him, she would have brought Him plain food; such as a piece of bread, or fish; or a little milk and honey; and she would have sat down with Mary at His feet and listened to His word.

Story of the Blind Beggar.

One Sabbath day Jesus was walking in Jerusalem, when He saw a blind beggar sitting down in the street.

This beggar was a young man. He had been born blind, and had been used from a child to sit in the street and beg. His parents were still living, but they let him beg his own bread.

Jesus had pity on this poor beggar. He cured him in quite a new way. He spat on the ground, and then mixed it with the dust, and with this wet dust, or clay, He made a plaster for the man's eyes; and said to him, "Go to the pool of Siloam and wash." There was a pond, or pool, in Jerusalem called Siloam.

The blind man could find his way through the streets by himself, for he had been used to walk alone. He went to the pool with the plaster over his eyes, and washed it off, and came back able to see.

Soon the neighbors saw him, and were surprised that he was no longer blind. These neighbors were people who lived near the street where the man used to beg; and they knew his face quite well. They said to each other, "Is not this the man who used to

THE LOST SHEEP.

sit by the way and beg?" Some said, "He is like him." But the beggar said, "I am the man who was blind and sat by the way and begged." Then the neighbors asked him, "How were his eyes opened?" The beggar answered, "A man called Jesus made clay and put it on my eyes, and told me to go to the pool of Siloam and wash; and I went, and I was made to see."

The neighbors said, "Where is that man?"

He said, "I do not know."

The neighbors knew that the Pharisees would say it was wrong to make clay on the Sabbath, as well as to cure a blind man.

They did not believe in Jesus, so they took the beggar to the Pharisees, as they were sitting to judge people.

The Pharisees said to the man, "How did you receive your sight?" The man replied, "Jesus put clay upon my eyes, and I washed, and do see."

Some of the Pharisees answered, "Jesus cannot be sent by God, because He has broken the Sabbath by making clay."

Other Pharisees said, "But how can a wicked man do such miracles?"

They asked the blind man, "What do you say of Jesus."

He replied, "I say, He is a prophet. If He were not sent by God, how could He open my eyes? Who ever heard of such a thing as a man giving sight to one who was born blind? If Jesus is a wicked man He could not have opened my eyes."

It was right of this young man to speak well of Jesus; but the Pharisees were so angry that they would have nothing to do with the man. They forbade him to enter the synagogue for a month.

Jesus heard how ill the poor man had been treated, and He went to look for him.

He knew the man could not be in the temple, for the Pharisees had forbidden him to go there. Jesus knew whether he should meet the man by the way, or whether He should find him in his own home. He knew the man well, but the man did not know Jesus, for he had never seen Him, as he was blind when Jesus first spoke to him.

Jesus said to him, "Dost thou believe on the Son of God?"

The man answered, "Who is He, Lord, that I might believe on Him?"

Jesus said, "Thou hast both seen Him, and it is He that talketh with thee."

The man replied, "Lord, I believe." And he worshiped Him.

This man was happy, for he had Jesus for his friend. He had spoken well of the Lord before wicked men; and one day the Lord will own him for His child before the holy angels.

Story of the Lost Sheep.

After Jesus had cured the blind beggar, He preached to the Pharisees.

He spoke these sweet words as he taught:

"I am the good shepherd; the good shepherd giveth His life for the sheep. I am the good shepherd; and I know My sheep and My sheep know Me."

That poor blind beggar was one of these sheep. Jesus knew him first, and afterward he knew Jesus. He must have felt glad when he heard those words about the shepherd and the sheep.

But the Pharisees were angry, and they said again that Jesus had a devil and was mad.

And other people said, "These are not the words of one who has a devil. Could He have opened the blind man's eyes, if He had a devil?"

The chief men among the Pharisees hated Jesus so much that they took up stones to stone Him; and would have killed Him, if He had not gone away secretly.

There were men called publicans. These men went about to get the public taxes for Cæsar, who was king at Rome; so they were called publicans. One of Jesus' apostles had once been a publican. This was Matthew. Jesus saw him once receiving money at a table by the side of the lake. That money was the public taxes. Jesus had said to Matthew, "Follow Me;" and he had come after Jesus.

Matthew had many friends among the publicans, and he wanted them to hear Jesus; so he made a great feast in his house, and invited the publicans, and he begged Jesus to come and talk to them.

When the Pharisees saw Him dining with the publicans and other great sinners, they were very angry and spoke against Jesus.

One name they called Him was, "The Friend of Sinners." The Pharisees were angry with Jesus for being a Friend to bad men: but we are glad that we have a Saviour who loves us. Jesus likes the name, "Friend of Sinners." He once told a little

JESUS THE FRIEND OF SINNERS.

And Jesus answering said unto them, They that are whole need not a physician; but they that are sick. I came not to call the righteous, but sinners to repentance.—ST. LUKE v: 31, 32.

parable to show His love to sinners. He said, "If a man had a hundred sheep and one of them went away, what would he do? Would he not leave the ninety-and-nine and go and look for the poor lost sheep? And when he had found it, he would put it on his shoulders and carry it home. And when he was come home

JESUS BLESSES LITTLE CHILDREN.

he would call his friends and neighbors together, and say, Rejoice with me, for I have found my sheep which was lost."

Children, do you understand this parable? It means that Jesus seeks for sinners, and brings them back to His own home, and tells the angels of God to rejoice with Him.

The proud Pharisees did not think they were lost sheep; but many poor publicans knew they were.

Jesus Blesses Little Children.

Children are the lambs of Jesus. Once some mothers brought their little ones to Him. The disciples wanted the mothers to take them away; but Jesus was much displeased with the disciples for telling the mothers to go; and He said,—

"Suffer the little children to come unto Me, and forbid them not; for of such is the kingdom of God." And then He took them up in His arms, and put His hands on them and blessed them.

He was kind to other people besides children. He was kind even to His enemies.

Once He was passing through Samaria on His way to Jerusalem with His disciples.

The people of Samaria did not like the Jews.

Jesus came near a village. He wished to sleep there; so He sent messengers to ask whether any one would let Him come to his house. I do not know who the messengers were, but I suppose they were some of the disciples.

Jesus waited outside the village till the messengers came back. Soon they returned.

They said, "No one will let you come to his house, because you are going to Jerusalem."

When the disciples heard that the Samaritans would not let them in, James and John spoke very angrily. They said to Jesus, "Let us command fire to come down from heaven, to burn up these Samaritans!"

Jesus replied, "You do not know what sort of spirit you have. The Son of Man is not come to kill men, but to save their lives."

How gentle Jesus always was!

But was not John very gentle, too!

Not at first; though afterward he was gentle like Jesus; for the Spirit of Jesus came into his heart; and then he was like the lamb and the dove.

It is wicked to wish to hurt those who offend us.

Jesus meekly went to another village, where the people were kind, and let Him come into a house with His disciples.

THE ROAD TO SAMARIA.

Story of the Rich Young Man.

Jesus was going on His way to Jerusalem.

One day a young man came running up to Him and knelt down at His feet. He was rich; and he was a ruler or lord—a great and honorable man. He wanted to save his soul, and he said, "Good Master, what good thing shall I do that I may have eternal life?" Jesus said, "If thou wilt enter into life, keep the commandments."

Then Jesus mentioned some of the commandments:—"Thou shalt not kill, nor steal, nor tell lies; Honor thy father and thy mother."

The young man replied, "I have obeyed all these commandments since I was a youth until now."

Had this young man really kept all God's commandments?

Oh, no! He thought he had, but he had not really; for every one has disobeyed God many times; no one can be saved by his own goodness. That was the reason that Jesus died for us; because we deserve to die and cannot save ourselves.

But this young man did not know he was a sinner. Yet Jesus looked at him and loved him.

He gave him another commandment, to try whether he would obey Him.

He said to him, "Go and sell that thou hast and give to the poor, and thou shalt have treasure in heaven; and come and follow Me."

The young man did not like to sell his fine house and garden, his fields and his furniture, and become poor like Jesus.

So he went away; but he was very sorry to go, for he wished to have eternal life, as well as the fine things of this world.

This young man ought to have obeyed Jesus, instead of going away.

When this sorrowful young man was gone, Jesus looked round about on His disciples and said, "How hard it is for the rich to enter the kingdom of God!"

The disciples were surprised to hear this, for they thought many rich people would go to heaven.

Peter said, "We have left all and followed Thee. What shall we have?"

Peter had left his fishing-boat and nets and many of his friends.

Jesus made this promise to Peter, and to all: "Every one that has forsaken houses, or brothers, or sisters, or father, or mother, or wife, or children, or lands, for my sake, shall receive a hundred times as much in this life, and afterward eternal life."

There are good men called missionaries, who have left their country to preach to the heathen.

THE RICH YOUNG MAN WAS SORROWFUL.

There are good men called martyrs, who have gone to prison and been burned for the sake of Jesus.

These missionaries and these martyrs shall wear bright crowns of glory when Jesus comes again.

Story of the Humble Publican and the Proud Pharisee.

Jesus was followed by a multitude as He passed through Jericho.

Most of them were poor; some were beggars, for Bartimeus was amongst the crowd, and the other beggar who had been blind.

There was a rich man who had never seen Jesus, and who wanted very much to see Him.

His name was Zaccheus.

He was a publican, or collector of public taxes, as Matthew the Apostle once had been.

But Zaccheus was set over the other publicans, and he was a very rich man.

Perhaps you think it was easy for him to get a sight of Jesus as He was passing out of the town; but there was one thing that made him fear that he should not be able to see Him. He was very short, and he was afraid tall men would stand before him, and hide Jesus from his sight.

So he thought, "If I could get up a tree, I could look down upon Jesus as He passed by."

He ran on some way, and then climbed a tree, and waited for the crowd to come near. It was a sycamore tree, with very large leaves, and Zaccheus may have supposed that he should be hidden among the leaves.

How much surprised he was—when Jesus passed by—to see Him look up and fix His eyes on him and say, "Zaccheus, make haste and come down; for to-day I must stay at thy house."

He saw that Jesus knew his name, and knew where he was, and where he lived, and all about him. He must now have felt sure that Jesus was God; for no one else could know all this without being told.

MODERN JERICHO.

Zaccheus made haste and ran to his house, and received his Lord there with great joy.

The proud Pharisees were watching all that Jesus did; and when they saw Him go into the publican's house they murmured; for they thought that all publicans were wicked. They said: "He has gone to visit a sinner."

They did not think that they themselves were much worse sinners; yet they really were: for proud people are the greatest of sinners. Zaccheus had committed many sins, and he now felt very sorry; and he wished to give up his sins and please God.

ZACCHEUS IN THE SYCAMORE TREE.

While the Pharisees were speaking against him and his Master, he stood and said,—

"Behold, Lord, I give half of all I possess to the poor; and if I have ever made any one pay more taxes than was right, I give him back four times as much."

Jesus was much pleased with Zaccheus, and said,—

"This day is salvation come to this house."

By this He meant that the family of Zaccheus would be saved, and that they would believe in Jesus, as well as their master.

Jesus said also, "The Son of Man is come to seek and to save that which was lost." Zaccheus was a poor lost sheep, and Jesus had found him and had brought him home, and the angels were rejoicing over him, though the Phari'ees were murmuring.

The Wonderful Story of Lazarus.

Before Jesus came to Jerusalem, He lived for a little while in a very quiet little place near the River Jordan.

While hidden there He received a message from two of His dearest friends. It was Martha and Mary who sent the message. This was all they said:

"He whom Thou lovest is sick."

Jesus knew that it was their brother Lazarus who was sick, for He loved him very much.

Two days afterward He crossed the River Jordan with His disciples, and went to Bethany. The disciples were afraid to go so near Jerusalem. But Thomas said, "Let us go that we may die with Him."

When Jesus came to Bethany He found that Lazarus had been dead four days. He knew this without being told. He had not come sooner, on purpose that He might raise Lazarus from his grave after he had been dead a long time.

Martha and Mary waited and longed for Jesus to come.

Four days passed, and at last Jesus came.

Martha and Mary did not think that He would make Lazarus alive again, for he had been dead so long; so they sat upon the ground and cried.

When Martha heard that Jesus was on the road a little way off, she came to Him and said, "If You had been here, my brother had not died; and even now You could make him alive."

Then Jesus said, "Your brother shall rise again."

"Yes," said Martha, "I know he will rise again at the last day, when all the dead people arise."

Martha was afraid that Jesus would not choose to make Lazarus alive soon; but she knew that He was able to do it.

She went back to the house, and found Mary still sitting on the ground, and a great many friends around her.

Martha whispered in her ear, and told her that Jesus wanted to speak to her. So Martha and Mary went together, and found Jesus waiting for them on the road.

Mary's friends went with her, and they cried; and Mary cried very much indeed; and when she saw Jesus she fell down at His feet and said, "Lord, if You had been here, my brother had not died."

378   MY MOTHER'S BIBLE STORIES.

Jesus was very sorry to see her so unhappy, and to see so many people crying: He felt very sad indeed, and He sighed very deeply. Jesus does not like to see any one in trouble, He is so kind.

Then Jesus said, "Where have you put Lazarus?"

Martha and Mary and their friends said, "Come and see;" and they showed Him the way. As Jesus walked along, the tears

THE RAISING OF LAZARUS.

And when He thus had spoken, He cried with a loud voice, Lazarus come forth. And he that was dead came forth, bound hand and foot with graveclothes; and his face was bound about with a napkin. Jesus saith unto them, Loose him, and let him go.—St. John xi: 43, 44.

rolled down His cheeks. At last they came to the grave. It was a cave in the rocks, and a very large stone had been rolled before it.

Then Jesus said, "Take away the stone."

Martha thought Jesus was going to look at Lazarus lying dead; and she said, "Do not go in: his flesh has a bad smell by this time. He has been dead four days." But Jesus told her to

THE SISTERS AT THE TOMB OF LAZARUS.

believe that He could make him alive. They then rolled away the stone.

Then Jesus lifted up His eyes to His Father in heaven and thanked him for helping Him to do wonderful things.

A great many people were standing by, looking at Jesus, and wondering what He would do.

Poor Martha and Mary were longing to see Lazarus alive again.

Then Jesus spoke loud and said, "Lazarus, come forth."

Lazarus heard, though he was dead; for the dead hear the voice of Jesus. He got up and walked to the door of the cavern. His hands were tied with cloths, and his feet wrapped round with cloths, and a cloth was over his face.

But Jesus said, "Undo the cloths."

How pleased Martha and Mary must have been to see his face again! How they must have thanked the Lord Jesus for His kindness!

The raising of Lazarus was the greatest of all Christ's miracles.

Many of the people who saw this miracle believed on Jesus, but others went and told the Pharisees.

Mary and the Precious Ointment.

The Pharisees met together to make new plans to kill Jesus.

As it was not yet the time for Him to die, He went and hid Himself in a village near the River Jordan.

The feast of the Passover was now almost come. Many people from the country came to Jerusalem. They expected to find Jesus there. As they stood together in the temple, they said to one another, "What do you think? Will He come to the feast?"

They were afraid He would not come; because they knew that the Pharisees intended to kill Him.

And did Jesus come to the Passover? Yes, He did; for that was His time to die. Only a week before His death He came to Bethany.

MARY ANOINTING THE FEET OF JESUS.

That village was nearly two miles from Jerusalem.

At Bethany Jesus saw again that little family,—Martha, Mary and Lazarus. But He did not sup with them that evening.

There was a man in Bethany named Simon. He had once been a leper. He now made a supper, and invited Jesus and His disciples. He invited Lazarus also. Numbers of people came to Bethany that evening to see Lazarus who had been raised from the dead, and Jesus who had raised him.

Martha was there, but not sitting at the table. She waited on her Lord.

Where was Mary?

She came in during supper-time with a box or bottle in her hand. It was made of a beautiful white stone called alabaster, and it was filled with a delicious scent made of a plant called spikenard.

As the bottle was sealed up she could not open it, so she broke off the neck, and poured the sweet ointment on the head of Jesus.

Then she knelt down and anointed His feet as He lay on the couch, and wiped them with her long hair.

The whole house was filled with the sweet smell of this ointment, and Jesus was pleased with this proof of Mary's love. But one man sitting at the table was much displeased. That man was Judas Iscariot. He said,—

"Why was this ointment wasted? Why was it not sold and the money given to the poor? It might have been sold for three hundred pence."

And could he think any ointment too precious to be poured upon Jesus? Though this bottle was worth nearly fifty dollars of our money, it was not too good for the Son of God. But Judas wanted the price, because he kept the purse where all the disciples put their money, and he was a thief, and often stole money out of that purse for himself.

Jesus knew why he spoke against Mary, and He took her part and said,—

"Trouble her not, for she hath kept this ointment for My burial. The poor you have always with you, and you can do them good whenever you like; but Me ye have not always. She has done what she could, and wherever My word is preached, what she has done shall be told."

This has come true; everybody who reads the history of Jesus, hears of Mary's anointing Him.

In less than a week afterward Jesus was buried.

Mary must have known that He was soon going to die and be buried, for she had so often sat at His feet and heard His word.

Christ's Royal Entrance into Jerusalem.

You have heard how Jesus sat at supper in the house of Simon the leper.

The next day he got ready to enter Jerusalem. He could easily have walked into the city, for it would have been a short walk of less than two miles.

But he chose to ride upon an ass, because God had said a long while before, that the Saviour when He came should ride upon an ass.

So on the first day of the week, He said to two of His disciples, "Go to the next village, and you will find an ass tied there and her colt with her. Loose them and bring them to me. If any one asks you why you loose them, say, 'The Lord hath need of them,' and the owner will let you have them."

So the two disciples set out, and they soon saw two asses tied up by the way, as if to be hired.

They began to loose the asses, as Jesus had directed them, when the owner saw them, and asked why they did so; and the disciples answered, "The Lord hath need of them." Then the owner let the asses be taken away.

The disciples brought them to Jesus.

Then the disciples spread their clothes on the colt, and set Jesus upon it, and it went quietly along with Jesus, though no one had ever ridden upon it.

A multitude of people followed Jesus as He rode, and spread their garments on the ground for the ass to tread upon, and cut down branches from the palm-trees and strewed them on the way. Thousands of voices shouted and sang:

"Blessed be the King that cometh in the name of the Lord!"

Such songs have seldom been heard on earth as were heard that day.

But there were men who felt no joy. They did not like to hear Jesus praised. These men were the Pharisees. They made up their minds to kill Jesus as soon as possible, though they had not yet decided how they should do it.

They would have killed Lazarus if they could, because it was through his being raised from the dead that so many people believed on Jesus.

Were not these men like Satan who was a murderer from the beginning?

Jesus Weeps Over Jerusalem.

As Jesus rode along He came to the edge of Mount Olivet. From that place He could see Jerusalem in all its beauty.

He stopped to look at the lovely city, and as He looked the tears flowed down His cheeks.

Why did He weep at the sight of the city? Was it because He thought of the cruel way in which He was going to be treated in that city?

Oh, no, He was not weeping for Himself, but for the people who were going to crucify Him.

He thought of the punishment that God would make them suffer.

He spoke to the city as if it could understand, and said:

"Thine enemies shall come one day and dig a deep ditch around thee, to prevent people getting out, and shall throw down thy walls upon the ground, and lay low thy children."

What love Jesus showed in weeping for the men who were going soon to kill Him!

PITY FOR THE UNFORTUNATE.

Then Jesus went on His way, and entered Jerusalem in the midst of the joyful multitude. The people in the city heard the shouts in the streets, and cried out: "Who is this?"

The multitude answered, "This is Jesus, the prophet of Nazareth!"

They did not say He was the Son of God, for very few believed on Him.

Jesus went first to the temple. Then He got off the ass, and entered the first court, where Gentiles might worship as well as Jews.

There he found a number of sheep and oxen, and cages full of doves; and men sitting by tables changing large pieces of money into many little pieces. He was much displeased with the men for selling animals and changing money. He drove them all out with their animals, and He overset the tables, so that the money rolled on the ground.

He did not overset the cages of the doves, but He told the sellers to take them away.

He knew that it was for sacrifices that the animals were sold; but He knew also that the temple was not the proper place for selling or for buying, and He said:

"My Father has said, 'My house shall be a house of prayer for all nations,' and you have made it a den of thieves."

The sellers cheated in selling, and so were thieves.

It was wonderful that the traders went out when Jesus sent them; but they had heard of His miracles, and they were afraid of Him.

When they were gone there came in blind people, groping their way, and lame people, leaning on their sticks; and Jesus cured them all.

And sweet young voices were heard singing, "Hosanna to the Son of David."

Hosanna means, "Lord, save us."

These children believed in Jesus as their Saviour.

The priests said very angrily to Jesus:

"Do you hear what these children are saying?"

THE FIVE VIRGINS.

Jesus answered, "Yes. And have you never read, 'Out of the mouth of babes God brings the best praise?'"

What a comfort it is for children to think that God likes their praises the best of all!

It was now evening;—Jesus looked around about on all things in the temple, and then left the city, and went back to Bethany with His disciples.

That night He slept in Bethany. We do not know in what house He slept, whether in the house of Martha, or in the house of Simon the leper, or in some other faithful man's house.

Story of the Widow and Her Mite.

It was now the last week of Jesus' life on earth.

He taught in the temple in the day, and at night He went to the Mount of Olives.

The last day that He was in the temple He told His enemies that they were soon going to be punished.

He cried out, "O Jerusalem, Jerusalem, how often would I have gathered thy children together even as a hen gathereth her chickens under her wings; and ye would not!"

When a hen sees a hawk in the air, ready to pounce upon her chickens, she calls them to come under her wings for safety.

How had Jesus called the Jews to come to Him?

He had often said, "Believe on Me, and I will save you from Satan and from death."

He had often said, "If you believe that I come from God you shall never die." But they would not believe on Him, they would not come to Him, and now they would soon perish.

Jesus went and sat in a court of the temple, where there were many large chests, into which people put what money they pleased.

The money was used by the priests in buying animals for sacrifices, and incense, and oil, and all that was wanted for the temple.

Many of the rich Pharisees came and put in large sums of money. Jesus could see their hearts and He knew they were proud of their gifts and liked to be praised.

At last a poor widow came and threw in two mites, which make half a cent.

Jesus knew that this was all the money that she had. It might have been the wages of one day's work, and would buy as much as fifteen cents would buy now. That poor woman may have had to go without food for one day; but she did not mind, for she loved God, and gave the money from her heart.

Jesus was much pleased with what she had done, and He called His disciples around Him, that He might speak about her.

He said: "That poor widow has given more than all the rich men; for after they had given much they had much left, but she cast in all that she had."

This poor widow was the last person that Jesus noticed in the temple, as far as we know. Does this not show how much Jesus loves the poor? After praising her, He left the temple, never to enter it again till He should be brought there as a prisoner.

The Evening on the Mount of Olives.

As Jesus went out of the temple, and passed through its beautiful courts, one of the disciples said to Him:

"See what large and fine stones these are here."

They were indeed large and fine blocks of marble, some were as big as a little room.

But Jesus seemed sad as He looked at them and said:

"Verily, I say unto you, The day will come when all these stones will be thrown down, and not one shall be left above another."

When He got to the Mount of Olives, He sat upon the side of the mount, and looked toward Jerusalem on the opposite hills. There He saw the beautiful temple like a mountain of snow, tinged with gold, rising up above the other fine buildings.

GOD'S CARE FOR US TAUGHT BY THE BEAUTIFUL LILY.

Four of His disciples came to Him as He sat. They were favorite disciples. Their names were Andrew, with the brother he once brought to Jesus—Simon Peter; James with his brother John, the most beloved of all the twelve. These four wanted to hear more about the throwing down of the stones of the temple. They wanted also to know when Jesus would come again.

That evening He told them how the enemies would come in a few years to destroy Jerusalem and the temple. He said: "There will be great anger from God upon these people, and some will be killed by the swords of their enemies, and the rest will be taken prisoners and carried away to other countries, and the heathen will tread down Jerusalem for many years."

All these things which Jesus spoke of have happened. The Romans were the nation who came to punish Jerusalem. After them the Turks came, and they have it still; and they have built a temple to Mahomet where once God's temple stood. At this day the enemies of God are treading down Jerusalem, and the Jews are wandering about in all lands, far from their own city. Many jews are in America.

Then Jesus spoke to the four disciples about His coming at the end of the world.

He said: "One day men shall see the Son of Man coming in a cloud with great power and glory."

But He did not tell them when He would come, for He said: "No man knows what day, or what hour the Son of Man will come; nor do the angels know that day—only My Father."

He told them not to delight in eating and drinking, and things of this world; but to watch and to pray. This was His last word,—"Watch!"

Judas Betrays His Master.

During the last week of the Lord's life, He spent His nights on Mount Olivet.

On one of those nights the chief priests and scribes came together to lay a plan for killing Him.

A WATER CARRIER IN THE STREETS OF JERUSALEM.

They assembled in the country house of the high-priest. It was amongst green fields, and rocks, and hills that the house was built, just outside Jerusalem, but not the same side as Mount Olivet.

These priests and scribes were very rich and great men, they were like lords in grandeur and splendor. Yet they were the children of Satan.

They said to each other: "How can we get hold of Jesus of Nazareth?"

One said: "We cannot seize Him in the day while He is teaching in the temple; for the people are so fond of Him that they would not let us."

Another said: "We must find out where He goes at night, and suddenly come upon Him, and carry Him off in the dark."

Another said: "But who will tell us where He goes at night?"

Another said: "Let us offer a reward to any one who will come and tell us. Let us promise to give him some money."

So these wicked men made known in Jerusalem, that they would reward any one who would show them where Jesus went at night.

Judas Iscariot heard of the reward. He loved money and had often stolen some out of the disciples' purse.

A few days before he had been very angry with Mary for pouring precious ointment on the feet of Jesus, instead of selling it and giving him the money to keep. But Jesus had praised Mary.

Then Judas had grown more angry. Satan put the horrible thought into his heart, "I will promise to show the priests where my Master goes at night, and so I shall get a great deal of money."

So he went to them and said: "What will you give me, and I will deliver Him to you?"

The wicked men felt very glad when they heard Judas say these words.

They promised to give Judas thirty pieces of silver.

Judas could not tell them yet at what hour he should come to fetch them; but he promised to watch for a time when the people were not near.

Very soon the time came. The next day was Thursday. In the morning Jesus stayed at Bethany.

His disciples knew that the Lord would eat the Passover that evening in Jerusalem; but they did not know in what house He would eat it.

So they came to ask Him.

Jesus desired Peter and John to go together to the city, and to walk along the streets till they met a man carrying a jug; then to go after him, till the man went into a house, and then to ask the master of that house for a room.

He told them to say to the master of the house:

"The Lord saith unto thee, I will keep the Passover at thy house with My disciples."

Jesus told Peter and John that the master of the house would lend them a room.

It all happened as Jesus had said.

Peter and John got everything ready in that room.

The chief food at that feast was a lamb.

It was to be roasted in an oven, and it was to be eaten with bitter herbs and a sort of bread called unleavened bread.

All these things Peter and John made ready. They also procured jugs of water and cups of wine.

When all was ready they returned to Bethany, and told their Master.

The Feast of the Passover.

It was on Thursday evening that Jesus walked for the last time to Jerusalem before He died.

He had walked many times along the green fields of Olivet, but now He should tread them no more as a sorrowful man.

Peter and John showed the other Apostles in what house they had prepared the feast.

They all went up a few steps, which led to the upper room, where the supper was spread.

Jesus knew that this was the last supper He should eat with His Apostles before He was killed.

The roasted lamb was on the table, and the Lamb of God would soon be on the cross.

There were seats around the table on which Christ and His Apostles could lie down; for this was the custom of the country.

John found a place close to Jesus.

He rested his head upon the Lord's bosom as he lay.

He knew that Jesus loved him most of all.

But there was a dispute among the Apostles that evening about who should be the greatest in the kingdom of God; for they still thought that Jesus would soon become King in Jerusalem, and shine there in all His glory, as He had once shone upon the holy mountain.

Jesus told them again how wrong it was to desire to be great, instead of being willing (as He was) to serve every one.

The time to begin supper was now come.

But before the Lord broke the bread He rose, and took off His loose upper garment, and wrapt a long towel around His waist.

Next He poured water from a jug into a basin, and then stooping low upon the ground, He began to wash His disciples' feet, and to wipe them with the towel around His waist.

Some of the disciples let Him wash their feet, but when Jesus came to Peter, he said:

"Lord, dost Thou wash my feet?"

Peter thought he was not worthy to be washed by Jesus.

He thought Jesus too great and glorious to wash his feet.

Jesus answered, "What I do thou knowest not now, but thou shalt know soon."

Yet Peter still thought that his Lord ought not to stoop so very low, and he said again, "Thou shalt never wash my feet."

Then Jesus said,

"If I wash thee not, thou hast no part with me."

Peter could not bear the thought of having no part with Jesus, so he said, "Wash not my feet only, but my hands and my head."

Jesus said to all His disciples, "Ye are all clean, all but one."

That one was Judas.

He had never been washed in Christ's blood by believing in Him. Yet Jesus washed his feet, as well as the feet of all the others.

When He had done, He took off the towel and put on His own garments, and sat down to tell the disciples why He had washed their feet.

He had promised Peter to tell him the reason soon.

The reason was that He wished to set them an example of love and humility.

He plainly said, "If I, your Lord and Master, have washed your feet, ye ought to wash one another's feet. For I have given you an example, that ye should do as I have done to you."

People in this country do not wash their feet in company, because they wear shoes; but there are many things we may do for the poor and sick, if we wish to be like Christ, and to please Him.

I have heard of a child who used to pick up sticks for the poor.

I have seen children making clothes for little babies, and knitting shawls for old women.

I have known children who saved their money to buy things for the poor.

There are children who like to take broth or pudding to the cottages of the poor; to bring their old toys to sick children.

Jesus Accuses Judas of His Treachery.

After washing the disciples' feet, Jesus sat down to supper.

He then gave thanks and poured out a cup of wine, and gave it to His disciples to drink, saying:

"Share it among you."

While the disciples were eating and drinking, Jesus looked very sorrowful.

What troubled Him most at that time was—not the thought of His own pain in dying,—but the thought of Judas' wickedness.

He said, "Verily, verily, one of you shall betray me."

Now all the disciples were very sorrowful.

They all began to say, Is it I? Is it I? Is it I?

Jesus replied, "He that dippeth his hand with me in the dish, the same shall betray me."

But several hands were then dipping their morsels of bread with Jesus in the dish, so no one knew which it was that would betray his Lord.

Then Jesus said, "Woe unto that man by whom the Son of Man is betrayed. It had been good for that man if he had not been born."

Then the disciples longed still more to know whom Jesus spoke of, and they looked at each other, wondering which it could be.

Simon Peter, seeing his friend John leaning on the bosom of Jesus, made him a sign to ask Jesus, and John whispered gently to his Lord, "Lord, who is it?"

Jesus replied, "He it is to whom I shall give the sop after I have dipped it."

Then he dipped a piece of bread in the dish and gave it to Judas.

When Judas had eaten the bread Satan entered again into his heart.

Satan had entered once before into his heart to make him strong to go to the priests and agree to show them where Jesus went at night.

And now the night was come, Satan entered into him again to make him strong to do the wicked thing he had promised.

Judas had now the courage to ask, "Is it I?" He well knew what the answer would be.

Jesus answered, "It is you. Do quickly what you mean to do."

The other disciples heard these words, but no one understood them, except Judas.

They thought that the Lord desired Judas to go quickly and buy things for the other days of the feast, or else to give something to the poor; for it was Judas who used to spend the money for the rest, as he took charge of the purse.

But Judas understood what Jesus meant, and he went straight to the palace of the high-priest.

He did not go to his country-house, but to a much finer palace in Jerusalem, where the high-priest used often to sit as a judge.

How glad were the high-priest and the other priests and elders to see Judas come again, and to hear him say,

"This very night I will bring you to my Master. He is going to the garden near Olivet. I will go up to Him and kiss Him to show you which He is."

They had much to do that evening in getting a number of people together, and in finding swords and sticks for them to carry in their hands.

They were much afraid lest, after all, Jesus should get away, as He had often done before.

But now His hour was come.

Jesus Rebukes Peter.

When Judas had left the room, Jesus began to talk with His disciples very tenderly and kindly, because He wanted to comfort them in their sorrow. He said, "Little children, yet a little while I am with you; but ye cannot come where I am going."

Peter did not know where Jesus was going. He thought he could go with his Master everywhere; and he wondered at hearing Him say, "Ye cannot come."

None of the disciples quite understood what Jesus meant, but Peter was the most ready to ask the Lord anything; so he said, "Lord, whither goest Thou?"

Jesus replied, "Thou canst not follow Me now to the place whither I am going, but thou shalt follow Me some day."

Then Peter thought that Jesus must be going to die; and he said, "Why cannot I follow Thee now; I will lay down my life for Thy sake!"

It was loving of Peter to feel ready to die with Jesus; but he did not know his own heart. He thought himself much braver than he really was; so Jesus gave him this solemn warning: "Wilt thou lay down thy life for My sake? Verily, verily, I say unto you, the cock shall not crow twice before thou hast denied Me thrice."

Peter would not believe that he could do such a wicked thing as to deny his Lord. So he went on declaring more earnestly than ever, "Though I should die with Thee, yet would I not deny Thee." All the rest joined with him in declaring that they would rather die than forsake Him.

Then Jesus told them that Satan wanted them, and meant to shake them with fear that night.

Soon He turned to Peter, and said, "Simon, Simon, I have prayed for thee."

How kind it was of Jesus to pray for Peter while He was so unhappy Himself; but Jesus never forgets any of His sheep, and He watches over them, when He knows the wolf is coming.

Did Peter at last believe that he should deny his Lord? Oh, no! he felt sure he never should, even if all the rest ran away from their Master; and he said, "Lord, I am ready to go with Thee to prison and to death."

The Sacrament.

It was a sorrowful supper that Jesus ate that night with His disciples.

Toward the end of the supper Jesus took bread and blessed and brake it, and gave it to His disciples. As He gave it, He said:

"Take, eat; this is My body which is given for you."

Did the disciples understand that the Lord's body would soon be broken or bruised on the Cross? They had heard Him say long before, "I am the true bread that came down from heaven."

Jesus said also, "This do in remembrance of Me."

Jesus gave His disciples another cup of wine, besides the cup He had given them at the beginning of the supper.

As He gave the cup He thanked God, and He said to His disciples, "Drink ye all of it; for this is My blood which is shed for you for the forgiveness of sins."

PETER'S DENIAL OF CHRIST.

People now meet together to eat bread and drink wine in remembrance of Jesus, because He said, "This do in remembrance of Me."

Children are not allowed to come to the Lord's table.

There are many grown-up people who do not wish to go to this supper.

But those who love Jesus come to His supper and remember His death for their sins.

Jesus saw how sad the disciples looked, as they ate and drank, and He said, "Let not your hearts be troubled; ye believe in God, believe also in Me. In My Father's house are many mansions. I go to prepare a place for you."

It is very sweet to know that there is so much room in God's house above. There is a mansion, or place for every one who loves Jesus."

The disciples did not love one another much, though they loved their Lord.

They often disputed together who should be the greatest in God's kingdom.

Jesus told them how much He loved them. He said, "As the Father hath loved Me, so have I loved you." What great love the Father has to His Son! Such love Jesus has for us. He has shown it by dying for us. Jesus then said to His disciples, "This is my commandment, that ye love one another as I have loved you." This is the way to please Jesus, to love one another.

Then Jesus made a great promise to His disciples. He had been a Comforter to them while He was with them, and now He said, "I will send you another Comforter."

This Comforter was the Holy Ghost.

It is He who changes men's hearts, and makes them holy like Jesus, and fills them with happiness.

After making this great promise Jesus rose up from the supper and went down into the street. He was followed by His disciples, and He talked to them as they went along that evening. They passed through the streets for three miles.

During this last walk Jesus prayed for the last time with His disciples. He lifted up His eyes and spoke to His Father in heaven, while His disciples listened.

He prayed for them all—except Judas. For him He could not pray, because He knew he would be lost; but for all the rest He prayed that they might be with Him in glory.

After this long, last prayer, they passed over the bridge that led across the narrow stream of Kedron; and they reached the gate of Gethsemane. This was a garden to which Jesus had often gone in past days, and so Judas knew the place, and could lead the enemies to the spot.

The Agony in the Garden.

Jesus entered the garden of Gethsemane in the evening.

There were olive-trees in the garden.

He said to eight of his disciples:

"Sit here, while I go and pray a little further on."

There were now only three disciples with Him. They were Peter, with the two brothers, James and John.

He took these three with Him further on in the garden. They were His favorite disciples. They had once seen His glory on the mount. Now they were to see His agony in the garden.

While He was walking with them He felt very sorrowful. It was our sins that made Him feel so very, very sad.

He told His three friends how He felt; and He asked them to stay near Him and watch with Him and pray.

Then He left them, and went a little further on, and threw Himself down on His knees, bending His face toward the ground, and He began to pray.

Oh, how earnestly He prayed.

He said, "O My Father, if Thou be willing, take away this cup from Me! Yet not My will, but Thine be done!"

What was the cup He spoke of?

It was the cup of sorrow for our sins; and no one can tell how very bitter it was to drink; but the Father could not take it away; for He had promised that His Son should drink it; and His Son had promised long ago to drink it, and He could not break His word.

But who is this coming down from heaven, so bright and so glorious? It is an angel. He comes to comfort his Lord.

The angel had once seen his Lord in glory, and now He sees Him groaning upon the ground, and bathed in His own blood; for Jesus was in so great an agony of pain, that the blood came out of His skin, and fell down in great drops upon the cold earth. But still He prayed—the more pain He felt, the more He prayed.

The angel did not stay long with his suffering Lord.

Jesus rose up from prayer and went back to the three disciples, but He found them fast asleep.

They awoke when He came. Jesus spoke first to Peter, and said:

"Simon, why sleepest thou? Couldest thou not watch with Me one hour?"

Jesus wanted Peter to remember how he had promised to die with Him, and never to deny Him.

He told all three to watch and pray, and He went away again.

He spoke the same words in His prayer as before, and then returned to His three disciples, and found them asleep again.

When He spoke to them they did not know what to answer.

Then Jesus went away the third time and prayed again; and then returned and found the three disciples again asleep.

But this time Jesus did not tell them to watch, for He knew that His enemies were coming immediately to seize Him. So He said to the three disciples:

"The hour is come. Rise up, let us go; he that betrayeth Me is at hand."

And so indeed he was. Judas came up to his Lord, and kissed Him, as if he were pleased to find Him.

Jesus knew that he kissed Him to show the enemies which He was of the four, and He said:

"Judas, betrayest thou the Son of Man with a kiss?"

Just behind this wicked man there came a great multitude. They brought with them lanterns, swords, and great sticks. It was the chief priests and Pharisees who had sent these men to

ANGELS MINISTERING TO JESUS.

seize Jesus. Jesus went to meet His enemies, and said, "Whom do you seek?" They answered, "Jesus of Nazareth."

He replied, "I am He!"

Instantly they all went backward and fell to the ground; Judas and all the rest. Nor would they have ever risen up again, if Jesus had not permitted them to do so. But He did let them rise, and they arose as bold and hard as before they fell.

Again Jesus said: "Whom do ye seek?"

Again they replied, "Jesus of Nazareth."

Jesus answered, "I have told you that I am He." This time the men did not fall to the ground, but Jesus let them seize hold of Him, only He said first, "If you seek Me, let these go their way."

Whom did Jesus mean by *these?*

He meant the three disciples who were with Him. He asked that they might be allowed to go free. How kind to think of them in this hour of terror!

The enemies were so well pleased to get hold of Jesus that they did not mind letting the disciples escape. They held Him very fast that He might not get away.

Peter Draws His Sword in Defence of His Master.

Peter might have run away when the multitude laid hold of his Master; but he wished to be brave and to stay and fight for Him.

Jesus had allowed His apostles to take swords with them. They had only two between them, and Peter had one of these. He drew this sword out of its sheath, and struck a blow with it on a man who was seizing his Master. That man's name was Malchus, and he was the servant of the high-priest.

Peter no doubt wanted to cut the man's head in two, but all he was able to do was to cut off his right ear.

Peter might have got into much trouble for doing this, had not his Master stretched out His hand, and healed the man. This was the last use Jesus made of His hands before they were bound, and this was his last miracle—healing an enemy.

He said to Peter: "Put up thy sword in its sheath. Do you not know that if I were to pray to My Father He would send a great many angels to deliver Me? But the cup which My Father hath given Me, shall I not drink it?"

Then Jesus spake to His enemies and said: "Are you come out as against a thief, with swords and staves to take Me? Why did you not seize Me when I sat daily with you in the temple teaching?"

Jesus knew well the reason why they took Him now. It was because the hour was come for Satan to do his will, and to fight against Jesus.

Now the enemies bind the blessed hands which had just healed the servant, and now they lead the Lamb of God to the slaughter.

The way was very long from the garden to the palace of the high-priest. It was his great hall of judgment, and not the house where he lived; for *that* was in the country.

The chief priests and Pharisees did not sleep that night. They were all waiting for the blessed Lamb to be brought. Like hungry wolves, they thirsted for His blood.

The tramping of feet is heard in the street, and the murmuring of voices. Jesus is led into the great hall where the cruel men are assembled.

Peter saw the men lead his Master into the palace, and he longed to follow Him.

But how should he get in?

He saw his friend John go in with Jesus—for the woman who kept the door knew that John was an acquaintance of the high-priest. But poor Peter stood outside, fearing he should never get in.

Soon John came back and said to Peter:

"I have spoken to the woman at the door, and she will let you in."

Then Peter went in with John. They went into a great hall full of servants. Jesus was not in that room. He was in another room standing before His cruel judges—the priests and the Pharisees.

It was cold in the hall that night, and the servants had lighted a fire in the middle of the room, and were standing near it warming themselves.

Peter went to the fire and stood and warmed himself.

408   MY MOTHER'S BIBLE STORIES.

He wanted to know what would become of his Lord, and he hoped that no one would find out who he was; for he was afraid of being punished for being a disciple of Jesus.

He had quite forgotten all he had said that night about dying with Jesus.

The Trial and Mockery of Jesus.

While Peter was warming himself by the fire, Jesus was standing before his judges.

The high-priest Caiaphas was His chief judge.

How sad were the looks of the Son of Man that night! His body had been bathed in blood, His knees were weak and weary, and His face was worn by grief, and His eyes swollen by weeping. There never was a man so changed by sorrow. But His enemies felt no pity.

The high-priest asked Him, "What have you taught the people?"

Jesus answered, "I have always taught in the synagogues and in the temple, and those who heard Me know what I said. Why askest thou Me? Ask them who heard Me."

This was a right answer to make, for Jesus knew that the high-priest would not believe what He said. Yet a servant who stood by was so cruel as to strike Jesus with the palm of his hand, and to say, "Why do you answer the high-priest so?"

The high-priest ought to have commanded that servant to go out; but he was pleased with him for his wicked blow.

Jesus meekly answered, "If I have spoken wrong, tell Me what it is; but if I have spoken right, why do you strike Me?"

A great many persons now came into the room to witness against Jesus by saying they had heard Him speak wickedly about God and the temple. But these witnesses did not speak the truth, for one said one thing, and another just the contrary. It was a law of the Jews that witnesses were not to be believed unless two agreed in saying the same thing.

When the witnesses had done speaking, the high-priest stood up and said to Jesus,—

"What do you answer to the accusations of these men?"

But Jesus answered nothing.

Then the high-priest said very earnestly, "I entreat Thee to tell us whether Thou art the Son of God."

Jesus answered, "I am."

When Jesus had spoken these words, there was great confusion and noise in the place; for the high-priest pretended to be so unhappy that he tore his clothes; and all the priests and Pharisees cried out, "He deserves to die."

They would have liked to stone him to death that moment; but the Jews were not allowed to put people to death. The Romans had conquered the Jews and had sent a Roman judge to Jerusalem. It was the Roman judge who had the power to have people put to death.

But where was the Roman judge that night? He was asleep in his bed, for it was now the middle of the night. The Roman judge would not sit on his seat to judge till the morning came. So there were many hours for Jesus to wait before He could be taken before that judge. The name of that judge was Pontius Pilate.

And what became of Jesus during the rest of the night?

He was tormented by the servants who had charge of Him.

They knew that people called Him a prophet, so they mocked Him by putting a cloth over His eyes and then striking Him, and calling out, "Prophesy, who struck Thee?"

What horrid shouts of laughter must have filled the place as they mocked Him!

They did worse still; they were so bold and brutal as to spit in His face.

Yet not one angry word or look did He return for all these insults. He bore all like the Lamb of God.

Let us love Him who bore the mockings of that night for our sakes; and let us be ready to be mocked for His sake—if wicked men should do so—and let us copy His meekness and His patience.

Peter Denies His Master.

Peter was now in the hall of the palace.

At first he stood by the fire and warmed himself, and afterward he sat down among the servants.

While he was there the maid who kept the door came up to him, and fixed her eyes upon him (as if she wished to be sure that she made no mistake), and then she said to the servants around: "This man was also with Him." But Peter said, "Woman, I know Him not."

The other servants believed the woman, and asked him, "Art not thou one of His disciples?"

One of the servants felt certain that he was (for this man was a relation of Malchus, whose ear Peter cut off); and he said, "Did not I see thee in the garden with Jesus?"

Peter denied most positively that he knew anything about Jesus.

He now thought it would be best to go into the porch (or door-way) where no one might notice him. As he was going there, the cock crew. But this first crowing of the cock did not make Peter remember what his Lord had said.

He had now denied Him once, for though he had spoken to several people, all he had said was nearly at the same time.

Peter hoped not to be noticed in the porch; but he was disappointed; for while he was there, both a man and a maid declared he was one of the disciples; and Peter grew so frightened that he did more than deny his Lord; he swore he did not know Him.

As Peter found that he was noticed even in the porch, he thought he might as well return to the hall in the palace.

There a dreadful sight met his eyes.

His Lord was in the midst of the servants, being mocked, beaten, and blindfolded.

Peter was more than ever afraid lest he should be seized by the servants; so he tried to appear as if he did not care for his

Lord, though in his heart he loved Him so fondly. He began to talk away, as if he were not sorry; but his way of talking made the servants think he came from Galilee. Most of the disciples came from Galilee, and the people in Galilee spoke in a different tone of voice from those in Jerusalem.

The servants thought that as Peter came from Galilee, he might be a disciple of Jesus; and they said to him, "Surely, you are a Galilean, for your way of speaking betrays you."

Peter saw that they thought he was a disciple, so he denied again that he knew Jesus. This was his third denial. Now Peter cursed as well as swore.

In cursing, men wish all manner of harm to come upon themselves, if what they say is not true.

In the midst of this swearing and cursing, Peter heard the cock crow.

He did notice this second crowing. At the same moment he looked toward the place where Jesus was standing among the servants, being mocked, beaten, and spit upon.

The Lord, who had heard everything, turned round and looked upon Peter.

It was a look that made him remember that his Lord had said: "Before the cock crow twice, thou shalt deny Me thrice." It was a look that went to Peter's heart—it was a look so full of love and sorrow!

Peter could not stand that look, and he went out into the porch again. He went there, not to hide himself, but to weep. He wept most bitter tears as he thought of what he had said. He felt he had been so ungrateful to his Saviour.—so mean,—so cowardly!

How could he hope ever to be forgiven!

If he had prayed in the garden, this might not have happened!

Pontius Pilate.

Jesus spent one sad night in the high-priest's palace.

The next place to which He was taken was the Jewish council or Sanhedrim.

There were seventy-two men who met together very often to judge people by the law of the Jews, but they had not the power to put any one to death.

The seventy-two men were called honorable councillors.

The high-priest was their chief.

As soon as it was morning, very early, the honorable councillors came together to sit as judges in a great hall.

Jesus was led to this great hall near the temple. It was called the hall of the Sanhedrim.

Jesus had to pass through many streets before he reached the temple gate. He passed through the temple courts, and entered the great hall of the Sanhedrim.

How pale, how weary he must have looked as He stood before His seventy-two judges! His great enemy, Caiaphas the high-priest, was one of the councillors.

But Jesus had now His hands unbound; it may be that the servants who mocked Him had unbound them.

The council asked Him the same question as before, "Art Thou the Son of God?"

Jesus gave the same answer, "I am."

Then the council burst into a rage, and said, " Now we have heard Him say with His own mouth that He is the Son of God."

So they condemned Jesus to death.

Thus He was twice condemned by the Jews; first in the palace of Caiaphas, and then in the hall of the Sanhedrim.

The Jews now determined to bring Him to the Roman judge, Pontius Pilate, and to have Him put to death.

They thought it would be best to tell Pilate that Jesus had declared Himself a King, and would not obey the great king at Rome.

This was their sly plan. For they thought that as Pilate was a heathen, he would not punish Jesus for saying He was the Son of God.

They bound again the hands of Jesus, and then led Him to the Roman judgment hall.

A great crowd came with the prisoner. Most of the councillors and the chief priests with a multitude of servants hurried through the streets about seven in the morning.

The last sorrowful day of our Lord's life on earth was now begun.

Death of Judas the Traitor.

Judas heard that Jesus had been condemned by the Sanhedrim near the temple.

He had hoped that Jesus would not be condemned, for he did not wish Him to be killed.

Why then had he betrayed Him to His enemies? To get money.

The love of money led him to do the worst deed that was ever committed.

But could Judas enjoy his money now he had got it?

No! he wished to get rid of it, for he could not look at it without thinking of his wickedness.

But what could he do with it?

He might have thrown it away. That would not do, for he wanted the priests to know how he hated their money.

He thought he would return it to the chief priests and elders, who had given it to him.

He knew where to find them. Some were still in their hall near the temple,—the hall of the Sanhedrim.

Judas went there and found some of the priests.

He offered them the money, saying:

"I have sinned; for I have betrayed the innocent blood."

But they would not take it.

They were not sorry for Judas, nor ashamed of their own wickedness.

They said, "What is that to us?"

Yet they could not take the money, because they knew it had been given to get a man killed, and so it was the price of blood.

As the priests would not put out their hands to receive the thirty pieces of silver, Judas threw them on the floor, and went away. The priests picked up the money, and then talked together.

"What shall we do with these silver pieces?" said they. "We cannot put them into the treasury to buy sacrifices, because they are the price of blood," said one. "What shall we do, then?" said another.

At last one said, "We want a place to bury strangers in; for we cannot bury Gentiles with our own people the Jews. There is a field to be sold—shall we buy it?"

"Do you mean," said another, "the potter's field, that is full of holes, out of which clay has been dug to make jars and jugs?"

"Yes," said one; "it is the potter's field that I mean."

So they made haste to buy that field. It used to be called the potter's field, but now it had another name given to it,—"The Field of Blood," because it was bought with the price of blood.

There was another reason for the horrible name. In that field Judas shed his own blood. He went to the field, tied a rope around his neck and hanged himself.

We believe that he fastened this rope to a branch of a tree, and that the branch broke, and let Judas fall down a steep place; for we know that he fell headlong, and that his bowels gushed out.

Every one in Jerusalem heard of his horrible death, and called the place where he died, "The Field of Blood."

Satan brought Judas to this miserable end by tempting him to sin, and then by driving him to despair. Judas ought to have sought forgiveness for his horrible crime; but he had no faith, and he perished for ever. He went to his own place, even Satan's place, because he was Satan's child. His father's place was his own place.

Pilate Tries to Save the Life of Jesus.

The time has now come for Jesus to be brought before the great Roman judge, Pontius Pilate.

He had already been twice judged, first in the palace of the high-priest, and next in the hall of the Sanhedrim.

But in those places it was Jews who judged Him. He was now going to be judged by a Gentile. This Gentile was a heathen. He had been sent to Jerusalem by the great king at Rome, called Cæsar, and he had the power to have people put to death, if he chose to do so.

The Jews were very eager to have Jesus killed, and that was the reason they brought him to Pontius Pilate.

They brought Him with His hands bound, as a prisoner (for His hands had been unbound while He was mocked by the servants).

A great many priests and councillors accompanied Jesus through the courts of the temple to the door of the judgment-hall close by.

But when they arrived at the door they stopped and would not go in. The reason was that the judgment-hall belonged to heathens; and the Jews thought that if they entered a heathen place their bodies would become unholy, and that they should not be able to keep the Passover during the seven days that it lasted.

How careful these men were of their bodies; but they never thought about their souls.

When Pilate was told that the Jews would not come in, he went out to speak to them.

There he saw the meek prisoner standing. Of all the prisoners he had ever seen, he had never seen one like the gentle Jesus.

Pilate asked the Jews, "What have you to say against this man?"

They replied, "If He were not a bad man, we should not bring Him to you."

Pilate felt such pity for the prisoner that he did not like to judge Him; so he said, "Take Him away and judge Him yourselves."

They answered, "We are not allowed to put any one to death."

Then they began to accuse the innocent prisoner of all kinds of crimes.

One said, "He goes about the country setting people against the great King Cæsar, at Rome."

Another said, "He tells every one that He Himself is our king."

As soon as Pilate heard that Jesus said He was a king, he wanted to speak to Him alone.

So he went back to his judgment-hall, and desired his servants to bring Jesus in.

When He was brought, Pilate said, "Art Thou the King of the Jews?" Jesus answered, "I am."

Then Jesus told Pilate that He was not like the kings of this world, who have soldiers to fight for them, but that He was a king who taught people the truth.

Pilate wondered at His way of speaking, and he went out of the hall and said to the chief priests, "I find no fault in this man."

This speech made the Jews fiercer than ever; and they went on accusing Jesus of doing a great deal of harm.

"He has gone about the whole land speaking against Cæsar: He began by setting the people in Galilee against Cæsar, and now he is come here."

As soon as Pilate heard that word "Galilee," he remembered that Herod was the Governor of Galilee, and that Herod was now in Jerusalem.

Pilate said, "As the prisoner comes from Galilee, I will send Him to Herod, the Governor of Galilee." Pilate did not want to condemn Jesus; he wanted some one else to do it. That was his reason for sending Him to Herod.

Jesus was led along the streets to Herod's palace. He had to go a great way along the streets,—all faint and weary as He was.

Herod's palace was the grandest house in Jerusalem.

Herod was exceedingly glad when he heard that Jesus was come; for he had long wanted to see Him.

A great while ago he had heard of His miracles, and had thought He was John the Baptist risen from the dead.

Now he hoped to see whether He really was John the Baptist, and he hoped to see Him do a miracle (for John had never done any miracles).

Jesus was led into the room amongst a crowd of priests and scribes.

Herod asked Him a great many questions. Perhaps he asked Him whether He was John the Baptist,—but this we do not know.

He was much disappointed at getting no answers from Jesus.

The priests and the scribes stood near—accusing Him of having done many wicked things: but Jesus answered them nothing.

Then Herod and his soldiers mocked Him and dressed Him up in a white shining robe, and sent Him back to the judgment-hall.

Pilate was sorry to see Him return, for he had hoped that Herod would have done something to Him, and that he should see Him no more.

The Jews Ask for the Release of a Robber.

Pilate was surprised to see Jesus so meek and so silent, while His enemies were so fierce and so violent. He was very anxious to set Him free, and he thought of a plan that he hoped would succeed.

It was the custom for the Governor every year at the Passover to ask the Jews what prisoner he should release.

He knew that the chief priests and Pharisees hated Jesus, but he hoped that the people still admired Him for His miracles.

So he called all the people together in the street, and said, "Which shall I release to you—Barabbas or Jesus?"

This Barabbas was a very bad man.

He had refused to obey Cæsar, and he had committed robbery and murder.

Pilate tried to persuade the people to ask for Jesus, saying, "Shall not I release unto you the King of the Jews?"

The chief priests heard what Pilate said, and went about among the people, trying to set them against Jesus and to get them to ask for Barabbas.

While they were thus employed, Pilate ascended his judgment seat in the street, and sat down, waiting for the people's answer.

At that moment a messenger appeared. He came from Pilate's wife.

"Do nothing against the just man," said she, "for I have been very unhappy about Him last night in a dream."

Pilate when he heard of the dream was still more anxious not to condemn Jesus.

He called every one together, priests as well as people, and said, "Which of the two shall I release?"

Then arose the horrible yell of ten thousand voices, saying, "Barabbas!"

But Pilate still would not yield. "What, then, shall I do with Jesus?" he said.

Another burst of wicked voices, and a cry,—"Crucify Him! Crucify Him!"

Pilate tried once more to melt those cruel hearts, and asked, "What evil hath He done? I have not found that He deserves to die. Let me beat Him and set Him free."

But the priests and the people answered, with still louder voices:

"Crucify Him!"

Pilate felt that it would be very wicked to condemn Jesus when he had done nothing.

So he took some water in a basin, and washed his hands before all the people, saying, "I am innocent of the blood of this just person."

But was he innocent? and could water wash out the stain of guilt on his heart?

No! he ought rather to have let the people and the priests tear him in pieces than to condemn an innocent person.

The people cried out, "His blood be upon us and upon our children."

Then Pilate ordered Barabbas to be released, and gave up Jesus to be crucified.

THE JEWS REJECT CHRIST.

The Roman Soldiers Mock Jesus.

Jesus was now condemned to be crucified. But before He was led out to His cross He was scourged.

It was the cruel custom of the Romans to scourge before they crucified.

So Jesus was fastened to a post by both His hands, and then His back was scourged by Roman soldiers.

A scourge was far worse than a whip or a stick; for it was made of knotted ropes and sharp little bits of the bones of oxen.

Each stroke of the scourge brought blood, and left a bleeding stripe upon the back.

Many, many strokes were given by the fierce soldiers—as many as could be given—without killing the fainting prisoner.

When He had been scourged, He was taken by the soldiers into the great judgment-hall.

Six hundred soldiers crowded around the bleeding and trembling sufferer. They had no pity for His bleeding stripes. Their delight was in savage mockery.

They had heard Him called "The King of the Jews," and they thought it absurd and laughable that one so poor should be a king.

So they set about mocking Him.

They pulled off His blood-stained clothes, and dressed Him in purple and scarlet garments, such as kings wear.

They took prickly branches or thorns and plaited a crown, and placed it on His head, and put a reed in His hand for a sceptre.

Then they kneeled before Him, and said, "Hail (or rejoice), King of the Jews."

Then they spat upon His face, and they took the reed and beat Him on the head (to make the thorns pierce Him more); and they struck Him with their hands.

Pilate found Jesus in the hall, bearing this cruel treatment without a murmur, and he thought it would melt the hearts of His cruel enemies if they could see Him as He then looked.

So he went out to the people and desired Jesus to be brought forth for them all to see.

Jesus came, wearing the crown of thorns and the purple robe.

Pilate showed Him to the multitude, and said, "Behold the Man!"

The people might perhaps have pitied their Saviour, but the chief priests and scribes cried louder than ever, "Crucify Him!"

Pilate answered, "I find no fault in Him. Take Him and crucify Him yourselves."

Then the Jews replied, "He ought to die, because He made Himself the Son of God."

Pilate had not been told this before, and he was more than ever afraid.

He went on trying every way to release Jesus.

But when he said, "Behold your King," the Jews answered, "Away with Him! Crucify Him!"

"Shall I crucify your King?" asked Pilate.

The chief priests replied, "We have no king but Cæsar."

Pilate, seeing that he could not save Jesus, took Him back into the hall.

There the soldiers stripped Him of His kingly garments, and put on His own raiment; and then they led Him away to be crucified.

The Crucifixion.

Now Jesus set out on His last earthly journey.

His weak body was covered with bruises, blood, and stripes.

He had passed the night without sleep or food; He had been hurried about many miles along the streets; He had been mocked and tormented in four places; and had borne the abuse of men and the burden of our sins.

He was now brought so low that He could hardly drag Himself along; yet the soldiers in their cruelty placed upon His bleeding shoulders His heavy cross.

He would have been crushed by these two great pieces of wood, and He would have died by the way, if His enemies had not looked out for some one to help Him.

They were much too proud to bear the cross themselves; but they met a man named Simon coming up from the country to Jerusalem, and they laid hold on him, and made him bear the cross after Jesus. Simon did not know then what an honor it was to bear the cross.

There was not an angel in heaven who would not have flown down with joy to carry that cruel cross, to relieve Jesus of the weight.

There was a troop of women among the crowd. They came weeping along the way. Jesus heard their cries, and spoke tenderly to them.

He said, " Daughters of Jerusalem, weep not for Me, but weep for yourselves and for your children, for the days are coming when your children will say to the mountains, Fall on us, and to the hills, Cover us."

A day was coming when the Jews would wish to be crushed under mountains sooner than bear their enemies' cruelty.

Two prisoners were led with Jesus to be crucified. They were thieves, and they had done many wicked things.

The immense multitude passed with Jesus through the gate of Jerusalem.

It was the gate just on the opposite side to Mount Olivet and Gethsemane.

On this side there was a place called Golgotha or Calvary.

These words both mean the same thing, " The place of a skull."

It was the place of death, in the midst of fields and gardens.

Here they stopped. The soldiers gave Jesus a cup of wine mixed with a bitter stuff called gall, but He only tasted it, and refused to drink it.

Then they stripped Him of His clothes, which once before they had taken off when they mocked Him.

They laid the cross upon the ground and stretched the Lord upon it. Four soldiers hammered nails into His hands and feet, to fasten Him to the cross; then they lifted up that heavy cross, and with a violent jerk placed one end in a hole in the ground.

The thieves were treated in the same way. The cross of Jesus was in the midst between the crosses of the thieves. Pilate had

THE CRUCIFIXION.

Now there stood by the cross of Jesus his mother, and his mother's sister, Mary the wife of Cleophas, and Mary Magdalene. When Jesus therefore saw his mother, and the disciples standing by, whom he loved, he saith unto his mother, Woman, behold thy son!—ST. JOHN xix: 25, 26.

written these words on a label, and had desired it to be placed over the head of Jesus: "THIS IS THE KING OF THE JEWS."

The Jews read this writing as they passed by.

The chief priests were so much displeased that they said to Pilate, "Why did you write 'The King of the Jews?' You ought to have written, 'He *said* He was the King of the Jews.'"

But Pilate replied, "What I have written I have written."

Pilate meant that he would not change what he had written; for he really believed that Jesus was a king, though he had not the courage to keep to the truth, and to die rather than condemn the innocent.

The Agony on the Cross.

Before the Lord was stretched upon the cross, the soldiers stripped Him of His clothes.

There was His long tunic that He had worn close to His body. This must have been stained with bloody sweat. The four soldiers who nailed His hands and feet to the cross tore the tunic into four parts, and each soldier took one.

Then there was His upper garment, called His coat or vesture; but it was more like a cloak than a coat.

This vesture was a very curious garment, for it was made of one piece, and it had no seam or joining. Perhaps some of those women who loved Him had woven it for Him.

The soldiers thought it would be a pity to tear this valuable garment; so they said to each other, "Let us not tear it, but let us cast lots for it."

We are not told in what way they cast lots. Nor do we know what the soldier who got the garment did with it. Perhaps he wore it himself. We shall never see it, because it has been worn out long ago and thrown away.

The Lord had nothing in this world but His clothes, for He was very poor. Even His clothes were taken from Him before He died.

It was nine in the morning when He was crucified.

The first word He spoke on the cross was a prayer to His Father. It was a prayer for His murderers.

"Father, forgive them, for they know not what they do."

What love it showed to pray for those who had just nailed Him to the cross; and for all who were now mocking Him!

Calvary was very near Jerusalem, and numbers of people were always passing by.

These people mocked Jesus as they passed by.

THE FRIENDS OF JESUS WATCHING THE PROCESSION TO THE CROSS.

The soldiers mocked Him. The rulers mocked Him. The priests mocked Him. Even the thieves mocked Him.

And what did these mockers say? They said, "If Thou be the Son of God come down from the cross."

The mockers wagged their heads and pouted out their lips, to show how much they despised the crucified Saviour.

All this while, Jesus never answered a word to all the abuse and railing of the multitude.

One thief left off mocking and began to pray. He could not kneel, he could not turn his head towards Jesus, he could not lift up his hands in prayer, he could only speak; and this was his prayer:

"Lord, remember me when Thou comest into Thy Kingdom."

That thief had faith to believe that Jesus was a king and would come one day to reign in glory.

Jesus answered, "Verily, I say unto thee, this day shalt thou be with Me in Paradise."

He did not let the thief wait for the day of His coming again. He promised to make him happy that very day by taking him to Paradise, where He Himself was going very soon.

Death of Jesus.

There stood by the cross of Jesus a few of His friends. Some of these were women. Three had the name of Mary.

First, there was Mary the mother of Jesus; next, there was Mary the mother of the two Apostles, James and Jude; and last of all there was Mary Magdalene, out of whom the Lord had once cast seven devils.

These three Marys loved Jesus exceedingly.

His mother Mary had loved Him the longest, and now she felt grief pierce her heart like a sword (as old Simeon had said it would, when Jesus was a babe).

By the side of this blessed Mary stood the most beloved apostle, John. Jesus looked down from His cross upon His mother.

AT THE FOOT OF THE CROSS.

He felt how lonely she would be when He was gone (as her husband Joseph must now have been dead). He knew that John would be as kind as a son to her. So He said to His mother, while He looked towards John, "Behold thy Son."

And He said to John, "Behold thy mother."

John understood that the Lord had given him His own mother to be his mother, and so he took her afterwards to his own home that he might take care of her.

It was now twelve o'clock in the day, when the sun is generally very hot and bright. But in a moment all the brightness was turned into darkness. This darkness hid the face of the Son of God from His enemies. For three hours that blessed face was hid from the sight of men.

Then a voice was heard crying out in an agony of grief, "My God, My God, why hast Thou forsaken Me?"

It was the voice of Jesus, speaking to His Father.

Had His Father really forsaken Him? No; He was always with His well-beloved Son; but He seemed to hide His face, because Jesus was then bearing our sins. Soon He spoke again, saying, "I thirst."

THE BASIN OF VINEGAR.

Pain of body makes people thirsty, and Jesus was so full of pain.

There was a basin of vinegar standing near, for the soldiers to drink. A soldier, who heard the Saviour's cry, dipped a sponge into the vinegar, and stuck it on a branch of hyssop at the end of a reed, and in this way made it reach up to His lips.

But this vinegar was mixed with bitter stuff called gall, and the Saviour only tasted it, and then cried out, "It is finished."

The last words of Jesus were, "Father, into Thy hands I commend My spirit." He did not feel at the last as if God had forsaken Him. Then He bowed His head and died. It was three o'clock in the afternoon.

Jesus had been six hours hanging on that cross in agony
Now all His pain was over, and His joy was begun.

All sinners may come to Jesus and be saved; for Jesus came into the world to save sinners.

Dear children, He loves you. Go to Him, and thank Him for dying for you. He will hear your little prayer and He will save you.

The Seven Sayings of Jesus on the Cross.

I.

Jesus prayed for His murderers.

Father, forgive them, for they know not what they do.

II.

He saved a penitent.

To-day shalt thou be with Me in Paradise.

III.

He gave His mother to John.

Behold thy son! Behold thy mother!

_{These three sayings were about others.}
_{The last four sayings were about himself.}

IV.

He complained to God of His spirit's agony.

My God, My God, why hast Thou forsaken Me?

V.

He complained to men of His bodily pain.

I thirst.

VI.

He gave up His work to His Father.

It is finished.

VII.

He gave up Himself to His Father.

Father, into Thy hands I commend My spirit.

"*Truly, This Was the Son of God.*"

There were soldiers standing close to the cross when Jesus died. They heard His last cry to His Father; they saw Him bow His head and die; and they felt the shaking of the earth, and they trembled at the sudden darkness; and at length they cried out, "Truly, this was the Son of God."

The chief, or captain, of these soldiers was called a centurion. He was much struck by all he saw, and he said, "Certainly this was a righteous man." Many people who had come to look at Jesus as He died, went home beating their breasts with grief. They had much to be sorry for, when they remembered the cruel words they had spoken.

The women who loved Jesus had stood a good way off, and had heard His dying words. Now they gazed upon His dead body with hearts full of love and grief. Among these women were Mary Magdalene, and Mary (the mother of James and Jude), and Salome (the mother of James and John). There were many more besides, who had come with Jesus from Galilee, and who had shared their food with Him.

One of the soldiers had a spear in his hand; and he pushed the sharp point into the side of the Saviour's body. Blood and water flowed out of the cruel wound.

The beloved John was standing near the cross when his Lord was pierced; and he noticed it particularly because his heart had been washed in water and blood by believing in Jesus.

Do you know the verse—

>Rock of ages, cleft for me,
>Let me hide myself in Thee.
>Let the water and the blood,
>From Thy riven side which flowed,
>Be of sin the double cure,
>Cleanse me from its guilt and power.

Jesus was like the rock which Moses struck that water might flow out of it.

JESUS GIVETH THE WATER OF LIFE. (431)

Joseph of Arimathea.

After the soldier had pierced Jesus, a good man named Joseph came and begged the body, that he might give it a decent burial.

He was not a poor man; for if he had been poor he would not have been allowed to have the body. He was a very great and rich man and was called Joseph of Arimathea, because that was his native place.

He was counted a very honorable man, and was one of the seventy councillors.

Most of these seventy councillors hated Jesus, but Joseph loved Him. He did not join with the councillors in condemning Jesus in the morning, but did all he could to save him.

Joseph was much grieved when Jesus was crucified. He thought to himself, " I should like to get His body, and bury it in my garden, in a grave that I have had made for myself when I die." This was a kind thought. Joseph went quickly to ask Pilate to let him have the dead body.

Pilate was surprised to hear that Jesus was dead so soon, for people often live for several days when nailed upon the cross.

Pilate could hardly believe that Jesus was dead. He had forgotten perhaps that he had given the Jews leave to break His legs. But Jesus had died before the cruel soldiers came.

Pilate called for the centurion, who had taken the other soldiers to the cross.

" Is Jesus really dead? " said Pilate.

" Oh, yes," said the centurion. " He was dead when we came to the cross, and since then His body has been pierced."

Then Pilate told Joseph he might have the dead body. How glad Joseph was to get it! he was in great haste to bury it, before the sun set that evening: for the Sabbath began on Friday evening, and lasted till Saturday evening. Joseph made great haste to buy fine linen to wrap the body in.

A friend came with him to fetch the Saviour's body. This friend's name was Nicodemus.

He was one of the honorable councillors, and he was good like Joseph. Once he had been ashamed of Jesus, and had come to Him by night, when no one could see him; but now he was not ashamed, and he came boldly with Joseph to take away the beloved body; and he brought with him a quantity of sweet-smelling spices. The two friends, Joseph and Nicodemus, spread

THE WOMEN AT THE TOMB OF JESUS.

And very early in the morning, the first day of the week, they came unto the sepulchre at the rising of the sun.—ST. LUKE xvi: 2.

the sweet spices in the linen cloth, and wrapped their dear Lord in the white sheet.

Then they carried the precious burden to the garden, and laid it in Joseph's new tomb, where he himself had meant to be buried when he died; but no one had ever yet been laid there. The tomb was quite sweet and clean. It had been hewn out of a rock, and it was like a little room, and there were steps to go down into it.

In that clean quiet place, the friends laid the body of their Lord. They must have had servants to help them; for they rolled a very great stone to the mouth of the little cave. That stone was to keep out all who would hurt the precious body.

The women who loved Jesus saw all that was done. What joy they must have felt when they saw the two rich men show such respect to their dead Master!

They observed where He was laid, and they made up their minds to come again to anoint Him with more sweet ointment.

The Women and the Angel at the Tomb of Jesus.

Very early on Sunday morning, while it was still a little dark, some women entered Joseph's garden. These women carried jars in their arms full of the ointment which they had made in the night.

They were going to the tomb of Jesus to look for His dead body, and to spread the sweet ointment over it.

One of them was named Salome; she was the mother of the beloved John and of his brother James. Another of these women was Mary, the mother of two of the Apostles, named James and Jude. The other woman was also named Mary—and she was called Mary Magdalene. She loved her Lord very much, for He had been kind to her, and healed her of a cruel sickness.

As they went along, they talked about the tomb. One said to the other, "Did you see what a great stone was rolled to the door of the cave? How shall we get in, for all of us together would not be able to roll away so very large a stone?"

You see how much troubled they were about the stone. What would they have said, if they had known about the soldiers who had been watching all night round the tomb? They would have been more troubled than they were about the stone; but they did not know that soldiers had been stationed there.

Soon they came near the tomb; and then they saw that the stone was rolled away; by this time the soldiers also were all gone.

𝔍esus said "And I, if I be lifted up from the earth, shall draw all men unto me."

John xii. 32.

THE CROSS OF CHRIST.	(435)

Just before the women came a wonderful thing had happened.

There had been a great earthquake, and an angel had come from heaven and rolled away the stone, and sat upon it, and the Lord had risen from His grave.

The soldiers were so terrified that they had fallen down on the earth, and had lain there as if they had been dead; but presently they had strength to get up, and to run quickly to Jerusalem, to tell what had happened.

The three women knew nothing about all this.

They were afraid when they saw the stone was rolled away; for they thought the Pharisees had done it, and had stolen the Lord's body. But they went bravely into the tomb, and there they saw—not the Lord—but a bright angel.

He looked like a young man, and he wore a long, white garment. This was the angel who had rolled away the stone. His face was glorious like the lightning, and his garment was white as snow.

The women were frightened when they saw the angel.

But he spoke to them very kindly, and said, "Be not afraid, for ye seek Jesus of Nazareth, who was crucified. He is not here; for He is risen, as He said. Come, see the place where the Lord lay." The angel told them next what to do. He said, "Go quickly and tell His disciples and Peter that He is risen from the dead. He is going into Galilee, and He will see you there, as He said. Behold, I have told you!"

The poor women were still afraid after hearing these precious words; but they were also joyful, and they ran very quickly to tell the disciples. Nor did they stop to speak to any one by the way.

Jesus is Risen and Glorified.

You have heard how the women ran to tell the disciples. You remember there were three who came to the tomb at first—Mary (the mother of James and Jude), Salome (the mother of John), and Mary Magdalene.

THE BURIAL OF CHRIST.

Now, you must know that Mary Magdalene did not go into the tomb with the other two: for as soon as she saw that the stone was rolled away, she took fright and ran back immediately, and went to Peter and John, and said to them, "They have taken away the Lord out of the sepulchre, and we know not where they have lain Him."

Peter and John set out immediately, running to the tomb as fast as they could. Mary Magdalene could not run so very fast, and she followed them a good way behind.

John ran the fastest, and got to the tomb first. When he got there, he did not go in—he only stooped down and looked in.

And what did he see? He did not see the women. They were gone away. He did not see angels: he saw nothing but the linen clothes lying on the ground; those linen clothes that Joseph had wrapped round the Lord's body.

Soon Peter came up; he did more than look into the tomb; he went in; but he saw no angel; he saw nothing but the linen clothes on the floor; he observed that the cloth which had been wrapped around the head of Jesus was folded up neatly and placed by itself. He could not tell who had folded it up, but we think it must have been the angel.

When John saw that Peter had gone into the tomb, he went in also; and when he saw the linen clothes folded up, he believed that his dear Lord was indeed risen from the dead.

Peter and John did not stay in the empty tomb, but they walked back to their own home a little way off.

Now they understood what He meant when He said, "I shall arise again the third day."

Mary Magdalene did not go home with them. She stayed in the garden. She stood by the grave weeping. Then she stooped down and looked in, and what a wonderful sight she beheld!

She saw more than the clothes. She saw two angels dressed in white, sitting in the tomb. One was sitting in the place where the head of Jesus had once lain and the other angel was sitting where His feet had rested.

JESUS MEETS MARY IN THE GARDEN. (439)

The angels saw Mary, and they said to her kindly, "Woman, why weepest thou?" She replied, "Because they have taken away my Lord, and I know not where they have lain Him."

When she had said this she turned around and saw Jesus standing close to her; but she did not know who it was. Jesus said to her, "Why weepest thou? Whom seekest thou?"

Mary did not see who was speaking, and she thought it might be the gardener, so she answered, "Sir, if thou hast carried Him away tell we where thou hast lain Him, and I will come and take Him away." Jesus answered her by one word—"Mary!" She knew it was the Lord, and replied, "Master!"

Oh what joy she felt as she spoke that word!

But Jesus told her that He could not stay with her now, for He was going to ascend to His Father. Then He commanded her, saying, "Go to My brethren, and say, I ascend unto My Father and your Father, unto My God and your God."

Then Mary went again to the disciples, and told them she had seen the Lord, and had heard Him speak.

She was the first to see Jesus after He rose from the dead. She was the first to hear His voice.

The first words Jesus spoke, after rising from the dead were, "Why weepest thou?" These tender words showed that love was in His heart, even now that all His sorrows were over. Even now He feels for every one who is weeping; so that we may go when we are sad, and weep at His feet.

The first name He called was "Mary." He still knows the names of all His people, and writes them down in His book of Life. Would not you, dear little one, like to have your name written there?

Jesus Appears to His Disciples.

That Sunday was a very happy day when Jesus rose in the morning. How many people who had been weeping all Saturday were made happy on that Sunday!

Mary Magdalene and another Mary, and Salome, were the first people made happy. Then Peter and John were made happy, for though they did not see Jesus at the tomb, yet they believed. Then some other women were made happy, who saw two angels, though they also did not see Jesus. Next, Peter was comforted after his sin by seeing Jesus.

Now I am going to tell you of the happy Sunday evening which the disciples had.

In the evening two friends were walking home to a village in the country. They talked together about all that had happened, and were very sad. On the way Jesus Himself came up to them; but they did not know Him, though they had often seen Him before He was crucified. Jesus kindly asked them what made them so sad. Then one of the friends, named Cleopas, replied, "Have you not heard of the things that have happened in Jerusalem?"

Jesus said, "What things?"

They answered, "Everything about Jesus of Nazareth; how He was crucified, and how we hoped He would rise again. But though some women, who went early to the tomb, say they have seen angels who said He was alive, yet none of us have seen Him."

Then Jesus told them that they were foolish not to believe what the prophets had said about the Lord; and He explained to them a great deal of the Bible as they went along.

At last the two friends came to Em-ma-us, the village where they lived. They begged Jesus to come into their house, saying, "Abide with us, for it is evening."

So Jesus went in, and sat down with them to supper.

Then He took some bread and blessed it, and broke it in pieces, and gave them each some.

Perhaps they may have seen Him do this before He had been crucified; for while He was breaking the bread they knew that it was Jesus.

But immediately He disappeared from their sight.

Then they remembered how warm their hearts had felt while He was talking to them as they walked.

They did not sleep at their house that night; though it was late, they set out to return to Jerusalem, nearly eight miles off.

They went straight to the house where the eleven apostles met together, with others who loved Jesus.

But before they could tell about their walk with Jesus, the apostles cried out, "The Lord is risen, indeed, and hath appeared to Simon Peter!"

Then the two friends told about Jesus breaking bread at their house.

We only know the name of one of these friends—Cle-o-pas.

While they were thus rejoicing about Jesus, He Himself appeared!

Though the doors were locked to keep out their enemies, yet Jesus came in.

He stood in the midst of them, and said, "Peace be unto you."

But they were greatly frightened, for they could not believe they really saw Jesus; they thought He was a spirit without a body.

Then Jesus said, "Behold My hands and My feet! It is I Myself!"

Then He asked them to touch Him, that they might feel He had flesh and bones.

Then they looked at His blessed hands and feet that had been pierced with nails, and they saw the deep hole in His side, and they knew that it must be Jesus in His own body. Then they were glad.

While they were full of joy and wonder, Jesus said, "Have ye here any meat?"

They gave Him what they had—a piece of a broiled fish and a piece of a honeycomb.

Jesus ate this food before them to show them He was really alive, and that He had a real body.

Then Jesus talked a great deal to them.

He told His eleven Apostles that He was going to send them out to preach; and having said this, He breathed on them, and said, "Receive ye the Holy Ghost."

Such was the end of this glorious Sunday—the first day of the week, and the greatest day ever known on earth.

Doubting Thomas.

On that happy Sunday evening, when Jesus first came to His Apostles, one of them was absent. It was Thomas.

You remember his unbelieving speech when told of his Lord's appearance. For a whole week Thomas saw nothing of his Lord; nor is it mentioned that any one saw Him.

On the next Sunday evening, the disciples were again overjoyed by a visit from their Lord, in the same place as before.

Did Thomas do as he had said, and put his fingers and thrust his hand into the wounded places?

No; he could do nothing more than exclaim, "My Lord and my God!"

A little while after that second Sunday, Jesus appeared to seven disciples in Galilee by the lake of Gennesareth. That visit was at the dawn of day. It was by the side of that lake where Jesus once fed the multitude. There He fed His hungry apostles on fish of His own giving, prepared at a fire of His own lighting.

Then He asked Peter a question that grieved him—"Lovest thou Me?" That question repeated three times reminded him of the three times he had said, "I know not the man."

This meeting by the lake was the third time that Jesus showed Himself to His disciples after He was risen.

Jesus had another meeting with His apostles, and with a great many more besides.

It was on a mountain of Galilee. We know not what mountain.

How many people do you think came to see Jesus?

Five hundred people came from all parts of the land. When they were all ready, longing for His appearance, Jesus came. Some knew He was the Lord, but others were not sure at first.

What a happy meeting there must have been on that mountain-top!

No enemy of Jesus was there. All loved Him and worshiped Him.

How many who had once been blind now rejoiced to see His face! How many who had once been sunk in sin, were now washed clean in His blood!

But there will be a happier meeting some day. That will be when Jesus comes again. Oh, what a company there will be! not hundreds, but millions!

Now we meet to part again, but then we shall never part. We shall then be all like Christ—bright and glorious in our bodies, and without sin—never more to die.

Jesus Ascends into Heaven.

We have heard of the sweet visits Jesus paid His disciples after He rose from the dead. Sometimes it was to a room in Jerusalem He came—then it was by a lake in Galilee He was seen—and afterward on a mountain-top.

He stayed a little while in Galilee among the places where He used to preach and pray, and do wonders.

But He soon returned to Jerusalem, and His disciples also. He did not now live with them as He used to do, but He often saw them and talked with them.

Once He met them all in some place in Jerusalem. We think it was in the room where He had seen them first on that happy Sunday when He rose from the dead.

The disciples knew that their Lord was soon going to leave them. They wanted to know what they ought to do when He was gone. He said, "Stay in Jerusalem, and wait for the promise of the

CHRIST ASCENDS TO HEAVEN.

Father." This promise was the Comforter or Holy Ghost. Had not the disciples heard Jesus say, "The Father will send you another Comforter—the Holy Ghost?" Oh, yes, they had often heard this precious promise.

Then Jesus told them, that when they had received the Holy Ghost from heaven, they were to preach about Him. He told them to preach first at Jerusalem, to the very people who had cried out, "Crucify Him!" He said, "Tell them that their sins shall be forgiven."

After they had preached at Jerusalem, they were to go further. Jesus said, "Go ye into all the world, and teach all nations, and preach the Gospel to every creature."

After the disciples had preached, they were to baptize people, as John the Baptist used to do.

When any one believed in Jesus, the apostles were to baptize him with water, and to say, "I baptize thee in the name of the Father, the Son, and the Holy Ghost."

Jesus spent forty days upon the earth after He had risen from the dead.

One day He walked out with His disciples from Jerusalem. They went together to Mount Olivet. It was the last time they were to walk together upon earth.

When they came to Mount Olivet, Jesus stopped, with His disciples all around, and lifted up His hands over them, and blessed them.

While He was blessing them, He was lifted up from the earth, and carried up into heaven. The apostles looked up and tried to see their Master as long as they could; but soon a cloud hid Him from their sight; they could see Him no longer; He went up, till He took his place at the right hand of God upon His throne.

And there He sits now, glorious, blessed, beloved Saviour!

The disciples worshiped their Lord, and still looked up into the heavens. They soon heard voices speaking to them—they beheld two men in white garments, even angels.

The angels said, "Ye men of Galilee, why stand ye gazing up into heaven? This Jesus that is taken up from you into heaven, shall come in the same way as ye have seen Him go into heaven."

The disciples did not go on looking, but returned with great joy to Jerusalem.

They went continually to the Temple, and praised and blessed God.

They knew He was happy now; they knew that He would come again one day; they knew He would send them the Holy Ghost from heaven.

The Disciples Receive the Promised Comforter.

Do you not wish to know what the Apostles did after Jesus went up to heaven?

We know what they did; for a history has been written called the Acts of the Apostles.

It was Luke who wrote that history—the same Luke who wrote the history of Jesus called the Gospel of Luke. He was not one of the twelve apostles, but he knew a great deal about Jesus and His apostles, and the Holy Spirit taught him what to write.

You know there were eleven apostles who saw Jesus caught up to heaven. Two angels stood near, and comforted them by saying, "This same Jesus, which is taken up from you into heaven, shall so come in like manner as ye have seen Him go into heaven."

This sweet promise made them very joyful.

It was on Mount Olivet they were standing when Jesus was taken up out of their sight. They had only a mile to go to Jerusalem. They went there and so remained because Jesus had bid them wait in Jerusalem till He should send down the Holy Ghost.

It was now fifty days since Jesus rose. There was a feast of the Jews at that time, called "the feast of first-fruits," when the Jews brought their first sheaves of wheat to present to the Lord.

Thousands of Jews came up from all countries to keep this feast. One name for the feast was Pentecost. It was now just fifty days after the Passover. It was the first day of the week. On that day the believers in Jesus met together in the large room to pray.

It was early in the morning—about eight o'clock. Suddenly a great sound was heard. It was like the sound of a very strong, high wind. This great sound filled the place where they were sitting, and shook the whole house. There came also what looked like fire—divided into many parts, each part appearing to be a tongue of fire; and these came and sat on each person present, on the women as well as on the men.

The great noise which had shaken the house had been heard in all Jerusalem, and people came running toward the place. They could not all get into the house, but the people in the house could come out to those in the street. The bright tongues were still to be seen upon them. There were Jews who lived in other countries, as well as Gentiles, and they heard the believers speaking in the languages they spoke in the countries where they were born. They were very much astonished, and said, "How do these men of Galilee speak all these languages?" Some thought this was a miracle, and said to each other, "What is the meaning of it?" But others only mocked and said, "These men have drunk too much wine."

Then Peter stood up, and all the other apostles stood near him. He spoke in a very loud voice, that all the multitude might hear.

He began by saying, "These men are not drunken, as you suppose; for men do not get drunk so early in the morning. But," said he, "God has sent down His Holy Spirit, as He promised. Hear my words," cried out Peter; "Jesus of Nazareth, who did so many miracles among you, as you know, has been crucified by your wicked hands. But He has been raised from the dead and taken to God's right hand, and now He hath sent forth this which ye now see and hear."

CHRIST SHOWS HIMSELF TO THE TWO MARYS.

The multitude could see the brightness of the Spirit. Many now believed that Jesus was the Son of God, and felt very unhappy for having crucified Him; and they were pricked in their hearts, and came to the apostles, saying very sorrowfully, "What shall we do?"

Then Peter answered, "Repent and be baptized every one of you in the name of Jesus, for the forgiveness of your sins, and you shall receive the Holy Ghost."

Three thousand were baptized that day.

Then was fulfilled what John the Baptist once said: "I indeed baptize you with water unto repentance, but He that cometh after me shall baptize you with the Holy Ghost and with fire."—Matt. iii. 11.

The Lame Man at the Beautiful Gate.

The three thousand people who believed lived very happily. They went often to see each other, and they all loved one another, and they prayed together.

Some were very poor and some were very rich. Those who were rich sold their fine houses and gardens, and with the money they helped the poor people.

The appostles did a great many miracles.

Let us hear the account of one of these miracles.

Peter and John went up to the Temple one afternoon, about three o'clock, when the lamb was sacrificed on the altar. As they passed through a fine brass gate called Beautiful, they saw a poor beggar lying there. He was lame. He had been born with weak bones in his ankles and feet, so that he could never walk. He was now forty years old, and he had no hope of ever being cured. Every day his friends carried him to this gate, that he might beg money of the people passing through. In the evening his friends carried him home.

When he saw Peter and John coming through, he begged them to give him something. They stopped and said to the beggar,

"Look upon us." So the man looked, in great hopes of a little money. Then Peter said, "Silver and gold have I none, but such as I have give I thee: in the name of Jesus of Nazareth, rise up and walk." Then Peter took the beggar by his right hand and helped him to get up. But the man sprang from the ground with a leap, though before he could not stand; his feet and ankle-bones had been made strong in a moment!

The man followed Peter and John into the Temple, leaping as he went, and praising God. There were a great many people in the courts of the Temple who had come up to pray, and they saw the man leaping, and they knew him well as the beggar who had sat at the gate year after year.

The man was so fond of Peter and John that he held them fast, lest they should go away. People in the streets heard what had happened, and came in crowds to see the man. They looked at Peter and John, admiring them, and thinking they were very great men to do such a wonder.

But Peter and John did not want to be admired. They wanted everybody to praise the Saviour. So Peter stood up to preach in the Temple courts. He said, "Ye men of Israel, why do you look on us, as though by our own power and goodness we had made this man walk? It is through believing on Jesus that he was cured. You asked Pontius Pilate to have Jesus killed, and to let go the murderer Barabbas. But God raised Him from the dead, and took Him up to heaven, where He will stay till the happy time that God hath spoken of. Repent ye, therefore, and be converted, that your sins may be blotted out."

The Stoning of Stephen, the First Martyr.

There were now thousands and thousands of believers in Jesus. Among them were many poor people, who needed to be supplied with food. The apostles called the people together and told them to select seven good men to help in this work. These men were called deacons, and they had power to work miracles.

Stephen was the most remarkable of all the seven deacons. He was full of faith, and did great wonders among the people.

But the enemies of Jesus hated him the more for being so wonderful. Learned Jews went to him and disputed with him, but they found that Stephen was wiser than they were.

So they determined to bring him before the great council, called the Sanhedrim, and to bribe men to tell lies of him. And they went about among the people and tried to set them against him, by saying false things of him.

One day they came suddenly upon him and caught him, and brought him to the great hall of the Sanhedrim, close to the Temple, and set him before his judges.

False witnesses came in and said that Stephen had declared that Jesus of Nazareth would destroy the Temple. Stephen had never said this, for it was the Romans who would destroy the Temple.

After Stephen had been so falsely accused, the judges, who sat round, looked at him, and were surprised to see his face like the face of an angel, so bright—so glorious! But this sight did not turn the hearts of the wicked judges. They went on judging him.

The high priest was the chief among them. (It was not Caiaphas now who was high priest. He had been put out of his place.)

This high priest, after hearing the wicked men accuse him, said to Stephen, "Are these things so?"

Then Stephen began to defend himself against what the false witnesses had said of him. He made a very long speech; at last he told his judges that they had all been murderers of the Son of God.

This made them very angry. Stephen's words cut them to the heart, but did not make them repent. They gnashed upon him with their teeth.

He lifted up his eyes toward heaven and saw there the glory of God, and Jesus standing on His right hand.

Then He cried out, "Behold, I see the heavens opened, and Jesus standing on the right hand of God!"

Then they cried out with a loud voice, and stopped their ears, that they might not hear Stephen's blessed words, and they ran upon him all together (as the men of Nazareth had once hunted Jesus). They ran far from the Temple courts, all along the street that led to a gate of the city, near the brook Kedron; and when they got Stephen out, they took up great stones and threw them at him.

In order to hurl the stones with more force they took off their outer garments, and asked a young man named Saul to take care of them. He was an unbelieving young man, who was glad to see Stephen killed. Stephen went on praying all the time the stones were falling, calling out, "Lord Jesus, receive my spirit." At last, when bruised all over and ready to die, he kneeled down and said, "Lord, lay not this sin to their charge!" Thus with his last breath he asked God

THE GATE NEAR WHICH STEPHEN WAS STONED.

to forgive his cruel murderers. As soon as he had offered this prayer he fell asleep.

This was the death of the first martyr. Thousands and thousands of martyrs have died like him, praising God and praying for their enemies, and they will all come with Jesus to reign with Him in glory.

Story of Philip and the Ethiopian Prince.

God had a great work for Philip to do. He was to bring the gospel into Africa. There were then three parts of the world that were known to the people of that time: Asia, where Jesus had preached; Europe, where the gospel had not yet been preached; and Africa, where black people lived. To Africa God determined to send the gospel.

The angel told Philip to go down to the Philistines' country, at the lower corner of Canaan. Gaza was in that part, but Philip did not go near that town; he went to a desert place near it, on the way to Africa.

It must have seemed strange to Philip to hear he must go to a desert. He might wonder whom he could preach to in a desert. But he went.

While he was walking among the rocky hills he saw a very fine carriage going along. It was coming from Jerusalem. There were horses and servants. A great lord was sitting in the carriage reading. This great lord was the chief servant of a great queen called Candace. She was the queen of a hot country in Africa called Ethiopia, where the people are almost black.

This lord had the charge of all the queen's treasure, and he was called her treasurer. But we do not know his name.

The Spirit said to Philip, "Go near to that chariot;" and Philip went. He heard the treasurer reading out aloud. He had a scroll, and not a book, in his hand. On that scroll, or roll, were written the words of the prophet Isaiah.

Who would have thought that a lord from a heathen country would read the Word of God?

But this man had been up to Jerusalem to worship in the Temple. He had not been allowed to go further than the outer court of the Gentiles, but his prayers in that court were heard as much as the prayers of the priests in the Holy Place. He had brought back a greater treasure than all his gold and silver, even the words that God once spoke to Isaiah.

Philip had the courage to speak to this great lord. He said to him, "Do you understand what you are reading?"

If the treasurer had been a proud man he would have been affronted by that question from a poor stranger; but he was humble, and he answered: "How can I understand if I have no one to teach me?" And then he asked Philip to come and sit by him in his chariot. When Philip was sitting in the chariot the rich man showed him what he was reading. It was that sweet verse in the fifty-third chapter: "He is brought as a lamb to the slaughter, and as a sheep before her shearers is dumb, so he openeth not his mouth."

THE CHARIOT OF THE ETHIOPIAN LORD.

The treasurer, after having read this verse, said to Philip, "I do not know the meaning of this. Does the Prophet speak of himself, or of some other man?" Then Philip explained it all to him. He told him that Jesus was the lamb, and that He had lately been crucified in Jerusalem; and that He had been as meek to His enemies as a sheep that makes no noise when it is sheared. And he told him that Jesus had risen from His grave, and that He had desired His disciples to go and teach people of all countries, and to baptize them in His name. The treasurer listened very attentively, and wanted to know whether he might be baptized. Just at this moment the chariot passed by a stream. There are not many streams in the desert, and the treasurer was pleased to see water. He cried out, "Here is water; may I not be baptized?"

Philip said, "You may, if you believe with all your heart."

The treasurer replied, "I believe that Jesus Christ is the Son of God."

When Philip saw that he believed, he desired the driver to stop the horses; and Philip and the treasurer both got out and went together into the water. There Philip baptized this Gentile stranger.

As soon as they were come up out of the water the Spirit caught up Philip and took him to a place by the seaside.

The place where the Spirit left him was once called Ashdod. It was a place full of idols. Philip went along by the seaside, from place to place, preaching everywhere. At last he stopped at a fine city called Cæsarea, built by the Roman Emperor, and called after Cæsar.

The treasurer must have been sorry to lose his teacher, yet he was so happy in his Saviour that he went to his home full of joy, ready to teach Queen Candace and all her people. So the gospel came into Africa, where many people turned to Jesus.

The Wonderful Vision of Saul.

A very wonderful event is now to be related.

You remember there was a young man named Saul, who treated cruelly the disciples of Jesus. He kept the clothes of those who stoned the holy Stephen.

This young man thought he did right in ill-treating believers in Christ, for he thought Christ was a deceiver, and not really the Son of God. After he had done much harm in Jerusalem, he went to other cities to hurt the believers who lived in them.

There was a great city, called Damascus, more than a hundred miles from Jerusalem. He wished to go there. First, he got letters from the high-priest at Jerusalem, giving him leave to seize the believers in Damascus, and to bring them in chains to Jerusalem. He meant to show these letters to the chief Jews in Damascus. But on the way a very wonderful thing happened.

Saul was traveling with several men as his guard. They all arrived in sight of Damascus about noonday, when the sun is the brightest. There suddenly appeared a light from heaven brighter than the sun. This light was so dazzling that all the travelers fell down with their faces to the ground, quite unable to look up.

While thus lying prostrate, Saul heard a voice from heaven, saying, "Saul, Saul, why dost thou persecute Me?" Saul answered,

INTERIOR OF A HOUSE IN DAMASCUS.

"Who art Thou, Lord?" The voice replied, "I am Jesus, whom thou persecutest." Saul, still trembling and astonished, inquired, "Lord, what wouldst Thou have me to do?"

The voice replied, "Arise, and go into the city, and it shall be told thee what thou must do."

All this time the other men did not speak a word, but they could not hear what Jesus said to Saul, only they heard a sound.

After being struck to the ground they got up and stood by Saul, but Saul himself did not get up till Jesus said, "Rise, and stand upon thy feet." Then Saul arose, and opened his eyes—but behold!—he could not see—the dazzling light had blinded him. The men were not blinded, and they led Saul by the hand into the city. They took him to a lodging in a street called Straight, at the house of a man named Judas. There Saul sat down, quite blind, and he refused to eat or drink for three days. As he sat in darkness he was thinking of his sins against Jesus, and of his cruelty to His people.

He felt so grieved at all he had done that he could not eat. He thought of the poor creatures he had sent to prison—of those he had beaten—and of Stephen, who had been stoned before his eyes. "Oh, how could I be so wicked? I am the chief of sinners!" he exclaimed.

Ananias Appears to Saul in a Vision.

While Saul was in this sad state of blindness and misery, God sent him a dream, or vision. It was a comforting dream.

Saul saw a man in his dream whose name was Ananias. He came into the room, and put his hand on Saul, and said, "Receive thy sight." Till this dream came, how could Saul know that he should ever see again? He knew that he well deserved to be always blind. But he kept on praying to God for pardon.

While Saul was praying, there was a man in Damascus who had a dream. This man was the same Ananias that Saul had seen in his vision. He was a very good man, and he had heard that Saul was coming from Jerusalem to seize God's people, and to bind them in chains. He was much surprised when God said to him in a dream: "Get up, and go into Straight street, and find the house of a man called Judas, and ask for a man called Saul: for Saul is now praying to Me; and he has seen you in a dream coming in and putting your hand on him, that he may be able to see."

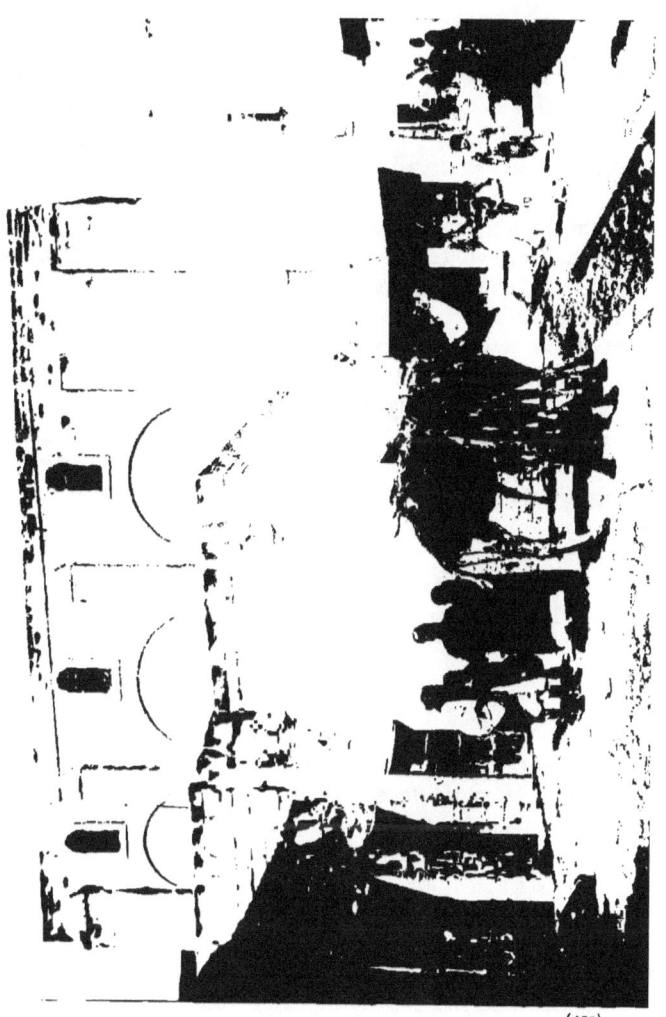

(459)

Ananias answered the Lord,—"Many people have told me of this man, and of how much harm he has done to the holy people in Jerusalem; and how he has come here with leave from the chief priests to bind all that call on the Lord Jesus."

But the Lord answered Ananias,—"Go thy way, for I have chosen him to tell many people about Me—Gentiles, and kings, and the children of Israel—and I shall show him that he must suffer a great deal for My sake."

Then Ananias went to Straight street, and entered into the house of Judas, and went up into Saul's room, and put his hands on Saul, and said, "Brother Saul, the Lord Jesus, who appeared to you as you came to this place, has sent me to you, that you may receive your sight." As he said this, something like scales fell from Saul's eyes, and he found he was able to see. Soon afterwards he was baptized, and then he ate food, and he grew strong again.

Saul stayed a good while in Damascus, and he became great friends with all the people of the Lord in the city. Those very people that he once meant to send to prison were now his dearest friends. He went to the synagogues, and preached there about Jesus Christ, that He was the Son of God.

The Jews grew very angry on hearing him praise Jesus so much. They were so angry that they determined to try to kill him. But Saul escaped the unbelieving Jews in Damascus, and after a journey of many days through the land of Israel, he arrived at Jerusalem. When he had last been there, what harm he had done in the city! But now he came to do good, and to save sinners by his preaching.

After staying some time, Saul told his friends that he must leave Jerusalem, for the Lord had commanded him to go away, because the Jews intended to kill him.

When the disciples heard this they were very anxious to send him away. They took him down secretly to the seaside. There was a fine town built in honor of the Roman Emperor Cæsar, and it was called Cæsarea. Saul had to go about a hundred miles to this town. He must at first have traveled by night to hide himself from the Jews.

What good man was living there who would be glad to see Saul? Philip, the deacon. Perhaps he had not seen Saul since the stoning of Stephen. How much changed Saul was since that time! That fierce, proud countenance was now gentle, afflicted, and humble.

But perhaps Saul had no time to visit Philip at Cæsarea, for his friends were in great haste to send him far away. There were ships embarking from Cæsarea. One was setting sail for Tarsus. That was his native place, and there Saul wished to go. How far was it off? Three hundred miles over the seas. Saul got into a ship. At last he came to land. He did not get out of the ship there; he had to sail twelve miles more up a river, till he came to a great mountain. Here was Tarsus, which was his home.

An Angel Delivers Peter from Prison.

At this time very great troubles came upon the saints in Jerusalem. Cæsar at Rome appointed Herod to be king of Jerusalem and of all the land.

This was not the Herod who had killed John the Baptist, and mocked Jesus the Saviour. That Herod had been sent far away by the Emperor Cæsar. This Herod was his nephew, and he was the grandson of the Herod who killed the babes of Bethlehem. What a wicked family these Herods were! This Herod commanded his soldiers to seize James, the brother of John, and to cut off his head with a sword.

So now John lost his brother. Those two brothers had been with Jesus on the mount of glory and in the garden of agony. James was one of the three favorites of the Lord, though John was the most beloved of all. He was the first of all the apostles to be killed for the sake of Jesus.

Herod saw that the Jews were pleased with him for killing James, so he thought he would kill Peter too; and he sent soldiers to seize him and to put him in prison; but, as he had heard of his once escaping from prison, he desired sixteen soldiers to guard him night and day.

Herod fixed the day when Peter was to be killed. The night before that terrible day the saints met together to pray for him. The other apostles had left Jerusalem, lest they also should be killed; but there were many saints still there. They met together in the house of a very good woman, named Mary. She was not one of the Marys we have heard of before. She was the sister of Barnabas who had once been kind to Saul.

Mary and her friends were sitting up all the night. Peter was quietly sleeping in prison. It was the beginning of summer, and it was warm. Peter had taken off his sandals and his upper garment, but he could not take off a chain from each hand, which was fastened to a soldier's hand on each side of him. Suddenly an angel made the dark prison brighter than the day. Yet Peter was so sound asleep that he did not wake, till the angel touched him, saying, "Rise up quickly." And as Peter arose, the chains fell off his hands.

Then the angel bade him tighten his clothes round his waist, put on his sandals, and wrap himself in his loose upper garment. All this time the soldiers slept.

The angel said, "Follow me." Peter followed, feeling as if he were dreaming. The angel led him past many soldiers that had been placed to watch outside, and brought him to the great iron gate. Though it had bolts and bars, it opened without key and without hand, as if it had opened itself.

The angel brought him down one street and then departed.

When Peter found himself alone he stopped to think of what had happened. He saw that God had set him free, and saved him from death. He had heard that the saints were sitting up at night to pray for him in Mary's house. So he went there. He knocked at the door of the porch, and Rhoda, the maid, came to the door. You know the history—how, when she heard Peter's voice outside, saying, "Let me in," her joy was so great that she forgot to open

RELEASED BY THE ANGEL.　　　　(463)

the door, but ran into the house to tell his friends that Peter was there—and how they would not believe her, but said it was some angel that took care of Peter.

Peter, however, went on knocking, till many friends rushed to the door and saw his face. They were inclined to make much noise in their joy, but Peter made a sign for them to be quiet, as the noise might have been heard by their enemies. When they were quiet, Peter told them how the Lord had delivered him. He then said, "Go and tell this to James and the brethren."

It was James the brother of Jude that he meant,—the same James that Saul had seen. Then Peter went away to some place that Herod did not know of.

Story of Paul and the Wicked Sorcerer.

Saul and Barnabas spent a whole year in Antioch, preaching to the Christians. While they were living at Antioch, the Holy Ghost said to the Christian teachers, "Let Barnabas and Saul go to the work I have called them to do." So the other Christian teachers prayed, and sent them out to preach to the heathen.

And they took with them a young man, named Mark. He was the nephew of Barnabas, and his uncle was fond of him, and liked to have him with him.

Saul and Barnabas sailed to Cyprus in a ship. They could easily get there in a day. When they landed at Salamis, the port, they found themselves among orange-groves and apricot gardens. The hills were covered with vines, and the green pastures were sprinkled over with milk-white flocks. But this sweet country was made hateful by the wicked ways of its people. The two apostles preached everywhere they could. They went all through the island preaching. The island is about one hundred miles long.

At the further end, there was a city called Paphos, where the governor lived. His name was Sergius Paulus. He was a Roman, and was king or governor under Cæsar at Rome—just as Pontius Pilate had been king in Jerusalem.

PAUL EXPELS THE EVIL SPIRIT.

But he was a much wiser man than Pilate. When he heard of the preaching of the wonderful strangers, he wanted to hear them and so he sent for them, that he might learn about the true God.

The two apostles went into the palace of the governor, hoping to lead him to believe in Jesus.

There was a very wicked man in the room. His name was Bar-jesus. He was a Jew, and had a Jewish name, meaning the "Son of Jesus," but he was really the son of Satan. This wicked Jew could not bear to hear of Jesus, and he tried to turn away the governor from believing in him. We do not know what he said, only that he spoke against the gospel.

Saul then turned towards him, and fixed his eyes upon him, saying, "O full of all cunning and mischief, thou child of the devil, thou enemy of all righteousness! the hand of the Lord is upon thee, and thou shalt be blind and not see the sun for a season."

Immediately this wicked man found himself in darkness, and he spread out his hands, looking for some one to lead him.

The governor, when he saw this miracle, believed in the Lord.

What a just punishment this sorcerer had! He tried to keep the governor in darkness of heart that he should not see the Light of the World. After this visit to Cyprus you will never hear Saul spoken of any more. From this time his name is Paul. No one knows why his name was changed; perhaps it was because Paul was a Roman name, and suited him, now he preached to the Romans and other Gentiles. Saul was only a Jewish name.

From Cyprus they went to Antioch in Pisidia, to Iconium, to Lystra. The apostles then determined to return to Jerusalem by the way they came.

Paul and Timothy.

When Paul and Barnabas were leaving Jerusalem they took with them several holy men. One of these was a prophet, called Silas. He became a great friend of Paul and he remained with him at Antioch when the other brethren went back to Jerusalem.

Barnabas took Mark with him and set sail for Cyprus, his own country, where he had once preached the gospel.

Paul chose for his companion Silas, the prophet, and he went to his own country, Tarsus, where he had once preached the gospel.

Here he found a young man named Timothy. He felt a great affection for Timothy. His mother was a Jewess. She had taught him to know the Scriptures when he was quite a child. His grandmother also had taught him. But he did not know about Jesus till Paul preached at Lystra. Paul heard a very good character of Timothy from all the Christians at Lystra. He wished very much to have him as a companion on his journey. Timothy was quite ready to go. These two were like father and son. Paul had no son of his own, and he was glad to have Timothy for his son. He called him his dearly beloved son.

Paul's Wonderful Dream.

These three friends traveled all about Asia together.

One day they came to a town called Troas. It was by the sea-coast.

One night Paul had a wonderful dream. He saw a man standing and speaking very earnestly to him, saying, "Come over and help us." He knew that the man came from Macedonia. Perhaps the man in the dream said where he came from, or perhaps Paul knew by his dress and language to what country he belonged. When Paul awoke he told his dream to his companions. How many companions had he? Two—Silas and Timothy. Now he had a third, named Luke.

We do not know where he first saw Luke. Paul must have been very glad to get Luke for a companion. Luke was a very learned, clever man, and he wrote this history we are reading from the Bible; it was Luke who wrote the Acts. He wrote also one of the histories of our Saviour, and for that reason he is called the "Evangelist"—for the four men who wrote the four histories of

Jesus are called the "Evangelists." Luke was a physician and doctor. Paul called him the "beloved physician."

The four friends set sail in a little ship. They were two days on the voyage. The second day they arrived at the sea-coast of Macedonia, the country of the man in the dream.

They went to a fine city called Philippi. It was built on a great plain close by a river. Very few Jews lived in this city, so there was no synagogue in it. But there was a little house for prayer close by the river-side.

On the Sabbath-day—which was Saturday—the four ministers went to this prayer-house. They found a few women at the prayer-meeting. The men, perhaps, would not come.

The ministers sat down and spoke to the women. There was one woman there who listened most attentively. Her name was Lydia.

After the service she spoke to Paul, and told him that she believed in Jesus, and that she wished to be baptized. Paul approved of her so well that he had her baptized; and also her family and servants.

Then Lydia asked the four ministers to do her a great favor. It was, to come to her house and live there as long as they stayed in Philippi.

Story of a Great Earthquake.

How happy and prosperous were Paul and his friends at Philippi! But soon there was a great change. The people persecuted these good men. They caught Paul and Silas, dragged them into the market place, beat them with rods, and cast them into prison. They put their feet in the stocks—that is, in holes in a board, so that they could not move. They could not lie down or stand up.

Paul and Silas were sitting in the stocks at night, when a sound was heard from their dungeon. Was it the voice of weeping and wailing? No, it was the voice of singing! And what was the singing about? It was the praises of God the prisoners were singing.

Suddenly a dreadful sound was heard—it was an earthquake.

So great was the earthquake that it shook the dungeon, opened the doors, and caused the chains to fall off from the prisoners. The apostles found that their feet were set free from the holes in the boards. They could easily run away. But they did not move, because they knew it was God's will they should stay. Nor did any of the prisoners escape, though they easily could.

The keeper was asleep, and was awakened by the earthquake. When he saw the doors standing open he felt sure the prisoners must be gone. He knew he had done wrong in sleeping, and he felt afraid that he should be condemned to die by the rulers. So he took out his sword, and was going to stab himself, when he heard a loud voice from the dungeon calling out, "Do thyself no harm, for we are all here." Great was his surprise. He called for a light, and sprang into the dungeon, and fell down trembling at the feet of Paul and Silas.

Immediately he brought them out of the dungeon, and said to them, "Sirs, what must I do to be saved?" He wanted now to save his soul. Paul and Silas answered, "Believe in the Lord Jesus Christ and thou shalt be saved."

The jailer had heard before that Jesus died to save him, and now he wished to be baptized. But first he washed the prisoners' stripes, and then was baptized with all his family.

The morning after the terrible earthquake, some men came to the prison with a message. They asked to see the jailer, and they said to him, "The judges desire you to let these two men go."

The jailer went and gave the message to Paul. He said, "The judges desire me to let you go. So depart, and go in peace."

But Paul would not go. He said, "I am a Roman." What did Paul mean by that? Was he not a Jew, born at Tarsus, not in Rome? Yes; but there were some men *called* Romans. It was a favor that the great Emperor at Rome gave to some men as a reward; for if a man was called a Roman, no judge could condemn him, unless he first proved him to be guilty, and called witnesses to show that he deserved punishment.

So the messengers went back to the judges and said, "Those prisoners are Romans, and they say that you have beaten them openly, and that you must now come and fetch them out yourselves."

Then the judges were frightened lest they should get into disgrace at Rome. They did not like going themselves to the prison, but to avoid disgrace they went.

Paul's Visit to Greece.

After their liberation Paul and Silas journeyed to other cities, leaving Luke and Timothy at Philippi. They arrived first at Thessalonica, the largest city in Macedonia. There were many spiteful, envious Jews at Thessalonica. They next journeyed about fifty miles before they reached Berea, a quiet city among the fruitful hills of Macedonia.

There were not many people in Berea, but they had a synagogue.

The Jews in Berea listened to the preaching about Jesus, and they looked in the books of the old prophets to see what was written there about Him.

Paul now made a long voyage, and after many days arrived at Athens, the most famous city of Greece. There never was a city with so many beautiful statues, pictures, temples, and altars. But most of the statues were the images of false gods, and all the temples were the houses of idols.

These Athenians were fond of hearing new things, so they thought they should like to hear Paul preach. But when they heard of the resurrection, some began to laugh; others said, "We will hear about this another day." Paul did not stay long with the scoffers of Athens; for he could do more good in other cities.

Paul set out on his journey to Corinth, a very large city about fifty miles off. Corinth was a far richer city than Athens. It was the capital of Greece. The chief pleasure in Athens was to talk

A SCENE IN A STREET OF DAMASCUS.

about new things; but the chief pleasure at Corinth was to feast and dance, and play at games.

Paul stayed at Corinth a year and a half, and went on teaching the word. Timothy joined Paul at Corinth. Paul at last set sail again.

He landed at Cæsarea, and went up to Jerusalem. He saw his friends there, and worshiped the Lord in His holy city. It must have been delightful to relate his wonderful history to the apostles who were there. But he did not stay long; he hastened back to Antioch in Syria, the city from which he had set out several years before.

Thus ended his second missionary journey. It had been indeed a blessed journey, for thousands of heathens had turned to God. In this journey the gospel was first preached in Europe, for Macedonia and Greece are in Europe.

Paul and Titus.

We have now read of two missionary journeys. The first when Paul set out with Barnabas and Mark. The second when he set out with Silas. From both these journeys he had returned safely, after suffering many afflictions.

It was Paul's chief delight to tell the heathen about Jesus; so after spending some time at Antioch with the brethren, he set out again.

One of his companions on this third journey was a young man named Titus. He was a Greek. His native city was Corinth, the capital of Greece, or Achaia. Paul loved Titus much, and called him his son. It seems he loved Timothy still more, for he called him his dearly beloved son.

Paul and Titus went through Little Asia. Little Asia was divided into provinces. One was called Cilicia. Tarsus was in Cilicia. There Paul was born; his relations lived there. It is probable Paul visited his native city.

He went afterwards into a province called Galatia. Those who lived there were a wild, warm-hearted people. Paul had visited Galatia some years before. The people were very fond of him at first, till false teachers came and set them against him for a time.

But they readily granted Paul's request. He had promised the brethren, that he would collect money for the poor saints in Jerusalem, who were in great distress. You remember there was a famine in most lands, and besides the famine there were persecutions at Jerusalem, so the poor saints were often in great distress.

When Paul left Galatia he went to other parts of Asia, and visited Lystra, which was dear to him as Timothy's birthplace.

He went through the province of Phrygia, and then went down towards the great city of Ephesus. He then returned to Jerusalem.

A Great Uproar in the Temple and on the Castle Stairs.

The day after Paul's arrival a great meeting was held in Jerusalem. The Apostle James was chief over the assembly: many elders were there. Christians brought large sums of money, collected in distant countries, for the saints in Jerusalem.

When they had presented these gifts, Paul began to address the assembly.

He told them the history of his travels, and of the conversions the Lord had wrought among the Gentiles. What praises flowed from the lips of the believers, when Paul had finished his speech!

Then some elders arose and began to give the apostles their advice. They had met with Jews who bore false witness of Paul, and who said he set people against the law of Moses. Was this true?

Some Jews from Asia (probably from the city of Ephesus), seeing Paul in the Temple, stirred up the people against him, and seized him, saying, "This Paul is the man who goes about speaking against the Temple; and he has now taken Gentiles into the Temple."

Paul had never done this.

But most people believed what the Jews from Asia said; and they all ran together into the Temple. They found Paul in the court of Israel, near the altar (where he had a right to be). They seized hold of him, and dragged him out of the court, down the steps. His enemies hurried him into the streets, and would soon have stoned him had they not been suddenly stopped in their wickedness.

There was a great tower just above the Temple, where a thousand Roman soldiers lodged. The captain heard that there was an uproar in the city, and he ran down in haste, with many soldiers, to the place where Paul was. He found the Jews beating him, but when these men saw the captain they left off beating Paul; for they knew they had no right to do so.

The chief captain came near and directed his soldiers to bind Paul, then he asked the people what he had done to make them so angry with him.

They gave so many answers to this question that the captain did not know what to believe. Some cried out one thing and some another, and there was such confusion that the captain desired the soldiers to take him into the tower, or castle.

The soldiers led him along till they came to the stairs that led to the castle. As they went up these stairs the people pushed the soldiers so much that Paul was lifted off his feet and carried up in the soldiers' arms. All the time the people, who were pressing up the stairs, kept crying out, "Away with him!" These people were ferocious as hounds ready to seize upon a harmless deer.

The captain had gone up the stairs first, for as Paul was on his way he saw the captain, and very respectfully said to him, "May I speak unto the people?"

The captain wanted to know who he was. Paul answered, "I am a Jew of Tarsus, and I beseech thee suffer me to speak unto the people." Then the captain gave leave for his prisoner to speak.

Paul stood on the stairs, rather near the top, and made a sign to the people below that he was going to speak.

THE SHIPWRECK OF PAUL. (475)

The fierce multitude wanted to hear him, wondering what he would say; and so they suddenly became quite silent.

Then Paul spoke. He told the multitude his history—how he once cruelly treated the Christians—and how he saw a light from heaven, and heard Jesus speak—and how he was made blind —and how Ananias restored his sight—and how he preached about Jesus in Jerusalem, till God said, "Depart, I will send thee far away to the Gentiles."

As soon as Paul had uttered these words, there arose such cries and shouts from the people beneath as you never heard. Amidst their yells they screamed, "Away with such a fellow from the earth; for it is not fit that he should live!" As they cried out, they took off their upper garments to prepare for stoning him, and they threw dust in the air, in their rage.

Paul's Escape from Scourging.

The captain began to think that Paul must have committed some very dreadful crime to make the Jews so angry with him. So he desired a centurion to take him into the castle, and to have him scourged till he should confess what he had done. What a horrible command this was! For what crime could Paul confess? He might have died under the scourge before he could confess. But he remembered that he was a Roman; that is, he had the privileges of a Roman citizen, though he was a Jew.

That privilege was not to be punished without being tried first, and found guilty.

The soldiers were binding Paul with straps of leather to the whipping-post, before beating him with rods, and the centurion was standing near; when Paul said to the centurion, "Is it lawful for you to scourge a man who is a Roman, and who has not been condemned?"

When the centurion heard this, he told the soldiers not to go on with their work, and he went to the captain and said, "You must take care what you do, for this man is a Roman."

Then the captain was quite frightened at having bound him with straps or thongs, and he went quickly to Paul, and said, "Tell me, Art thou a Roman?" Paul said, "Yes." The captain said, "I paid a great deal of money to be made a Roman."

"But I," said Paul, "was free-born." He meant that his father had the privilege, and so he, his son, inherited it from him.

The captain then sent away the soldiers, and made them put up their straps and their rods.

But he thought it best to let Paul sleep in the castle that night, for had he sent him back, the Jews might have torn him in pieces.

The captain was very anxious to do what was right to Paul as a Roman citizen. He thought it would be best to let his own nation judge him. So he sent a message to the councillors of the Sanhedrim to come to their hall in the morning.

Paul stood before the council, and looked at them earnestly. He knew many of them, for he himself had once belonged to the council, and had helped in condemning Stephen.

His first words were—"Men and brethren, I have lived before God as my conscience showed me was right."

Paul spent another night in the castle, but it was a joyful night; for the Lord came and stood near him, and said, "Be of good cheer, Paul; for as thou hast been My witness at Jerusalem, so thou shalt be My witness at Rome."

Now Paul knew that his enemies would not be able to kill him, and that he would go to that great city, Rome—the grandest city in all the world, where Cæsar, the emperor of the world, reigned.

Paul had long wished to go to Rome, that he might speak for Jesus there, and turn many to the Lord. But he did not yet know how he was to get there.

Paul Speaks Before King Agrippa.

Soon after this Paul was taken to Cæsarea. He remained in prison while Festus, the governor, waited for a ship to carry the prisoner to Rome.

While Festus waited, a king came to see him. He was the son of the old Herod who is called Herod the Great in history.

His name was Herod Agrippa, but he is generally called Agrippa only.

He was a very great man—greater then Festus, for he was a king who could do what he would, while Festus was only a governor under Cæsar.

Agrippa brought with him his sister, Bernice.

Agrippa paid a very long visit to Festus.

One day Festus said to him, "I should like you to see a man I have here in prison, named Paul. The Jews hate him very much, yet I cannot find that he has done anything wrong. They chiefly quarrel with him about one Jesus, whom the Jews say is dead, and who Paul says is alive. I would have taken him to Jerusalem to be judged, but he wishes to go to Rome, to be judged by Cæsar."

Agrippa said he would like to hear the man speak.

"To-morrow," said Festus, "you shall hear him."

The next day King Agrippa came into the great court, accompanied by the Princess Bernice, dressed in a very grand manner.

All the chief men came also.

Then Festus commanded that Paul should be brought forth. He came with his chains on his hands, a poor prisoner, mean and low in his appearance, but with Christ in his heart.

There were no accusers this time to speak first, so Agrippa commanded Paul to begin.

The prisoner stretched forth his chained hand, and spoke respectfully, saying, "King Agrippa." Then he told his history to the king, declaring how he had seen Jesus, as a light brighter than the sun, and how he had heard His voice.

"Therefore," said he, "I tell every one that Jesus died and rose again."

When Festus heard him speak of rising from the dead, he cried out in a loud voice that Paul was mad.

Paul replied, "I am not mad, most noble Festus! but speak forth the words of truth; and the king has heard about these things."

Then Agrippa said, "You almost persuade me to be a Christian."

Paul gave him the most beautiful, loving answer,—"I would that you were not only *almost*, but *altogether* such as I am, except these chains." These were the chains upon his hands.

Then the king and the great people arose from their seats, and went into another room.

They said to one another, "This man has done nothing to deserve death or even chains."

Agrippa said to Festus, "If he had not asked to be judged by Cæsar, he might have been set free."

But was Agrippa ever *quite* persuaded to be a Christian? No, never. He heard the truth, but he did not follow it at the moment he heard it.

At last a ship came to Cæsarea in which Paul could sail toward Rome.

He was given in charge of a centurion named Julius; there was a great storm at sea, and day after day the ship continued to be tossed by the waves. Finally it was wrecked near an island, called Melita. The shipwrecked men were all saved. The chief man of Melita was called Publius. He was very kind to Paul.

At the end of three months, the spring was come, and the sea was smooth. The centurion hired a ship to take the whole party to the shores of Rome.

The day came for the centurion to lead his prisoner to Rome. He took him along a well-paved road, very near the sea-coast. Every twenty miles there was a kind of inn for the travelers to rest.

On the road Paul met some friends, who had come from Rome on purpose to welcome him. Seeing them pleased his heart so much that he thanked God and took courage.

At last he arrived at Rome, with a troop of loving friends around him, as well as the soldier to whom he was chained.

Paul's Life in Rome.

When Paul arrived in Rome, where did he go? As he was a prisoner, he ought to have been taken to the place where the soldiers lived. It was a great square with buildings on every side, and a great ditch outside. But he was not taken to that noisy, crowded place, like the other prisoners.

He was allowed to live in a lodging of his own, though he was always to be chained to a soldier.

Do you ask how it was that Paul could pay for a lodging? I suppose it was through the kindness of his friends in Rome. There were a great many in Rome who loved Paul very much.

When he had been three days in Rome, he sent a message to the chief Jews in the city. The message was—to ask them to come see him in his lodging.

They were soon on their way to see Paul. They had often heard of him, but very few had ever seen him; and they must have longed to see such a wonderful man.

They found him weak and worn, bowed down with age and sorrow, but full of love and kindness. The soldier was chained to his arm.

Paul thought these Jews might have heard from other Jews that he had done something wicked.

He assured them that he had done nothing to deserve being in chains. All he had done to offend the Jews was to preach about the resurrection.

This is the last thing said of Paul in the Bible. Luke did not write any more of Paul's history. Still we learn from other books that he was at last beheaded at Rome. We know that he wished to die for Jesus, and he had his wish. He will rise again, and reign with Jesus when he comes. How bright he will shine among the saints! for he turned many to righteousness.

www.ingramcontent.com/pod-product-compliance
Lightning Source LLC
Chambersburg PA
CBHW022100300426
44117CB00007B/530